THE KING'S MOUNTAIN MEN

THE STORY OF THE BATTLE,
WITH SKETCHES OF THE AMERICAN
SOLDIERS WHO TOOK PART

By

KATHERINE KEOGH WHITE

Southern Historical Press, Inc.
Greenville, South Carolina

This volume was reproduced
from a personal copy located in
the Publishers private library

Please direct all correspondence and book orders to:
SOUTHERN HISTORICAL PRESS, Inc.
PO Box 1267
Greenville, SC   29602-1267

Originally printed: Dayton, VA. 1924
ISBN #978-1-63914-131-9
Printed in the United States of America

PREFACE

The list in this book, of the heroes who won the battle of King's Mountain, does not assume to be complete. So far as I am aware, no rosters are in existence. Historians are not agreed as to the number of the Americans who were in the expedition. The general opinion is that it was between one thousand and twelve hundred. I had this number in mind when I began a search for the names of the individual soldiers, and an authentic record in each instance of the soldier's service, in the war of the Revolution. While investigating county records, land grants, pension statements, and other sources of information, I came upon many stories of their lives, especially in the records of Washington county, Tennessee, in 1777-1780. These stories, so full of human interest, often begin before the date of the battle. The narratives introduce us to a life of tragedy as well as romance, on the inland frontier of Virginia and the Carolinas, wild savages and ferocious beasts menacing them at all times. Nowhere else in the American States were the souls of men more nearly strained to the breaking-point. Without official permission and without assurance of reward, these heroes of the frontier came together as brothers and neighbors, and formed a volunteer army to protect their families and their country.

In this book I aim to bring out the human interest which is so overlooked in the admirable histories of the American Revolution. Thus I present, without change, the letters written to Lyman Draper by James Sevier, Gilbert Christian, John Sevier, and William Martin. Not only do these letters afford proof of military service by some of the frontiersmen, but they throw direct light on the expedition itself and on other combats with their enemy.

Emphasis is placed on the state of Franklin, or Frankland. The attempt to establish this commonwealth was an outburst of indignation on the part of the volunteers. Fresh from their victory at King's Mountain, they found themselves without a government and without a country that recognized them. Once more they were forced to band together, this time to make a government for themselves, while defending their loved ones from Indians, tories, and escaped criminals. It is this unflagging loyalty which makes these heroes as brave and courageous as the "Immortal six hundred that walked in the valley of death."

I am under special obligations to the histories of Southwest Virginia, the Carolinas, Georgia, and Tennessee. As these works have been of service to me, so do I hope that the present volume may be helpful to others who engage in research. I also extend my most appreciative thanks to Miss Mary Rothrock, librarian of the Lawson McGhee Free Library, Knoxville, Tennessee, for her aid, and particularly for giving me free access to the valuable Calvin McClung Historical Collection of the said library.

Katherine Keogh White

CONTENTS

SECTION ONE

PREFACE

SECTION TWO

Personal Sketches of King's Mountain Soldiers

APPENDIX

Tennessee Revolutionary Pensioners List

BIBLIOGRAPHY

INDEX

SECTION ONE

THE BATTLE OF KING'S MOUNTAIN

The volunteer army that fought at King's Mountain October 7, 1870, puts us in mind of the three hundred Spartans under Leonidas who defended the pass of Thermopylae 2261 years earlier, or of the six hundred who rode into "the valley of death" at Balaklava in the Crimean war. American history affords no other instance of a thousand frontiersmen coming together of their own free will to make themselves into a volunteer army. The only equipment of the soldier in that expedition was his trusty Dechard rifle with its accessories, his sure-footed mountain horse, and his pocketful of parched corn. These men knew little of professional warfare, but they did know how to keep tories and Indians from their settlement.

When Patrick Ferguson, England's sharpshooter colonel, sent them word that unless they came on to join him and the king he would march over the mountains and hang everyone of them, they at once declared that they would have a voice in the matter. They determined to take care of him, and they performed their task effectually.

Another aspect of this notable expedition is worthy of remark. The returned soldiers had no time to wait for words of praise and promises of reward. They had to hurry back by the nearest path to their wives, children, and the old men and boys who were left to protect the settlements from the Indians. They were just in time to beat off a thousand Indians who were on the march, having learned that the fighting men had gone to King's Mountain.

At King's Mountain these soldiers had trapped and annihilated a British army more numerous than themselves. Yet they came near being reprimanded by the Continental Congress for taking the warpath without express permission. If they had failed there might have been trouble, but all is well that ends well. So in time the state governments of Virginia and North Carolina and the central government as well gave official recognition to the leaders and men who gained one c the most momentous victories of the Revolution.

King's Mountain battle took place at a time when the American cause was looking desperate. Failure after failure had come to the American arms in the South. The engagement at Musgrove's Mill, about two months earlier, was indeed rather a victory for the whigs, some of the King's Mountain men taking part in it. While trying to harass the British the Americans fell into a trap, yet they fought off their enemy and escaped with all the prisoners they had taken. Ferguson chased them to the Blue Ridge and then sent the insolent letter which caused his ruin.

The following is the letter to General Gates, commander in the South in the latter half of 1780, and found in the North Carolina Records. It was written by Colonels Shelby, Sevier, Cleveland, Campbell, Winston, and Hampton, who asked for a trained officer to lead them.

Rutherford county, Camp near Gilbert Town,

October 4, 1780

Sir:

We have collected at this place about 1500 good men, drawn from Washington, Surry, Wilkes, Burk of North Carolina, and Washington County, Virginia, and expect to be joined in a few days by Colonel Williams of South Carolina with about a thousand more. As we have at this place called out Militia without any order from the executive of our different States, and with the view of expelling out of this part of the country the enemy, we think such a body of men worthy of your attention and would request you to send a General Officer immediately to take the command of such troops as may embody in this quarter. Our troops being Militia, and but little acquainted with discipline, we would wish him to be a gentleman of address, and be able to keep a proper discipline, without disgusting the soldiery. Every assistance in our power shall be given the Officer you may think proper to take command of us. It is the wish of such of us as are acquainted with General Davidson, and Colonel Morgan (if in service) that one of these Gentlemen may be appointed to this command.

We are in great need of ammunition, and hope you will endeavor to have us properly furnished.

Colonel McDowell will wait on you with this, who can inform you of the present situation of the enemy, and such other particulars respecting our troops as you may think necessary.

Your most obedient and very able servants,

> Benj. Cleveland
> Isaac Shelby
> John Sevier
> Andw. Hampton
> Wm. Campbell
> Jo. Winston

At the close of the very day the above letter was written, Campbell was nominated by Shelby as temporary commander, on the ground that he was the only Virginian of regimental rank. During the next two days the leaders picked out the best men with the best horses and rifles, and then took Ferguson's trail 910 strong. The men on foot and those with poor horses were told to follow.

In their rapid advance the mountain men could not spare the time to deal with a large body of tories forming to join Ferguson. Passing this force they were joined at Cowpens by 60 men from Lincoln county under Colonel Hambright. They were also joined by an equal number of South Carolina men under Major Chronicle and by a band under Colonel Williams of the same state. During thirty-six hours the riflemen never alighted but once and then at Cowpens. They had little to eat but parched corn. A persistent rain made them wrap their guns and ammunition in sacks, blankets, and even their hunting shirts. It was necessary to keep their powder dry, even though their bodies were drenched by the cold downpour. When they at length caught up with Ferguson, they went into the fight with neither rest nor refreshment.

The battle lasted only an hour. The haughty Ferguson was slain and his army wiped out of existence, though stationed on the flat summit of a low ridge.

II.

WATAUGA AND ITS RECORDS

The "Back Country" as the land beyond the Blue Ridge was styled, in the colonial days, was not colonized after the manner of the seaboard plantations.

The early settler on the Holston trailed his way hither through forest and along the watercourses, using sometimes the Indian lane and sometimes the path of the elk and the deer. When he found a spot to his liking he set up a bark shelter, or looked up a cavern or some other place of safety until he could build a log cabin.

In this way came John Hunnicut, the first white settler, and William Been, the second arrival, the former placing his cabin high on the flank of a mountain, the latter building at the mouth of Boone Creek, and in his new habitation was born his son, Russell, the first white native of Tennessee.

Next came the defiant Regulators to escape the vengeance of the royal governor of North Carolina. With them were many indented servants from the low country. They came singly, or in small groups. Virginia, South Carolina, and even Pennsylvania, were represented in this influx. Not all these people were saints, neither were all of them sinners.

The settlers of Carter Valley in Hawkins were certain they were in Virginia, yet knew they were on the lands of the Cherokees. The same opinion was held in the settlements on the Watauga and the Nollichucky. All these people lived under a government they called the Watauga Association. It was founded by Jacob Brown, who came from South Carolina and afterward fought at King's Mountain.

In 1772 the over-mountain people were designated as squatters, and were ordered to vacate. But it has never been at all easy to eject the American pioneer from land he has cleared by hard labor. This was true of the Watauga settlers. Their leaders made gifts to the Indians who agreed to let them stay if there were no further encroachment. The pleased settlers called a constitutional convention. It is significant that they adopted the laws of Virginia, although a majority of them were from the

Carolinas. Their court of five magistrates, with a sheriff
and a clerk, continued until 1775, the year in which the
American Revolution began. The Watauga Association
then transformed itself into the Washington District of
North Carolina. John Carter was made chairman of its
Committee of Safety. When news came of the Declaration of Independence, Washington District sent a petition
asking annexation to the Provincial Congress at
Halifax, North Carolina. North Carolina failed to return an answer, yet John Carter, John Sevier, Charles
Robertson, and John Hall appeared as delegates at Halifax and were accorded seats.

All the men signing the petition were frontier soldiers, and nearly all fought at King's Mountain. The
names found in the North Carolina Records are William
Been, Jacob Brown, John Carter (chairman), Zachary
Isbell, John Jones, Robert Lucas, James Robertson,
George Russell, James Smith, James Stephenson, William Tatham (clerk), and Jacob Womack.

The names following constitute the complete list.
The original, in the state archives at Raleigh, bears this
indorsement: "Received August 22, 1776."

Barley, John
Barton, Joshua, Sr.
Bates, Henry, Sr.
Bates, Henry, Jr.
Bates, William
Blair, Hugh
Bostin, Joud, Sr.
Bowyer, Lew (attorney)
Brokes, or Brooks, William
Brown, John
Brown, Joseph
Brown, Joseph (2)
Buller, Joseph
Bumper, Job
Calvit, Frederick
Calvit, Joseph
Carter, Landon
Chuckinbeard, John
Clark, William
Cooper, James
Cox, Abraham
Cox, Edward
Cox, John, Sr.
Cox, John, Jr.

Cox, William
Crockett, David
Crockett, William
Cunningham, Christo-
  pher, Sr.
Cunningham, Christo-
  pher, Jr.
Davis, John
Dedmon, Thomas
Dodd, William
Dunham, John
Dunham, Joseph
Durroon, Rice
Easley, James
Fletcher, Richard
Goodan, Drury
Greer, Alexander
Greer, Andrew
Greer, Joseph
Grimes, Joseph
Hail, John
Hawkins, Matt
Hickey, David
Hider, Michael

Hightower, Oldham
Hix, Abednego
Hodge, Ambrose
Hopson, Edward
Houghton, Joshua
Houghton, Thomas
Hughes, David
Hughes, Thomas
Hutann, George
Jones, Lewis
King, John
Luske, Joseph
McCartney, Charles
McCormick, John
Mitchell, Joab
Mitchell, Mark
Moore, John
Morris, Daniel
Morris, Gideon
Morris, Groves
Morris, Shardick
Mosely, Robert
Nave, John
Nave, Teeler

Norton, Richard
Overall, William
Pebeer, Elias
Reeves, William
Roberson, John
Roberson, William
Robertson, Elijah
Robertson, Mark
Rose, Ossa
Sevier, John
Sevier, Robert
Sevier, Valentine
Sherill, Adam
Sherill, Samuel, Sr.
Sherill, Samuel, Jr.
Shote, Emanuel
Siler, Henry
Simpson, Thomas
Tipton, Jonathan
Vaughn, Frederick
Waddell, John
Williams, Jarrett
Wilson, Isaac
Womack, Jacob

In 1777 the General Assembly of North Carolina took over Washington District, forming it into Washington county, the boundaries being coextensive with those of the present state of Tennessee. The new county was included with the Salisbury Judicial District. Courts were organized, a land office was opened, civil and military officers were appointed, and this new political division was ready for business. In the court records of 1777-80 we see again many of the names in the preceding list.

I now give the records for the years indicated, for the purpose of exhibiting the human interest in them, and the rigid justice dealt out to high and low alike. The original manuscript is in the archives of the Tennessee Historical Society. It was donated by John Allison, author of "Dropped Stitches in Tennessee History."

At a Court begun and held for the County of Washington on the 23rd February, 1778.

Present, John Carter, Chairman

John Sevier
Jacob Womack

John McMahan
Benjamin Gist

Robert Lucas	John Chisholm
And. Greer	Joseph Wilson
John Shelby	William Cobb
George Russel	James Stuart
William Been	Michael Woods
Zachariah Isbell	Richard White
John McNabb	Benjamin Wilson
Thomas Houghton	James Robertson
William Clark	Valentine Sevier

Took the oath as prescribed by Law and proceed to Business accordingly.

Adjourned till to-morrow ten o'clock.
Tuesday met according to adjournment.
John Sevier chosen clerk for the county.
Valentine Sevier, Sheriff.
James Stuart, surveyor.
John Carter, Entry-taker.
John McMahon, Register.
Jacob Womack Stray master.
Adjourned till to-morrow at nine o'clock.
Wednesday met according to adjournment.

Ord. that Amos Bird and John Smith be Jurors to attend the next Supreme Court at Salisbury.

Elijah Robertson, vs. Robert Sevier for an assualty —ordered that Robert Sevier be bound to his good behavior and enter Recognizance with two securities in the sum of ten pounds himself (and five pounds each of his security) for his good behavior for the Time and Term of Twelve Months.

William Parker and William McNabb entered themselves Robert Sevier's security for his good behavior.

Ordered that James Maulden, Josiah Hoskins, and John Higgins be appointed to assess all the taxable property lying above the Iron Mountain in this county.

Ordered that Benjamin Cobb, Soloman Smith, and William Archer be appointed to assess all the taxable property of the people.

Thursday—Ordered that John McNabb be appointed Coroner of the County. Court adjourned till court in course.

> John Carter
> John McNabb
> Mich. Woods.
> George Russell
> Benj. Wilson
> Robert Lucas

At court begun and held on the 25th day of May 1778 at the house of Charles Robertson.

Present

Richard White	Michael Woods
Jacob Womack	Joseph Wilson
Thomas Houghton	John McNabb
John Chisholm	William Clark
Benjamin Gist, Esq.	George Wilson

State vs. Zekle

Ordered that the defendant be committed to Gaol Immediately and to be Kept in custody until he can be conviently delivered to a Continental Officer.

Monday—May Court.

Wm. Aiken	Jacob Brown
Jas. Hollis	David Hughs (ab)
Amos Bird	Joseph Fowler (ab)
John Nave	Robert Shurley (ab)
Arthur Cobb	Jas. Grimes
John Dunham	Robt. Blackburn
Peter McLamee	John Clark
John Patterson (ab)	Hosea Stout
Nathaniel Clark	Andrew Bunton (ab)
Jas. Wilson	John Hoskins
Drury Godlin	Ning Hoskins
Chas. Gentry (ab)	

Grand Jurymen

Tuesday met according to adjournment.

Ordered that David Hickey be fined five pounds for insulting the Court.

Charles Robertson, Jr., entered security for paying the same at laying next par. Leasy.

Tuesday, 26th May.

Emmanuel Carter presented to the court four pounds, five shillings and four pence being the residue left of the price after deducting constable fees, and paying John Chisholm 2 lbs., 14 of a certain horse and saddle by Order of Colonel Carter belonging to Robert——who made his escape from Emmanuel Carter after being committed to Gaol on suspicion of horse stealing and said money ordered to be left in the hands of the clerk.

May court—Tuesday 26, 1778.

State vs. Jacob Brown.

Ordered that Jacob Brown give security for one hundred pounds for himself and two securities in the sum of fifty pounds each.

William Clark, Esq. and John Nave entered themselves security for the defendant's good behavior for twelve months towards the State and especially Amos Bird.

Anne Buller maid oath that attended at court in behalf of Amos Bird pltff. vs. Jacob Brown defdt. three days and supposed to be 25 miles and allowed one day for returning home.

John Shurley attended two days at court in behalf of Amos Bird plftt. and Jacob Brown defdt. supposed to be 14 miles.

On motion it is ordered that Joseph Bullar give security for his personal appearance at the next court, himself one hundred pounds and two securities in the sum of fifty pounds each. Edward Hopson and William Trimble acknowledged themselves as security.

Tuesday 26, May.

Ordered that Zeckle be discharged by the sheriff he the said ————— having enlisted in the Continental army.

James Grimes' earmark a crop in the left ear and under keel in the same, also a slit in the ear, and the same is ordered to be recorded.

Ordered that the Clerk cause the Sheriff to summons a jury or jurys to try the defendants, Cavits entered with Entry-taker and returned to the Court, and that they make a report to next court according to act of Assembly.

State vs. James Bradly.

Ordered that defdt. enter security for his appearance at next court in the sum of fifty pounds for himself and two securities in the sum of twenty-five pounds each. Thomas Price and Joseph Bullar acknowledged themselves his security.

Ordered that John Tye be summoned to appear next court vs. Shadrack Moory.

Ordered that Jas. English be summoned as witness for Shadrack Moory next court.

William Bayley Smith vs. James Smith.

Judgmt. accdg. to acct. proved. Land ordered to be sold and the accounts on James Books' condemed to use of pltff.

John Sevier vs. Richard Davis.

Attchmt. dis. pltffs cost.

State vs. Elijah ————.

It is the opinion of the court that the dfdt. be committed to the District gaol for further trial and that dfdt. be immediately confined or give sufficient security for his appearance at the next term of the Supreme Court to be held in the District of Salisbury for the sum of one thousand pounds for himself and five pounds each for security.

Thomas Price, William McNabb, Esqrs. came into court and acknowledged themselves the dfdts security for his appearance at the superior court to be held at Salisbury the 5th of September next to be levied of their goods and chattels.

Charles Robertson came in court and acknowledged the conveyance of 640 acres of land unto Matthew Talbot and the same is ordered recorded. (Matthew Talbot was a King's Mountain man, and his cabin and mill were built on Gap creek).

Charles Robertson, Esqur. came into court and acknowledged the conveyance of 115 acres of land unto Matthew Arthur and the same is ordered to be recorded.

The last will and testament of John Cox, decd., was duly proved by the oaths of Colonel Carter and Emanuel Carter, and the same to be recorded.

May 27, 1778.

Ordered that a Commission be directed to Isaac Shelby and James Montgomery Esqurs. to take the deposition of Robert Caldwell and Edmund Waring in behalf of Elijah ————.

On motion it appears that ———— and ———— and

———— did feloniously steal a certain bay gelding from Samuel Sherill Sen. Ordered if Samuel Sherill can find property of said thieves, he take the same into possession, leaving bond if the thieves come back so the court can take it over. (This Samuel Sherrill, Sr., was the father of "Bonny Kate," John Sevier's second wife.)

Court adjourns until Court in course.

> Charles Robertson
> Robert Lucas
> John McNabb
> William McNabb
> Benjamin Wilson

August Term 1778.

Present

Jacob Womack	Benjamin Gist
Joseph Wilson	John Shelly
Thomas Houghton	Mishl. Woods
Andrew Greer	Joseph Walton
William Been	Wm. McNabb
William Clark	John McNabb
Zachr. Isbell	Robt. Lucas
Benjamin Wilson	William Cobb

State vs. Shadrack Morris.

It is the opinion of the court that the defendant give security for his good behavior in the sum of two hundred pounds himself and two securities in the sum of one hundred pounds each for his good behavior for twelve months. Shadrack Morris came into Court and acknowledged himself indebted in the sum of 200 pounds. John Gibson and John Durham acknowledged themselves indebted to the sum of 100 pounds each. To be levied on their goods and chattels.

William Cocke by his Council Waightsil Avery his Attorney moved to be admitted to the office of Clerk of County Court of Washington county, which motion was rejected by the Court, knowing John Sevier was entitled to the office.

25th August, 1778.

The Sheriff returns here in court a certain declaration in the trespass and ejectment at the suit of Samuel Saveall on the demise of George Wilfong and Cathrine Adams. Against Simpleton Spendall. With a certain notice on the back of the declaration a copy whereof was served by the sheriff upon John Redding, as tenant defendant instead of the said Simpleton Spendall. Otherwise John would be turned out of possession.

On motion of Atty Waighstil Avery for John Redding. It being the opinion of the court that the suit be dismist.

On petition of Amos Gavin setting forth that he has built a grist mill on Roan creek, he the only proprietor of the land on one side of the Creek, and James Mandan owns the land on the other side, and that the said James be summoned to appear in next court to answer said petition which is commanded that the said James be summoned.

State to Moses Crawford—It is the opinion of the court that the defendant be imprisoned during the present war with Great Britain and the Sheriff take the whole of his estate into custody, which be valued by a jury at the next court, and that one half of the said estate, be kept by said Sheriff for the use of the State, and the other half be remitted to the family of the Defdt. (Crawford was one of the deserters, on the march to the battle of King's Mountain.)

640 acres of land from Charles Robertson to Joshua Houghton, proved by Thomas Houghton.

587 acres of land by Charles Robertson to Thomas Houghton, Esqur.

Samuel Tate ordered to pay 2 percent to the Chairman for insulting the Court.

States evidence—Elizabeth Shoat sworn
Edward Shoat

Dfts. Evidence—Jean Williams, Jurat.
Lidia Cross

It is the opinion of the court, John Rodgers be sent to the Supreme Court.

Motion of Samuel Tate to confirm a judgment of Washington Court of Virginia that Ann Newland should serve a certain time mend. in sd. court.

Is the opinion of the court that the said order is illegal and the said Ann Newland be set free and discharged being no longer a servant.

Samuel Tate came into court and prayed an appeal to the Supreme court, which was granted. (Samuel Tate, like Shylock, wanted his pound of flesh.)

Joshua Bolden vs. John Rice.
Verdict for the Defdt.

27th, August, 1778

Ordered that John Sevier, clerk, be admitted to take 30 lbs. for his service.

Ordered that Valentine Sevier, Sheriff, be allowed for his exofficio services the sum of 50 lbs.

Ordered the John Sevier be pd. 60 lbs. for his exofficio services for the year of 1778.

Ordered that William Ward be allowed 30 lbs for summoning 26 people to give an inventory of their estates.

Ordered Emanuel Carter 3 lbs for summoning 40 to appear.

Ordered Samuel Lyle, 4 lbs. for summoning 60 to appear.

Ordered John Smith, 4 lbs for summoning 65 to appear.

State vs. Henry Box.

Opinion of the court that Henry Box be discharged.

Ephraim Dunlap motion to send Isaac Butler to the Continental army to serve three years or during the war.

On hearing the facts the court ordered Isaac Butler to be jailed until they could deliver him to a Continental Officer.

The court had Clark to certify that Ephraim Dunlap was a gentleman of honesty, probity, good behavior, and well qualified to act as an atto.

Aug. 27, 1778.

Benjamin Rodgers vs. Peter Ford.

Caveat returned by the Sheriff, settled and agreed. All fees paid. Val Sevier, Abraham Sevier, Julius Robinson, Zachriah White, Dempsey Ward, Andrew Thompson, Gideon Morris, Robert Sevier, Jermiah Duncan, came into court and took the oath of Allegiance.

Ordered that the sheriff make the sale of six head of Creatures taken by John Sevier from Joseph Box called the property of Zekiah Collins, wheel right, and make return of money arising from the sale thereof to the Treasurer.

Isaac Buller was ordered to apprehend two deserters, Joshua Williams and a certain Dyer.

320 acres of land from John Moore to Cleaver Barksill, and the same to be recorded.

Joshua Buller, by his council Waightsil Avery being before the court moved to be discharged from comitment of Michael Woods and William Clark, Esqurs; Justices of the peace to the Goals of the said county in order to be turned over to the Continental Service for three years or during the war.

Upon the information of facts, the court is of the opinion that Joseph Buller ought to be discharged, and he is therefore here discharged.

Aug. 26, 1778.

Ordered that Amos Bird and John Smith to attend the next supreme court as Jurymen.

Ord. that Margaret White an Orphan girl be bound unto Baptist McNabb until the said girl comes to the age of 18, he the said Baptist conforming to the laws maid and provided for the same.

Controversy between Robert Young and Evan Shelby defendant should not be received.

Michael Hider vs in law Amos Bird.

The jury find for the plaintiff—Warrant issued accordingly. My fees paid.

Bartley Hinson vs Caveat on land Robert Patterson. The jury for the plaintiff. Ord. that warrant issue.

McNabb vs. Z. White

Motion ord. that a commission issue to Andrew Greer and John Shelby, Esq. to take the disposition of Elias Lane on behalf of Zachary White that the same be given in the above suit.

State vs. Moses Crawford.

A summons from under the hand of Wm. Clarke, Esq. one of the Justices of peace for said county requiring Moses Crawford to appear before this court the first day of the present setting thereof and take the oath of Allegiance to this State is returned into court here by John Smith Constable executed on the said Crawford. The said Moses Crawford shall be permitted to remain within the State and that the said Moses for the offense aforesaid hath incurred the penalties that shall be subject to all the disa. in such case enacted and provided in the 9th section of an act entitled an act of the General Assembly of the State of North Carolina declaring what crime and practices vs. the State shall be Treason or Misprison for Treason and providing punishment adequate to crimes of both Classes and for preventing the dangers that may arise from persons disaffected to the State.

James Daniel vs. Evan Shelby.

Verdict for Shelby. Ord. that warrant be issued accordingly.

The State vs. John Rodgers.

Defend. brought for trial and upon the trial pleads not guilty.

Ord. that the sheriff summon Amos Bird, John Clark, Isaac Johnson, Danl. Kennedy, Wm. Trimble, Francis Hughes, John Nave, Joseph English, Adam Wilson, John Russell, Pharoah Cobb, Benj. Cobb, Josiah Hoskins, Philip Shelly, John Hoskins, Solomon Smith, Samuel Henry, Jonas and Little to serve on the Grand Jury at our next term of court.

Christopher Cunningham came into court and took the oath of Allegiance.

Joseph Denton, David Hickey, Michael Hider came in court and took the oath of Allegiance.

Michael Hider by his att. Luke Bowyer prayed a continuance of his suit vs. Amos Bird until next court. Granted.

James Denton had the earmarks of his cattle recorded.

Ord. that Thomas Price and William Blevins be sumd. to appear at next term of court to prove the convey. of the Watagua Purchase to Charles Robertson on behalf of the people living thereon.

Christopher Cunningham was indebted to the court for 100 lbs. to appear as witness for the State vs Elijah Robertson in behalf of the State. (Elijah Robertson was up for being inimical to the State.)

Joseph Tipton, Charles Robertson (Buffalo) Hugh Henry, Jno. Hughs, Saml. Denton, Geo. Little, Jas. Denton, John Cunningham, Thom. Little, John Brown, Sr., John Brown, Jr., William Reeves, Jacob Chamberlain, Gorden Reeves, came in court and took the oath of Allegiance to the State.

November Term, 1778. Met at the dwelling house of Matthew Talbert.

Present

John Carter, Chairman.

Charles Robertson	Joseph Wilson
John McNabb	William McNabb
Thomas Houghton	William Clark
James Stuart	Benjamin Gist

The first business was to admit Ephraim Dunlap to practice law in this court, he producing his licence signed by Samuel Spencer and Samuel Ashe, Chief Justice for the state.

Ord. Jacob Womack, Jesse Walton, Geo. Russell, Joseph Willson, Zach. Isbell, and Benjamin Gist appointed to lay off the place for erecting the Court house, prison stocks, and the said return is ord. filed in the court office.

Michael Bacon and James Pearce leave to build mills on Limestone creek, but they both to build on their own land.

William McNabb, stray msater.

John Brown sold 358 acres to Humphrey Gibson.

Ord. that Pheba Collins have three creatures returned to her that was ord. by the court to be sold by the Sheriff, the creatures supposed to belong to Hezekiah Collins.

Ord. that Betsy Fauling and John Chisam Esq. have leave of administration on the estate of William Fauling, Decd. they first giving bond.

Danl. Kennedy, John Nave, Benja. Cobb, Solomon Smith, Saml. Henry, Jonas Little, Caleb Odull, Jas. Hollis, Ed Smith, Hum. Gibson, Jas. Pearce, John Moore, Matt Little, Jas. Mauldin, Julius Robertson, James Henry, and William Asher Jurymen.

Ord. that Hump. Gibson be fined 10 lbs. for swearing in court.

Ord. Amos Bird, John Clark, Francis Hughes, Joseph English, Adam Wilson, Pharoah Cobb, Josiah Hoskins, Phillip Shelly, and John Hoskins be fined accord. to law for not attending the Grand Jury.

24th Nov. 1778.

Present

Jas. Wilson, Benjam. Gist, James Stuart, John Mc-

Mahon, Wm. Clark, Thomas Houghton, Jesse Walton, Charles Robertson, Wm. and John McNabb.

Jacob Brown sold 400 acres of land to Peter Mc-Name. recorded.

Jacob Brown sold 663 acres of land to Wm. Ritchey recorded.

Charles Robertson, 340 acres of land to John Mc-Mahon, recorded.

Jacob Brown, 370 acres of land to Wm. Clark, recorded.

Jacob Brown, 80 acres to Wm. Clark.

Jacob Brown, 669 acres to Emanuel Carter recorded.

Jacob Brown, 350 acres to Isaac Wilson, recorded.

Ann Choate admr. of Thomas Choate entered Exekl. Smith, Jas. Hollis, and Robert Sevier her security to the sum of 3000 lbs.

County of Tryon did. postm. to two Justices of peace take the disposition of Danl. Shipman and Jacob Shipman, in behalf of John Robertson defdt, in a suit with Peter McLane, plttf. on a caveat.

Ord. Joel Callahan serve as Constable. (He was one of John Sevier's captains in the King's Mountain battle.)

Ord. Davis Fain serve as constable.

Ord. Nathl. Clark serve as constable.

Caleb Hunter—Prin. Recog. 200 lbs.

Ashel Rawlings Security each 100 lbs.

Wm. Hitchie.

Void on condition that sd Caleb Hunter makes his appearance at the next term of court and not depart without leave.

State vs. John Gibson, Pleads not guilty.

Emanl. Carter and Austin Choate witness for the State—sworn. The court on hearing the facts ordered his appearance at the next term of court in the sum of 250 lbs. and two security 125 lbs. each.

Ed Rice and Jesse Bonds goes his security. Void if John Gibson makes his personal appearance at next court, and not depart without leave.

25th Nov. Jacob Brown, 220 acres of land to Wm. Nelson, recorded.

And 389 acres to same.

And 460 acres to Elijah Nelson.

Ord. that Richard Woolidge pay the sum of 20 lbs. for not doing his duty in taking care of James Mauldin, who was committed to his charge as constable.

Ord. that Benjm. Cobb fined 31 lbs. for not attending the G. Jury.

Ord. the Ded. potestatem to 2 justice in the State of South Carolina, to take depo. of Solomon in behalf of John Gilliland in a suit on a caveat John Shurley pltff. Jno. Gilliland defdt.

Jacob Brown 300 acres of land to John Heoms, and 202 acres to Cornealius O'Neal, and 673 acres to John Woods, and 182 acres to Moses Crawford and ord. recd.

Henry Lyles 376 acres to Joshua Houghton, Charles Robertson, 376 acres to Henry Lyles.

Michl. Woods received 182 from Moses Crawford.

Court Adjourns.

26, Nov. 1778.

Present the Worshipful

Jesse Walton, Wm. Clark, Michl. Woods, Thomas Houghton, Wm. McNabb, Rich. White Esqrs.

John Carter, Esq., Chairman

Jacob Brown proved by the oath of John Smith the conveyance of 3 certain Tracts of Territorys of land as in the deed prescribed conveyed to Brown by Oconostoto, the Tennessee warrior, Breed Slave Catcher, Artacullacullah, and Chenastoy, Chiefs of the Cherokee Nation and same is ord. recorded.

Road be laid from forks of Indian creek to or near Jacob Brown, John Nave, and Robert Young. (Robert Young shot Ferguson on King's Mountain.)

Jonathan Douglas vs. Jemima Chancy.

Emanl. Carter, Valentine Sevier witness for pltff.

Henry Lyle, Jas. Hollis, Hump Gibson, Joseph Duncan, Jos. Bullar, Nathl. Clark, Chris Cunningham, John Gilliland, Wm. Nelson, Chris Cunningham, Jr., Jas. Melican and Robert Young jurymen.

We of the jury do find for the plttf twenty pounds dam: Nathl. Clarke foreman.

Baptist McNabb vs. Zachariah White, debt.

Non Suit.

Ord. that Eph. Dunlap be fined 5 dollars for insulting the court, especially Richard White.

David McNabb vs. Andrew Greer, debt.

Judg., for 41 lbs. 13 sh. 4 pence according to acct. filed.

Adjourn.

27th Court met.

Present the Worshipful
John Carter, Chairman

Thos. Houghton, Wm. McNabb, Chris. Cunningham, Michael Woods, Esqrs.

Ord. John Sevier be appointed Trustee for the county.

Robert Young vs. Evan Shelby, Caveat.

The jury make return that a certain Big spring Run ought to be the line and that the survey run a paralell line with sd. spring Run, and it is consid. that ord be issued accord.

Ord. that Richd. Willson, Isaac Johnson, Thomas Gillespie, David McCord, Jesse Been, John Trimble, Samuel Culberson, Michael Bacon, John B. McMahon, John Gillaland, Jas. Stinson be summoned for next court as jury.

Valentine Sevier Entd. himself, Jno. Carter, and Charles Robertson, his security, in the sum of three thousand pounds for his faithful discharge of the public monies that may be delivered into his hands from the different Tax Gatherers for the year of 1778.

John Sevier Entd. himself with John Carter and Charles Robertson his security in the sum of one thousand pounds for his faithful discharge as County Trustee.

Cleavers Barksdale, Deputy Sheriff for the county.

Charles Robertson overseer of road from Little Ford on the Holston to Matthew Talbert's on the Watagua.

(Part of the 1779 Record missing at this point.)

Monday, Feb. 22, 1779.

Thomas Jonathan, had his ear mark on his crops record.

Joseph Tipton, 445 acres of land to Robert Young, record.

Charles Robertson, 487 acres to Robert Young, record.

Chas. Robertson, 400 acres to John Been, record.

Matthew Talbert, Jacob Brown, Jno. Stuart, Wm. Trimble, Isaiah Hamilton, Robert Young, Jr., Samuel and Adam Sherrell, Robert Cullwell, Jas. Grimes, Joseph Tipton Chris. Taylor Robert Blackburn, Wm. Nelson, Nathl. Clark, and John Nave jurymen.

Sworn.

On petition of Michl. Bacon setting forth that three children, to-wit: a boy named Charles Hill, aged 6 years, a girl named ————Craft aged 9 years and a boy named Achilles Craft were orphan children and desired that the girl and the youngest boy should be bound to himself and the oldest bound to some tradesman.

The court have considered that Michl. Bacon keep sd. two youngest children, in his possn. and that sd Michl. also take the oldest boy who is now out of his custody at this time into his custody also.

Ord. Stephen ———— a deserter be confined and sent to District Goal of Salisbury or delivered to some Continental officer.

Uriah Hunt fined for insulting the court.

State vs. John Holley Sr. on tryal for being inimical to the common cause pleads not guilty.

Sam. Matthews, Dicey Matthews, Caleb Hunter witness for the State.

The court on hearing the facts and the testimony of the witness it is of the opinion of the court that dfdt. be sent to the superior court for further trial.

Tuesday 23, Feb. 1779.

State vs. George Lewis for treason vs. the State, Wm. Williams, Elizabeth English witness for the State, sworn.

On hearing the facts and considering the testimony of the witness, it is the opinion of the court that dfdt. be sent to District Goal, it appears to the court that sd. Lewis is a spie or an officer from Florida out of the English Army.

State vs. John Holley, Jr., for treason, Caleb Hunter witness for the State. It is the opinion that the dfdt. is not guilty, and is ord. discharged.

State vs. Jonathan Holley for treason, on hearing the facts the court ord. discharge of Holley.

State vs. Thomas Barker for treason. On hearing the facts the court ord. discharges.

State vs. Alexr. Choatwood for treason, the court ord. his discharge.

State vs. William Bryant for treason, the court ord. his discharge.

State vs. Francis Holley for treason, the court ord. his discharge.

Robert Cullwell fined for insulting the coutt.

Ord. that the negroes now in the possession of Adam Wilson, Esq., the property of John Holley, Sr., be delivered to the wife of John Holley, Sr. In case she gives bond and sufficient security to the sum of 5000 pounds for her safe keeping and delivering the negroes and other personal property of John Holley whenever demanded by proper authority in behalf of the State of North Carolina. Otherwise the Sheriff take the negroes and other personal property into his possession.

John Holley, Thomas Barker, William Storey, Jonathan Holley, and John McMahin go the security of 5000 for Rebecca Holley.

Ord. Rich. Willson serve as constable.

Ord. John Redding serve as constable.

Wm. McNabb to Elijah Robertson 206 acres of land so recorded.

Ord. Joel Callahan be summed to appear in next court to show why a fine of 10 lb. shall not be award for refusing to serve as constable.

Charles Robertson, 420 acres to William Been, recorded.

Charles Robertson, to 560 acres to William Been, recorded.

George Lumkins sold Jo a negro fellow 20 years and Dianah a negro wench, and same is recorded.

Rob. Shurley, fined for insulting the court.

R. Culwell fined for insulting the court.

Court adjourned.

Court Met 24 day

Present John Carter, Chairman; Ben Willson, Andrew Greer, John McNabb, Thomas Houghton, Jesse Walton Esqrs.

State vs. Moses Crawford, Treason.

James Greeleem Chas. Adkins, John Smith, State witness. Sworn.

The court on hearing the facts and the testimony of witness prd. Moses Crawford to the Goal for further tryal.

The above ordered vs. Crawford Reed.

Chas. Robertson, to Chris. Cunningham land, also four others, of 530, 300, 640, 390 acres to Rob. Lucas and 300 acres to Edw. Lucas.

On motion of Moses Crawford by his council L. Bowyer that the order for sending Crawford to the Salisbury Goal be reconsidered and Moses be discharged on taking the State Oath, and giving bond and security in the sum of 10,000 lbs. The court on condg. the case do permit sd. Moses to remain and be discharged, he giving such bond and taking the Oath. John Russell, John Redding, John Smith, Robt. Cullwell, John Stuart, Aron B——son and William Story jointly go Moses Crawford's security.

Void on condition that Moses Crawford be of peaceable and good behavior in all cases especially toward the good and safety of the Independant State of North Carolina, also United States of America. Moses Crawford took the oath of allegiance to the State of North Carolina, and is so recorded.

Thursday, 25.

Valentine Sevier, Jr., 360 acres of land to Valentine Sevier, Sr., recorded. Peter McName came in court and gave the names of delinquents in taxes. Robert Cullwell fined for insulting the court.

On motion of John Holly by his council Ephm. Dunlap that he be requitted from being sent to the Salisbury Goal for Treason on his giving bond for twenty thousand pounds with security, for good behavior in all cases whatsoever. The Court is of the opinion that Holley may ————and be discharged he giving bail accordingly.

John Clark, Robt. Cullwell, Isaiah Hamilton, James Moore, and Jonathan Holley jointly go Holley's bail. Void on condition John Holley be of good and peaceable behavior in all cases whatever, especially towards the good and safety of the State of North Carolina, also Independent States of America.

(He does not take the Oath of Allegiance, and later his bondmen give him up and he is sentenced to the Goal for a year, and his estate was confiscated. He was not a Tory, but stood for a principle as he saw it.)

Amos Bird vs. Michael Hider in land dispute the Court ordered that Bird and Hider have their land resurveyed.

Wm. Brockus vs. Wm. Fauling, Henry Hickey, Jesse Been and Elizabeth Craig were witness.

Wm. Ward and Joseph Tipton were summoned for not serving as constables.

Thomas Young and Evan Edwards to serve as constables.

Jacob Brown, 176 acres to James Grimes.

Joseph Bullar to Michael Bacon 143 acres of land.

Valentine Sevier vs. Isaac Ruddell attachment, judg. and orde to acct. proved. 58 lbs.

State vs. Andrew Greer.

John Carter and Robert Lanier. On attachment.
It is the opinion of the court the attachment is illegal and ought not to lye.

Court, 24th day of May, 1779.

Present the Worshipful: John Carter, Charles Robertson, John McNabb, Geo. Russell, Rob Lucas, Thos. Houghton, Benj. Gist, Jas. Stuart, Wm. McNabb, Wm. Cobb, Valentine Sevier appointed Sheriff.

The last will and Testament of Rebecca Vandepool was proven by Thos. Houghton, and James Grissome, and the same recorded..

Thomas Hardeman has his mark for creatures recorded.

Teter Nave have leave to administrative on the estate of Abraham Vanderpool, give bond and security for the same.

Tuesday, 25 May, 1779.

Charles Robertson, 400 acres to William Sharp, recorded.

Charles Robertson, 480 acres to Garrett Fitzgerald.

State vs. Dick, Stealing a bell.

Defdt. pleads not guilty.

Wm. Thornton witness for the State.

Ben Dick gives security for appearance at court, 500 lbs. Robert Bayley and Chas. England were the securities.

Benj. Holley, High Treason, Jesse Walton and Jesse Bond witness for the State.

Ord. that John Murphy be fined the sum of twenty pounds for ill treatment of his father, Patrick Murphy.

Ord. that Patrick Murphy be fined for 20 lbs., for insulting Zachariah Isbell a member sitting on the bench.

State vs. Patrick Murphy for stealing two hogs the property of Zach Isbell and Thomas Evans. Jas. Crawford and Wm. Murphy witness for the State, John Smith, Richard Travillian and John Redding witness for Murphy. Sworn. The Court ord. that Murphy pay to Zach Isbell for his hog 26 lbs., and for Evans hog 10 lbs. and receive on his bare back well laid on by the Sheriff, 20 lashes.

Matthew Talbert, Jr., was made Deputy surveyor under Jas. Stuart, Esq.

Wednesday, 26.

Present the Worshipful, Jesse Walton, Zach. Isbell, Wm. Clark, John McNabb, John Chisholm.

James Jones and Thomas Young appointed constables.

Court ord. John Bond do keep and take care of George and Mary Bond, orphans, until properly bound to him as prescribed by law.

Ord. that the depo of George Kilham in county of Burke be taken in behalf of John Nave in suit with James Greelee.

Ord. that the depo. of John Colter of Washington county, Virginia be taken in behalf of John Nave in suit against John Clark.

Ord. Jas. Roddy, Ligh Hoskins and Jesse Hoskins assess taxable property lying above Iron Mountain and return to Richard White.

Ord. Matt Talbert Sr., Andrew Taylor, Clevers Barksdell assess below the Iron Mountain including the waters of Brush creek and Watagua, and also on the N. of Watagua make returns to Thomas Houghton.

Ord. that Wm. Been, Jr., Jarrett Fitzgerald, Pharoah Cobb assess all below Iron Mountain as far as the Big Limestone, extending as far North as Browns line, and make returns to William Cobb.

Ord. Jacob Brown, John Woods, Jonathan Tipton assess all below Iron Mountain as far as the Big Limestone, extending as far North as Browns line, and make returns to Wm. Clark.

Ord. that Henry Earnest, Sealy Rawlings, and Samuel Lyles assess all below Big Limestone on the North side of Chucky, and all below John Sevier's Mill Creek on North side of Nolachucky, and make return to Jos. Willson, Esq.

Ord. that John Robertson, Bradley Gambril, James Abbott and Valentine Little, serve as constable.

Court adjourned.

Thurs. 27

David Robertson vs. Barnabas Anderson, Cavit.

Jury find for the Dftd. Ord issue accdly.

Garrot Fitzgerald vs. Thomas Titsworth, Cavit agreed.

Martin Armstrong vs. John Caviack. Dis. by order of pltff.

David Robertson vs. Wm. Ritche. Cavit jury find for pltff. The court ordered a new tryal.

William Nelson vs. Samuel Handly. Cavit Jury find for Pltff. Ord. issue accdgly.

Edward Hughes vs. James Grimes, cavit Dismd by ord. of pltff.

Daniel Keith vs. David Fain, Cavit jury find for pltff.

John Gilahan vs. Charles McCartney, cavit Dismisd. by ord. of pltff. All my fees paid.

Alexr. Duglass vs. Jacob Vance, cavit jury find for pltff.

John Nave vs. John Clark, cavit jury find spl. verdict cond for pltff.

Nathl. Clark vs. John Stuart, cavit jury find for pltff.

James McCord vs. Wm. Ritchee. Cavit jury find for pltff. The dfdt. pleads for new tryal, court decided with the jury.

John Shurley vs. John Gilliland, cavit jury find for pltff ord acco.

William Story vs. Henry Massingill, cavit jury find for pltff.

William Ritchee prays an appeal to the Superior court in his suit with McCord on a cavit. Court granted the appeal.

Joseph Fowler serves as a constable.

Charles Robertson, 240 acres of land to Christopher Cunningham—if not entered before.

Wm. Ritchee proved his earmark for cattle. Recorded.

Ord. take the depo. of David Looney and Jas. McCain on behalf of Peter Huffman, defdt. in a suit with William Cocke, on a cavit.

John Dunham vs. John Colter, cavit jury find for the pltff ord. issues accdg.

John Holley vs. Richard Travillian, cavit jury find for the pltff. rd. issue accdg.

James Charters vs. Jacob Womack, cavit Agd. by ord. of pltff.

Philip Mulky vs. Wm. Cobb. Cavit agreed by ord. of pltff.

Jacob Vance vs. Jas. Moore, cavit Dis. by order of pltff.

Wm. Thornton vs. David Huckky, cavit jury find for pltff.

Charles Duncan vs. Samuel Fain, jury find for pltff ord. issue accdgly.

Elija Robertson to appear in court. John Gilliland his security.

Elisha Bauding to appear in court, Wm. Flanary and Jas. Wray his security.

Ord. that James Millican be fined 24 lb. for insulting the court.

On petition of Joseph Campbell it is ord. that he be discharged from payment of any public or county tax.

Robert Bayley came in court and delivered Ben Duke Middleton who he was security for the last court, and B. Middleton is brought into custody.

James Hollis came in court and proved by his oath with an acct. of 28 lb; 13 sh. 4 p. against the estate of Wm. Rauling decd.

Samuel Tate Prin. in the sum of 1000 lb. Robert Sevier and James Wray his security. Void on condition that Tate makes his personal appearance in our next court to answer such things as shall there and then be objected against him.

Samuel Henry vs. Andrew Greer. Debt on Inqy.

Jas. Hollis, Thomas Gillespie, Peter McName, John Casady, Wm. Ritchey, Joseph Duncan, Christ Taylor, John Dunham, Bednego Inman, Jonathan Edwards, Charles Gentry, jurymen.

Jury find for the plaintiff 58 ℔, 14 sh., 9 p.

Andrew Greer vs. David Josb. Cavit—The court orders a new tryal.

Andrew Taylor vs. John McNabb. Cavit jury find for pltff orders to issue accdg.

John Dunham vs. Abel Lanham, cavit jury find for the pltff.

George Wilfong, Admr. vs. John Clark. Cavit jury find for the pltff. Court orders that orders for warrant issue accdg.

John Clark came into court and prayed for an appeal for his suit George Wilfong vs. him on a cavit which appeal was granted.

George Wilfong was Admr. of Philip Adams decd.

Court adjourn.

26th. Present, John Carter Cha., Charles Robertson, And. Greer, Thomas Houghton, Wm. Clark, Geo. Russell, Zach. White.

Ord. that the sheriff collect from William Moore four fold, his taxable property being appraised by best information that John Woods, Jacob Brown, and Jonathan Tipton Assessors could get to the sum of Eight thousand pounds.

Andrew Greer vs. Howel Doddy. Cavit Jury find for Defdt.

Wm. Cocke vs. Peter Hufman. Cavit jury find for defdt.

Philip Mulcky vs. Pharoah Cobb. Cavit Disd. by order of pltff.

Ord. that the sheriff take and receive 8 dollars per day on juries on Cavits. Also 8 shillings for each juryman that he shall summon also each juryman shall and may be entitled to receive 32 shillings per day for his attendance to try such cavits.

Andrew Taylor vs. John McNabb. Cavit jury find for pltff. Defdt. pleads for a new tryal. The court on considering the case order a new tryal.

Ord. that the Sheriff seize all the property of Jacob and Benjamin Holley, and also the property of George Underwood.

Ord. that the Sheriff seize all the property of Isham Yearly.

Ord. that a depo. of Colonel Charles McDowell on behalf of John McNabb Esq. Defdt. in a suit with Andrew Taylor.

Wm. Ward proved he worked 4 days as constable.

John Sevier, Jesse Walton, Zachariah Isbell entered in recognizance to the Governor with Valentine Sevier, Andrew Greer and Charles Robertson Esqr. their security in the sum of two hundred and fifty thousand pounds for faithful discharge as commissioners of confiscated estates.

Aug. 1779.

Justice Joseph Wilson, Benj. Gist, Michl. Woods, Wm. Been, Chas. Robertson, Jesse Walton, John Chisholm, Thomas Houghton, Esqrs.

Spruce McCay, Esq., moved to this court that he might be admitted as an attorney to practice the law in this court. The court admitted Spruce McCay after he produced his license from Hon. Sam Ashe.

David Hughes vs. Lazarus Cotton ,Attamt.

William Trimble vs. Eduard Hogan, Attach.

Henry Earnest proved his earmarks and was recorded.

Ord. that John McFarling have leave to Admin. on the estate of James Richardson.

Tuesday morning.

John Carter, Cha., Jos. Willson, Benjm. Gist, John McNabb, Wm. Clark, and Zach. Isbell.

Ord. that Adam Willson, Robert Willson, Jas. Stinson, Jos. Gist, and James Rodgers appointed to lay off a road most convenient and best way from the court house of Washington down to Benj. Gist, and make return at our next court. Charles Robertson, 300 acres of land to William Sharp, and 600 acres to the same.

Ord. that Robert Sevier be admitted to keep an ordinary in this county at the court house.

Wm. Cobb, Joseph Willson, Thomas Houghton, make a report of taxable property. Robert Lusk to appear in court, Samuel Lyle and Wm. Thornton his security.

Jonathan Edwards vs. David Stoderd, the deft. is discharged.

State vs. George Dayley. The sd. George called and failing to appear the court therefore ord. that Scire of Facious issue vs him returnable next term of court.

Ord. that Andrew Greer open a road from Col. Sevier's on the Watagua to within 2 miles of Solomon Smith. Edward Smith open a road from Double Creek to Ning Hoskins. End of August term, 1779.

Nov. 22, 1779.

Present: John McNabb, Benj. Gist, and John McMahon.

Ord. that Matthew Talbert, Jonathan Tipton, Francis Hughes, William Ritchey, Samuel Williams, Andrew Taylor, James Stinson, Godfrey Isbell be summoned to show cause why they did not attend the Grand Jury acco to summons.

George Webb, 580 acres of land from Shad Morris.

George Webb, 480 acres of land from Benjamin Pyburn and Mico proved by oath of David Webb.

James English to erect a grist mill on his place.

Jacob Dyck ord. into the custody of the sheriff.

Wm. Marlin proved his ear mark recorded.

William Richard Davie Esq. produced license from the Hon. Samuel Ashe and John William empowering to practice in several counties in this State, he is permitted to practice and plead in this court.

Charles Robertson, 580 acres of land to Shadrack Morriss.

Jacob Dyck appeared and is discharged from his recognizance.

George Vinson, Hugh Fulton, and Isaac Taylor appointed surveyors.

Benj. Cobb, Solomon Smith, John Higgons, Josiah Hoskins, James Mauldin allowed 4 dollars a day for assessing 1778.

Fauling Admr. vs. Brocken. Jury, Peter McCaine, Zach Dillinham, Quilla Lane, Samuel Williams, John Gillaland, James Stinson, James Hollis, Jonathan Tipton, John Clark, Wm. Ritchey, Daniel Henderson, James Romine. The jury finds 2000 lb. damages.

John Nave vs. John Clark the jury finds no damages.

John Webb vs. Wm. Cobb. Cavit continued to May court.

Ord. Robert Young to open a road from court house to Robert Young's place. Ord. Wm. and John Moore, John Ritchey open a road from Burke's line to the head of Buffalo creek.

(This ends the 1779 records, and I give 1780 until the last before the King's Mountain battle.)

February Term, 1780

At a court begun and held at the court house February, 1780. Present the Worshipful John Carter, Cha., And Greer, Thomas Houghton, John McNabb, Charles Robertson, Joseph Willson and William Been.

On motion that John Carter should resign his office as Entry Taker. The court have taken the same under consideration and do receive the resignation. The court appoints Landon Carter Entry-taker. His securities were John Sevier, William Cocke, Charles Robertson and John Carter.

Sarah Cullwell have leave to administering the estate of Robert Cullwell Decd. Andrew Greer and Charles Robertson her security.

William Cocke is given license to practice and plead in this court.

Ord. if Joseph Buller does not build a mill on his land on Limestone within the time limited, William Hutton shall have leave to build a mill on his land on Limestone.

Ord. William Been build a mill on Boone Creek.

Jacob Fitzgerald, Pharoah Cobb, Valentine Little, made oath how many days they served in assessing.

Ord. that the clerk certify that Thomas Hardiman is a person of good character.

Charles Robertson, 640 acres to Jarrett Fitzgerald.

Ord. Druary Goodin be appointed guardian of William Hardin.

May Term 1780

Present, the Worshipful John McNabb, Joseph Willson, George Russell, Jesse Walton.

Ord. that Joseph English, Thomas Gillaspy and Thomas Davis be appointed to appraise the Estate of Robert Culwell Decd. and return report to court.

The Last Will and Testament of Joab Mitchell, Decd.

was proven by oath of John Colter, Richard Mitchell, and James Colter, and the same is ord. to be recorded.

Ord. that Mary Mitchell have leave of administration on the Estate of Joab Mitchell. Mark Mitchell and George Russell her security.

The court have appointed Wm. Been, Thomas Hardiman and George Russell to appraise Joab Mitchell Estate.

Samuel Weaver came in court and voluntarily confest that he had been in the English army in several engagements against the Americans during his stay with the enemy, etc. The Court taken the same in consideration do order Samuel Weaver be sent to the superior court for further tryal.

Isom Yearly came into court and confest that he had been inimical to the common cause of Liberty. The court orders him sent to the Superior Court for tryal.

A power of attorney from John Maglohlin to Moses Linville was proven by the oath of Joseph Willson, Esq.

A bill of sale from Joseph Fowler to David Blackwell for Ten head of hogs.

Agnes Woods have leave of administration on the estate of John Woods. David Hughes and Peter McName her security.

John Hamilton, John Nave, Peter McName, Saml. Williams, Christ Cunningham, Asel Rawlings, Christo. Taylor, John Delaney, Francis Hamilton, Simon Bundy, Matthew Talbert, William Campbell, Joseph Bullard, Robert Gentry, Grand Jurymen, sworn and charged. Matthew Talbert Foreman.

Thomas Brandon appointed Constable to serve jury.

State vs. William Nelson. For passing Counterfeit money. John Ritchey, James Elliott, Robert Gentry, and Chris. Cunningham witness. The court on considering the case sent him on to the Superior Court for tryal.

Ord. that James Stuart have leave to build a grist mill on his entry land on Little Limestone, adjoining the entry land of David Hughes, and the same to be a public mill.

James English vs. Aron Pinson. Case. Robert Lusk, Henry Nave, Jacob Brown, John Waddle, Isaiah Martin, Thos. Talbert, Joshua Green, Hugh Henry, Moses Moore, Adam Willson, Henry Massingill, James McAdams sworn. The suit dis. by the plaintiff.

Wm. Nelson Prin. 20,000 lbs., Robert Sevier, John Chisolm, and John Waddle his security in the sum of 10,000 lbs. each.   Void on condition the Prin. appear at the next term of Superior court.

William Cocke vs. Peter McName. Debt. The jury find for plaintiff and assess damages four hundred pounds and six pence costs from which judgement the defdt. appeals.

Samuel Weaver, Jr., Prin., for the sum of 10,000 lbs. Samuel Weaver, Sr., John Bullard, Joseph Nation are his security for 5,000 lbs. each on condition Sam Weaver, Jr., appear at the next Superior court.

Isam Irby given bail for security of twenty thousand pounds with two security, Peter McName, John Ritchey, Benjamin Inman are witness for McName.

Wed. 24.

Present the Worshipful Thos. Houghton, And Greer, Benj. Gist, John McNabb, Wm. Clark and Zachariah Isbell.

Ord. that Thomas Brandon be sumd. to appear at the next court to show why he did not serve as constable to Grand jury.

Valentine Sevier vs. George Dayley. Debt. A jury to-wit: Davis Job, Jas Wray, William McAdoo, Martin Maney, Julius Roberts, Jacob Brown, Jonathan Tipton, Samuel Tate, Robt. Lusk, John Jones, William Cox, Hosea Rose, Sworn. The Jury assess two hundred pounds damages and six pence costs.

The State vs. Mary Greer. Indictmt. Capias to issue, defdt. (Issued.)

Thomas Early vs. Thomas Lott and Elza Robertson. Debt. The jury on the aforesaid tryal—Dismst by plaintiff.

The State vs. Samuel Tate. Indictment true bill and defdt gave bail for appearance next court.

State vs. William McAdoo. Indictment. True Bill Capias to issue defdt—Issued.

The State vs. James Delaney. Indictment Not a true Bill.

Ord. that James Roddy, John Diggons, and Richard Willson be appointed assessors of the Roane District, and that Andrew Willson be appointed constable to warn the inhabitants, and Richard White be appointed to receive the inventory of the same.

Ord. that John Shelby esq. be appointed to receive the inventorys of the taxable property of Captains Mc-Nabb, Val. Sevier company that Saml. Culberson, Robt. McFee, Ralph Humphreys be appointed assessors for the same, also Eml. Carter be appointed constable to notify people.

Ord. that George Russell esq. be appointed to receive the inventorys of the taxable property of Captain Been's company, and that Thomas Hardiman, John Russell, and Arthur Cobb assess the same, and that Bradley Gambrill be constable to notify people.

Ord. that Jesse Walton esq. be appointed to receive the inventorys of the Taxable property belonging to Captain Brown, William Isbell and Patterson's company, that John Nave, Alexander Moore, William Murphy be assessors, and that John Bond be appointed to notify people

Ord. that Joseph Willson esq. be appointed to take the inventorys of the Taxable property within the companys of Trimble, Willson, Gest, Stinson, Davies, that Samuel Moore, John Alexander, and Adam Willson be the assessors and that Thomas Brandon be the constable to notify the people.

Ord. that the inventory of the estate of William Moore now be given in to the Clerk by Jacob Brown, Jonathan Tipton and John Woods assessors, should be received, and that the Clerk shall give instructions to the Sheriff to collect to the amount of the sum that shall be found to be Due on the same and no more.

Elisha Baulding appeared and was discharged by proclamation.

Valentine Sevier appointed Sheriff for the year.

Valentine Sevier, Sheriff, is allowed for his service for the year of 1779 the sum of one thousand pounds.

John Sevier, Clerk, is allowed for his service for the year of 1779 the sum of seven hundred pounds.

The State vs. John Odull. Indictment. Not a true Bill.

Samuel Tate, Prin. in the sum of 10,000 lbs. Andrew Greer, Joseph Bullard, his security, each 5,000 lbs. for his appearance at the next term of court.

James Milican in the sum of 5,000 lbs. witness for State vs. Tate. Sub. for Sam Tate, Collering Coleson, and John Grimes.

Court adjourned.

Thursday the 25th.

Present the Worshipful Jesse Walton, Thomas Houghton, James Start, John McNabb, Andrew Greer.

Ord. that Deds. issue to the county of Burke to take the depo. of Charles Wakefield and Mary Inman in behalf of Amos Bird in a suit depending with Samuel Sherrill.

Ord. that a Ded. issue to take the Depo. of Henry Francis in regard to a suit Samuel Crawford vs. Samuel Williams.

Ord. that a Ded. be issue to the county of Burke to take the Depo. of Charles Wakefield in behalf of Samuel Sherrill in a suit vs. Amos Bird.

Ord. that John B. McMahon, Joseph Culberson, William Clark, Jr., John Clark, Jr., Ebenezer Byram be appointed Constable.

John Odull Prin in the sum of 1000 lbs. Wm. Cox, and Julius Robertson, his security to the sum of 500 lbs. each for his appearance at next term of court.

Ord. that John Sevier be appointed Trustee for the county.

Ord. that Jesse Walton, James Start, Thomas Houghton, esqs. be and is appointed to settle with Sheriff and Trustee for the county for the collections for the years of 1778, 1779 and make a report to next court.

August Term. (This is the last term before the King's Mountain battle.)

Held on the 28th day of August, 1780.

Present the Worshipful Jesse Walton, Thomas Houghton, John McNabb, Zachariah Isbell, esqs.

Thomas Hardiman, William Stone, John Russell assessors. Have returned their inventory of the taxable property within their District, and the same is received.

Ord. that new ord. issue to the assessors of Roan's creek District, appointing the same as before, and that they make a return at our next court.

Present John McNabb and Benjamin Gist, Esqs.

Entry-taker returns a bond from John Bearden unto William Campbell, sd. Bearden caviting 100 acres of Land and No. 2567, and it is ordered that order is for tryal issue.

Ralph Humphrey, Joshua Houghton, James Roddy, Jon. Tipton, James Stinson, William Tremble, John

Wood, James Lackey, Thomas Hardeman, Joseph Greer, Abraham Denton, George Gillaspy, Adam Willson, Pharoah Cobb, Jurymen Sworn.

Ord. that Deds. issue to take the depo. of Ann Mc-Adoo on behalf of Mary Greer, pltff. vs. William McAdoo defdt.

Edmund Williams and Samuel Lyle sworn and appointed to attend the Grand jury.

Thomas Jonachin paid 9 dollars for the recording his mark.

George Dayley, Prin. to the sum of 20,000 lbs. and his two security were Joseph Buller and John Smith, 10,-000 lbs. each for his appearance in next court.

Moses Johnson, Prin. 20,000 lbs. Jos. England and James Crawford, 10,000 lbs. each.

Ord. that George Dayly be entitled to take and receive his creatures and other property now in the hands of Alex McFarling and Michl. Carter, the said George Dayley having entered into security as required by the court.

Ord. that Moses Johnson be entitled to take and receive his creatures and other property now in the hands of Hickey sd Moses giving bond to the court.

Ord. that a fine of 100 lbs be imposed on John Chisolm, Esq. for being guilty of striking and beating Abraham Denton in the court yard. Also disquieting the peace and decorum of the Court, and that the Clerk issue an execution for the same.

State vs. John Redding. For speaking word treasonable and inimical to the common cause of liberty. Samuel Matthews witness for the State. The Defdt. pleads not guilty at his tryal. The court hearing the facts of the case, decides he give bond for the next term of Court. John Redding Prin. for the sum 20,000 lbs., and John Bullar and John Clark, each 10,000 lbs. security for his appearance.

Ord. that John Been, Benjam. Cobb, and George Russell review a way for a road from Chaots Ford on the Holston to the Cherokee Ford, or elsewhere on the Big Limestone, and make a report to our next.

State vs. James Delaney. Stealing Sheep—True Bill

State vs. John Redding. Treason—True Bill.

Ord. that Abraham Denton be allowed to build a grist mill on Sinking Creek on his own land, and he shall be entitled to toll allowed for public mill.

Ord. that Isaac Lane be appointed constable.

Ord. that ———— of John Francis and Marry Carr on behalf of Walter Carr pltff. vs. Hezekiah Chaney, defdt.

State vs. John Shelby. Indict Manslaughter. True Bill.

The Court taking the same under consideration and duly considering the same in the most mature and deliberate manner are of the opinion that the defendant John Shelby, be acquitted.

Wednesday.

John Russell made oath that he served four days in assessing the taxable property in the District he was appointed. He was allowed sixty dollars pr. day.

Robert Sevier vs. Thomas Morrison. Attachment.

The court having taken under consideration the appointment of Comissioners for the county, to be Judges of the different kinds of paper emissions in circulating in this county, or may be hereafter agreeabled to an act of Assembly in that case made and provided in order to prevent frauds and imposition that may be committed in said county, and for the purpose of detecting and suppressing Vices of this kind, have appointed John Sevier, William Cobb, Thomas Houghton, and Andrew Greer, Esqs. to be the Judges of all such monies and have accordingly taken an oath for the performance of said trust.

State vs. Emanl Carter. For failing to serve as constable.

Ordered that Isaac Taylor, son of Andrew, be appointed constable. Court adjourned till Court in course.

Thos. Houghton
William Cobb
Charles Robertson
Andrew Greer

The next term of court was November 17, 1780, about six weeks after the battle of King's Mountain.

In the expedition to King's Mountain, the soldiers under Sevier were taken from Washington county, North

Carolina, those under William Campbell from Washington county, Virginia, Shelby getting the greater part of his from Sullivan county. There were, of course, many from other places, but the larger number came from the localities mentioned.

The records of the November term show how the personnel of the settlements on the Tennessee side was already changing by the coming hither of King's Mountain men from other places. Among the names which now appear are those of Charles and Robert Allison, John Newman, John Trimble, Jacob and David Reynolds, Robert Blackburn, and Samuel and John Wear.

Watauga Old Fields is what is now Elizabethton in Carter county, Tennessee. It was an Indian village when Andrew Greer, a hunter, first came here. There is an old cemetery where it is thought Indians were buried. John Carter settled a half-mile above the town, and the place is still in the family. Three miles above is the grant to John Nave, likewise still owned by his descendants. The same fact is true in many other instances. Charles Robertson, so prominent in the early records, lived on Sinking Creek. The mill that Baptist McNabb built on Buffalo Creek was the first in the settlement, Matthew Talbert building the second. Valentine Sevier lived in Watauga Old Fields, but his son John lived in the Jacob Brown settlement on the Nollichucky. This extended below the mouth of Big Limestone, and was the farthest of the frontier bases. There were forts at Brown's and Eaton's stations, in the fork of the North Branch of the Holston, on Beaver two miles from the Virginia line, and at Womack's and Gillespie's stations. John Shelby also had a fort. Out of these defenses came the men who united with the militia from Washington county, Virginia, and fought the Cherokees at Island Flat in 1776.

Jonesboro is the oldest town in Tennessee, although it was a county seat when Washington was formed in 1779. As originally laid out, Washington began at the northwest corner of Wilkes county, the line following the Great Iron Mountain to the hunting grounds of the over-hill Cherokees, then along the Unaka Range to where the trading path crosses from the Valleys of the over-hill country, then to the line of South Carolina, then due west to the Mississippi, then up that river to a point due west from the starting point.

Sullivan county was taken from Washington in 1780. The first court met in the house of Moses Looney, a King's

Mountain man, and all the justices were his comrades. They were Isaac Shelby, David Looney, William Christie, John Dunham, William Wallace, Samuel Smith, John Rhea, the clerk, Nathaniel Clark, the sheriff, and John Adair, the entry-taker who let Shelby and Sevier have the state's money to finance the expedition.

At court begun and held in the court house on the 17th day of November 1780. Present, Worshipful Charles Robertson, Chairman, William McNabb, John McNabb, Thomas Houghton, Jessie Walton, and Benjamin Gist, Esqs.

Josias Martin came into court and made oath that the ear mark of his cattle, sheep, and hogs is a smooth crop in the left ear, and in the right ear a half crop, and the tail cropt off the hogs, and the same is ordered to be recorded.

Joseph Wilson being summoned as Garnishee of James Robertson by Martin Maney declares on oath that he has one hundred dollars and ninety dollars in his hands and judgement is given against the Garnishee for the same.

A power of attorney from Wm. McBride to Robert Wilson investigating him with certain lands, &c., is proved by the oath of Joseph Wilson, Esq. and the same to be recorded.

Charles Allison, John Newman, Robert Allison, and Daniel Kennedy took the oath appointed by law for Justice of Peace, and took their seats accordingly.

The muncupative will of John Bullard, Decd. Duly proven by the oaths of Joseph Nation, Elinor Nation, and Anne Bullar, and the same is ordered to be recorded. Court adjourned until tomorrow at nine o'clock.

Met according to adjournment.

Present, John Carter, Chairman; Chas. Robertson, Benj. Gist, Wm. McNabb, Thos. H. Houghton, Jos. Willson, Chas. Allison, Godfrey Isbell, Daniel Kennedy and Rich. White, Esqs.

The list of Taxables for the Roane District is retd. by Richd. White Esq., and is recd by the Court.

The Court ordered that Mrs. Hannah Millican do receive forty bushels of corn that was the property of Philip Shelby, being corn due to James Millican Decd. from sd. Shelby for serving as substitute in behalf of Shelby.

Wm. Murphy, John Nave, and Alex Moore Assessors made their return and is recd by the Court.

Wm. Murphy and John Nave made oath that they served five days assessing and is allowed.

Joseph England, Prin. ....10,000 pounds

Jas. Stinson, Sectv., ... 5,000 pounds

Jas. Carr, Sectv., ... 5,000 pounds

On condition the principal be of good behavior and make his personal appearance at the next term of our Court.

George Dayley, and Joseph Bullar, Jos. England, James Crawford, and John Smith his security is Discharged from their recognizance entered into last Court.

Moses Johnstone, and Joseph Bullar, Jos. England, Jas. Crawford and John Smith his security is discharged from their recognizance entered into last court.

Joseph Keeny, Prin., ... 40,000 pounds

Joseph Bullar, Joseph Dunham, Sectv. 20,000 pounds each. On condition principal appear in next Court.

James Gibson, in the sum of 5,000 pounds.

Jesse Green, in the sum of 5,000 pounds.

Jas. Robertson, in the sum of 5,000 pounds.

Wm. Greer, 5,000.

On condition they appear at next court to give testimony vs. Joseph Keeny. Court adjourned to meet tomorrow morning at nine o'clock.

Wednesday morning met.

Present, Jesse Walton, Wm. McNabb, Charles Robertson, Thos. Houghton and James Stuart Esqs.

State vs. Jas. Ray. Recognizance for being inimical to the State.

Joseph Carter witness for the State, (sworn) Chas. England witness for Defdt. (Sworn.)

The Court order defendant to enter recognizance for his appearance in next court.

Jas. Ray, Prin. ....20,000 pounds

Wm. Cox, James ———— secty. each 10,000.

On condition the principal be of good behavior **and** make his personal appearance at next Court.

Samuel Tate, Prin. 10,000

Jos. Bullard, Drury Goodin, Sectys, each 5,000.

On condition Prin. makes his appearance at court.

The State vs. Humphrey Gibson, on Recog. for being inimical to the State, &cc.

James Ray witness for the State sworn.

Court order Defdt to enter to recog. for his appearance next Court.

Humphry Gibson, prin. 20,000

Jos. Dunham, Jos. Bullard each, 10,000 lb.

Condition Prin. appear at next term of court.

Joseph Bullard and his security Joseph Brown is released from the Recognizance entered into before Chas. Robertson for Joseph Bullar appearance.

Ord. that the Commissioners advertize and sell the properties of James Crawford and Thomas Barker, the sd Crawford and Barker being found and taken in arms against the State. (They were going to hang Crawford and Barker right after the King's Mountain battle, but Colonel Sevier interceded for them and saved them.)

Adjourn Court until tomorrow at nine o'clock.

Court met. Present, Thos. Houghton, Jesse Walton, Wm. McNabb, Esqs.

Luke Bowyer vs. John Shelby in debt.

John Shelby, Edward Sweeton, Judgmt. according to specialty & costs.

Philip Connoway vs. Godfrey Isbell attachmt. The sheriff returned that the same is levied on a parcel of corn in the hands of Wm. Hatcher. Judgmt. for lb. 4,000 and courts order of sale. The pltff. agreed to take the corn and allow give to the judgmt. for same.

Wm. Cannon vs. Wm. Murphy, Jr., on attachmt. The sheriff return the same levied on a rifle gun,—ordered to be dismist.

Robert Blackburn vs. George Hamilton, attachmt. Dismist for want of prosecution.

John Trimble vs. Geo. Hamilton, attachmt. Dismist for want of prosecution.

The Court have elected Cleavers Barksdale high Sheriff for the year of 1780.

Ord. that John Holley go and take away a bay horse with a star on his face being the sd. Holly's property taken away from him by a certain Thomas Mitchell.

Ordered that Cap. John Paterson deliver unto John Holly a certain rifle gun the property of John Holly. (This Holly was a Royalist, and the whigs were confiscating his property, but the Court stood by him until they decided the justice of the case.)

John Black have leave of Administration on the estate of Michael Mahoney decd. (Michael Mahoney was one of Sevier's soldiers killed in the King's Mountain battle.)

John Black, Prin. _____10,000 lb.

Charles Robertson, Richd. Minton security each, 5,-000. Recd 23 dolls. On condition that John Black make a faithful administration on the estate of Michael Mahoney.

Court order Joab Reynolds, Joseph Lovelady do have their arms, ammunition, &cc., delivered to them again which was taken by Captain Nathaniel Davis. Reynolds pays 8 dollars (first time dollars appear)

Ordered by the Court that Joseph Keena be entitled to take and receive his property taken by James Gibson, &cc.

Ordered that James Boilstone have his mare returned that was taken by Cap. Patterson.

Cleavers Barksdale have entered himself with Charles Robertson & Jesse Walton, his securitys, in the sum of thirty thousand pounds for his faithful discharge of his office as high Sheriff for this county for the year of 1780.

John Sevier entered himself with Charles Robertson in the sum of five thousand pounds for his faithful performance as Trustee for the year of 1780.

John Chisolm, Esq. took the oath of deputy surveyor under James Stuart, Esq. (Chisolm was a soldier of fortune, was in King's Mountain, and the one that really caused Governor Blount's impeachment.)

Court adjourned until Court in course.

Thomas Houghton
Jno. McNabb
Benj. Gist
Wm. McNabb
James Stuart
Jno. Chisolm

February Term, 1781

At a court begun and held at the Court House on Monday 26th day of Feb. 1781. Present the Worshipful

Chas. Robertson, Thos. Houghton, Jno. McNabb, **Jos.** Wilson, George Russell & Robert Allison, Esqs.

Ordered by the court all those who gave and entered into recognizance last Court be recognized until next Court.

A bill of sale from Sarah Resinor to Robt. Paris for a black mare and some other creatures, both horses and cattle as therein mentioned was duly acknowledged by sd. Sarah Risinor and is ordered to be recorded.

Daniel Higdon came into Court and proved himself by the oaths of several credible witnesses, also by the certificates of sundry gentlemen that the sd Daniel Higdon is a zealous and good friend to his country, and that the court do earnestly recommend it unto Mr. James Roddy to deliver unto the sd. Daniel Higdon a certain negro man named James which he, the sd Roddy's company took from Henry Grimes, proviso that sd Higdon do well and truly prove his property of sd slave.

Rebecca Lowery, Prin. ....15,000 lbs.

Saml & Jno. Wier, Security 7,000

Void on condition Rebecca Lowery do make a lawful administrative on the estate of Robert Lowery.

John Trimble vs. Geo. Hamilton, Attachmt.

James Grimes being summoned as Garnishee declares on oath that there is several things in his house which was attached by Jos. Pearson, a deputed constable, and returns made to this court, which effects are ordered to be sold, to first discharge sd. James Grimes' debt to the sum of 802 pounds and cost; if any over plus to be subject to the discharge of John Trimble's debt being the sum of 1600 pounds and cost.

Robert Blackburn vs. John Allison, Attachment dismissed.

John Allison vs. Francis Baker, Stealing corn. The court on hearing the testimony of the witness and considering the facts are of the opinion that defdt receive five lashes on his bair back.

Hannah Milican have leave of administration on the estate of James Milican.

Hannah Milican, Prin. .... 10,000 pounds

Jno. Lyle & Jno. McNabb, security 5,000 pounds each. Void on condition Hannah make a lawful administration on the estate of James Milican.

James Stuart vs. John Highes, attachmt. Judgmt by Default and order of sale.

Memo. that Wm. Ritche gave his list of taxable property 150 acres of land which sd land is given in by James Stuart, and it is ordered that the clerk do not charge Ritche with the same.

Court adjourned until 9 o'clock in the morning.

Tuesday morning met according to adjournment.

Edward Smith appeared this day and is released from his recognizance for his appearance to this session.

Jos. England, Prin. .... 10,000 lbs.

James Carr and John Burrows .... 5,000 lbs each
To appear in August Court.

On condition principal appear the next court &c.
Jos Keena, Prin. .... 40,000 lb.
Jesse Walton & security each 20,000
Jas. Ray, Prin. 20,000
Jas. Carr & Wm. Cox each 10,000
Samuel Tate, Prin. 10,000
.... security each 5,000
Void on condition prin. appear at next court.

Ordered that Matthews Paramore be appointed Overseer of the road now to be cut out from the Court House to the branch at the corner of Danl. Harrison's fence.

Chas. Hays to be Overseer of the road to be cut out from Danl. Harrison's to John Howard on Lick creek.

Ordered that the property taken from Mary Dyckes be restored to her and that the Commissioners order the same to be given up. The property from Ann Hughes to be restored to her, and the Commissioners order the same be given up. (Dyckes was the Tory, and this court was not going to let his wife suffer for her husband's bad deeds because she always tried to do the right way, so the court fined Jesse Greer one hundred pounds, because he refused to give Mrs. Dyckes her property in the contempt of Court orders.)

Nath. Evans, Prin. 10,000
Jas. Allison and Jas. Anderson each 5,000
on condition the Prin. appear in next term of court.

James Gibson being brought into court for throwing out speeches against the Court, to-wit, saying that the Court was perjured and would not do justice and other glaring insults—The court on considering the matter are of opinion: That the said James Gibson is guilty of flagrant breach of peace and for the same, and the glaring and daring insults offered to the Court do order that the said James Gibson be fined the sum of fifteen thousand pounds and be kept in custody till the same be paid. (This trouble began in 1780 with Gibson being too free in speech. Those days you could not "throw out speeches" against any part of the Court.)

Patrick Murphy, Prin. .... lb. 10,000

Charles Robertson & Jesse Walton each 5,000

Jas Alliott, Jas. Anderson, Nathl. Evans & Wm. Fain each in 10,000 pounds to appear and give testimony vs. John Holly &c.

Ord. that Sci. facias issue to summon Elisha Nelson, Drury Woodin & Thos. Brandon to show cause, if any they have, why judgement shall not be awarded against them towit, for two thousand pounds against Elisha Nelson and one thousand each against Drury Woodin and Thos. Brandon.

Ordered Joseph Buller, Alex. Moore & James Allison appointed to view and mark a road from the court house to English's mill on Horse Creek and make a report at next term of Court. Ordered that James Allison be appointed overseer of the road from the Court house to the Wattaugo River.

Ordered that Benjm. Cobb be appointed overseer of the road from the Wattaugo river to the county line.

Court adjourned till Court in course.

Jesse Walton
Robt. Allison
Danl. Kennedy
John Newman
George Russell
Thos. Houghton
Joseph Wilson

May Term, 1781

At court begun and held at the Court House the 28th of May 1781, present the Worshipful Charles Robertson, Jesse Walton, Jno. McNabb, Andrew Greer, Danl. Kennedy & Valentine Sevier Esqs.

State vs. Davis Hickky, Misprision of Treason. Wm. Henry, Hugh Henry, Jas. Milican witness for the State sworn. The court are of the opinion that the defdt. was guilty of a flagrant breach of the peace vs. the State &cc., and do fine him 2500 pounds and give security for his good behavior for one year and one day.

Ord. Sci Facias issue vs. Christopher Cunningham and Robert Orr to show cause at the next court why a conditional judgment of five thousand pounds each shall not be confirmed against them for not appearing this court according to their recognizance entered in before Jno. McNabb Esq.

Ralph Humphrey came into court and took the oath of Justice of peace, and took seat accordingly.

A bill of sale from Wm. Cox to Thomas Hardeman for the conveyance and delivery of a certain Negro man slave named Jupiter was proven by the oath of Wm. Cox and John Chisolm Esq. and the same is ordered to be recorded. Left 40 dollars to pay fee.

State vs. John Boyd, Misdemeanors. The court on considering the matter are of the opinion that the Dfdt. be fined two thousand pounds and imprisoned for the term of six months and given security in the sum of forty thousand pounds. Witness for the State, Sworn Martha Miller, Mary Baker, Francis Baker, Jas. Wyley, Martha Miller, Jr., Rich. Mintom.

The last Will & Testimony of John Drewy Chews was duly proven by the oaths of Sarah Calhoun, Martha Parsons, and swear they also see John Calhoun and Lucrecy Calhoun signed the sd will as Witness in the presence of the Testator and by his consent, and the same is ordered to be recorded. Also the above will declaring Margaret Calhoun and Edward Mitcheson his extras and as there appears that the sd Executrix who was left in care of the sd estate and the children of the Testator is in necessity and want of said estate to support and maintain the said children thereon. The court order that Margaret Calhoun one of the executors do take and receive all or any part of the sd John Drury Chews estate whereever the same may be found.

John Boyd, Prin. 20,000

John Allison and Davis Stuart each 5,000. Void on condition that John Boyd confine and keep himself on his plantation which the sd Boyd now lives upon with family for the term and time of six months from this date. (John Boyd had a young family, so the court knew he was badly needed at home.)

The last will and Testament of Nathl. Davis Esq. was duly proven by the oaths of Robert Davis and Mary Davis and the same is ordered to be recorded. Ordered that Danl. Kennedy, James Willson and Joseph Willson, Esq., appointed to appraise the estate of Robert Lowery decd.

Court adjourned till tomorow at nine o'clock.

Mildred Bond gives bond to administration of her husband's estate, Jesse Walton and Cap. Samuel Williams security to forty thousand pounds. Court appoint Edward Rice, Joseph Reed and John Woods to appraise the estate.

The State vs. Joseph Bullard, warrant. The court order that Joseph Bullard give security for his good behavior for twelve months in the sum of ten thousand pounds with two securities, five thousand pounds each. John Nave and John Reding securities. Void on condition Joseph Bullard peaceful in behavior for twelve months.

The State vs. John Denton, warrant. Court orders to give security for good behavior for twelve months and give security in the sum of 10,000 pounds and two securities in the sum of 5,000 pounds each. Charles Robertson and James Pearce his securities. Void if the Prin. is peaceable and good behavior for one year.

Ordered that Samuel Tate be fined the sum of ten thousand pounds for contempt of court issue Fi Facious vs. his estate for the same.

Jas. Ray, prin. 10,000

Joseph Bullard and Abram Wood, 2,000 each.

Ralph Humphrey, Robert McAfee and Samuel Culberson made return of taxable property in their district, the same recorded.

Ordered Rich. Minton serve as constable in the room of John B. McMahon.

The State vs. Jesse Green. Warrant for stealing a gun from Thomas Brown. Mary Dunham, Thos. Brown, Jesse Gentry, witness for the State sworn. Nath. Evans for the pltff sworn.

It is the opinion of the Court that the defdt is not guilty and that Thomas Brown prosecutor, Thomas Brown pay the cost.

The State vs. Pat. Murphy, stealing a bell. Ordered to appear at next court.

Patrick Murphy, Prin. 10,000

Charles Robertson and Jos. Bullard, security 5,000 each.

Charles West was duly qualified as deputy Surveyor of this county under James Stuart.

Ordered that Jesse Greer be fined the sum of one thousand pounds for contempt offered the court in refusing to deliver the Widow Dyckes her property as directed by the order of the court.

Ordered that a grist mill now already built by Bartholew Woods be considered as a public grist mill and that the sd Woods be entitled to take such a toll and have the rights and immunities as other public grist mills within the District.

Cleavers Barksdale being appointed Sheriff enters bond for his faithful discharge of sd office in the sum of one hundred thousand pounds and Charles Robertson and Edmund Williams fifty thousand each as security.

Ordered that George Bundy & Reuben Bundy orphans of Simon Bundy decd be bound to William Wells, the sd Wells entering into the rules and forms and laws made and provided in that case.

Bradley Gambell made oath he served two days as constable in notifying the inhabitants of Wm. Been's District.

Elisha Nelson, Prin. 10,000.

Bradley Gambell and Robert Campbell securities 5,000 each.

Ord that the Tavern keepers in this county sell at the following prices to-wit, viz:

A Dinner, 20 dol.

Breakfast or supper, 15 dol.

Corn or oats pr. gallon, 12 dol.

Pasture, 6 dol.

Stabledge 12 dol. with hay or fodder lodging, 6 dol.

W. I. Rum, 20 dol.

Peach Brandy, 80 dol.

Whisky, pr. qrt., 48 dol.

Taffea Rum, 100 dollars pr qt.

Court Adjourned.

Wesday 30th day.

James Eadens vs. Henry Grimes, attachment.

Richard Mitchell an orphan the son of Joab Mitchell decd. came into court and made choice of Charles Robertson, Esq., as his guardian, and the court has appointed him his guardian.

John Callahan is appointed surveyor of that part of the road wherein James Allison was overseer before, from Samuel Fain's house unto John Been's Ford. That the Hands still continue to work under James Allison, to include Robert Allison and so down to George Russell's including the waters of Sinking Creek and across the sd road from thence four miles from the same and all the inhabitants within the upper and lower end of the sd line extending the four mile out.

Ordered that Chris. Taylor and John Sevier be appointed to view and mark off a publick road from the Court house to John Sevier's mill.

Ordered that a publick road be laid from the court house to the head of Indian Creek, and that Cap. Vo. Sevier, Thos. Houghton, Esq., Robert Young, Jr., and Jno. McMahan be commissioners to lay off the same as soon as possible, and that Andr. Greer, Esq., Joseph Tipton, and Cap. Samuel Williams is to be overseers to have the same cut out and kept in repair and that Cap. Sevier's company and Cap. McNabb's company as high up as McNabb's mill, and Cap. Saml. Williams company except but what is on Little Limestone to be liable to work thereon.

Ordered that Isaiah Hamilton be surveyor of the road from the court house to John Sevier's Mill and that the lands on the south side Big Limestone as far up as Robert Allison, Esq. and as low down as Charles Allison's Esq. and from thence straight across including all the inhabitants on the north side of Cherokee Creek up as far as George Carrs and that the same be cut immediately.

Ordered that James Allison have leave to keep a tavern at the Court House for one year and have entered John Sevier and Valentine Sevier as securities for the same.

Ordered that Isaiah Hamilton have leave to keep Tavern at his house for one year and entered Val. Sevier and James Allison as his securities.

Ordered that Valentine Sevier be payed four thousand for being sheriff for 1780.

Ordered that Richd. Minton have leave to keep a Tavern at the Court House for one year and have entered Jacob Brown and Saml. Williams as securities.

Ord. that Joseph Reed, Wm. Meek, Isaac Taylor, son of Andrew Taylor, ... Wilson. (Richard White to add Christian name) and William Miller do serve as constables.

Justices and assessors appointed for the year of 1781:

1st District, Richard White, Esq., Jas. Roddy, Jesse Hoskins, ... Bowman.

2nd District, Thos. Houghton, Esq., William Cox, James Henry, Andrew Taylor.

3rd District, Wm. Cobb, Esq., Thos. Hardiman, Thos. Jonchin, Wm. Cocke.

4th District, Wm. Clark, Esq., Jno. Woods, Michl. Woods, Jacob Brown.

5th District, Joseph Willson, Esq., Anthony Moore, Robert Wier, Abraham Hoskins. And that the 1st District Andrew Willson, 2nd Isaac Taylor son of Andrew, 3rd Wm. Frame, 4th Wm. Meek & Joseph Bond, 5th William Moore and Abraham Hill be appointed constables to notify people.

Ord. that Anderson Smith be appointed to serve as constable.

Court adjourned till court in course.

> Charles Robertson
> Andw. Greer
> Ralph Humphrey
> Zach Isbell
> Jess. Walton
> Tho. Houghton

August Term 1781

Present the Worshipful Chas. Robertson, Cha.; Thos. Houghton, Danl. Kennedy, Charles Allison, Wm. McNabb, Benjm. Gist, Jos. Willson, Richard White and John Newman, Esq.

Grand Jurymen present

Edm. Williams	Saml. Williams
Andrew Taylor	Adam Willson
Martha Berymore	Thos. Hardimen
Jas. Roddy	Chris Taylor
Corne. Bowman	Alexr Galbreath
Wm. Murphy	John Alexander
Joshua Houghton	Samuel Wier
Jacob Brown	Moses Moore
Mich. Woods	

Sworn—Order to appear in the morning.

Petit Jurymen present

Robert Erwin	Robert Been
David McNabb	Charles Young
Isaac Taylor	Jesse Bounds
David Lyle	James Campbell
Alexdr. Anderson	Josiah Martin
Jonathan Tipton	William Bryant

Ord. to appear in the morning at 9 o'clock.

Charles (?) to administration on the estate of Cristopher Cunningham decd.

A bill of sale of a slave Jupiter to Cato West by Thomas Hardeman to be recorded.

A bill of sale from Michael Massingill to Cato West, a negro boy named John eight years old, to be recorded.

Court adjourned till tomorrow morning at nine o'clock.

Tuesday 28th May, 1781.

Thomas Talbot is appointed commissioner to collect Tax for 1780 and 1781.

Thomas Talbot securities Colo. Ralph Humphreys and Cleavers Barksdale.

The court order that the clerk certify to the General Assembly Danl. Dunn is an infirm man an object of charity and they recommend that he may be discharged from paying public taxes for the county.

Order that the sheriff forbear collecting a fine of ten thousand pounds inflicted upon Samuel Tate the last court.

Thomas Talbot have taken the oaths appointed for public officers, he to act a deputy sheriff under C. Barksdale, Esq.

Wm. Deal vs. Jeptha Higson, on suspicion of stealing of creatures from pltff. Discharged by the court, fees payed.

Mrs. Frances Lyle, Jas. Stuart & James Houston have leave of administration on the estate of John Lyle decd. and securities are Danl. Kennedy, Charles Allison & Jno. McNabb.

Geo. Russell, Esq., David Robertson, William Allison, and William Young is appointed to view and mark a road from Bartholm Woods' mill to John Been's and report to court.

Charles Robertson have leave to administration on the estate of Edward Hampton.

The State vs. John Hoskings for being the accessary to the death of James Millican.

John Hoskings give security for the sum of 10,000 pounds. Cleve Barksdale and Ruth Hoskings securities.

Landon Carter has leave of administration on the estate of Colonel Carter decd. have entered Valentine Sevier, Thomas Houghton, and Charles Robertson securities in the sum of five hundred thousand pounds for his faithful administration, &cc.

The State vs. James ————. Misdemeanor. The court ordered dfdt to be discharged.

Ord that the clerk certify to the county court of Frederick in commonwealth of Virginia that Wm. Reeve is a man of peaceful character and honest behavior and that his wife Mary Reeves who is the daughter of Peter Wolf decd. who formerly lived in the county of Frederick of the Commonwealth of Virginia is now living.

It is recommended by the Court that David McNabb and others who have the negroes or any of them belonging to Mrs. Maberry in there possession to immediately give them up to her, she proving her property.

Court adjourned till tomorrow morning at nine Wednesday 29th.

Memo. to summon Robert Paris, Robert Hood, William Storey in behalf of Durham against Green Bashin and Mitchell.

The State vs. Zachariah Isbell. Indictmt. and abusing Samuel Crawford. The defdt pleads not guilty.

Zachariah Isbell prin ....10,000 pounds
Andrew and Jacob Brown secuty. .... 5,000 each

The State vs. Patrick Murphy. Stealing a bell. Defdt. pleads not guilty.

A jury to wit John Newman, David Lyle, Jacob Brown, Alexander Anderson, Robert Been, James Allison, Thos. Mitchell, Jesse Green, Robert Gentry & James Stinson passed on the tryal. The jury find the defdt not guilty.

Charles Robertson conveyed two hundred and eighty acres to John Odull and the same is registered.

James Stuart vs. James Crawford. Inquiry.

A jury to-wit Matthew Paramore, Robert Gentry, Thomas Mitchell, Benjm. Inman, Jesse Green, Alexander Anderson, Charles Gentry, John Nowland, Adam Porter, Joshua Greer, James Gibson passed on the sd tryal. M. Paramore Cha.

We of the jury do find for the Defdt. S. McCay attorney for the pltff. prays the court for leave to offer reasons for an arrest of Judgement.

Court adjourned till tomorrow morning at 8 o'clock, Friday, 31st.

Ord. by the court the sheriff employ some workmen to repair the house the court is held, also prepare a table for the Clerk, a kind of bar for the attorneys, and some benches for the jury to sit on, and have same done by next term of Court.

Ord. that Thomas Hall give security for his good behavior for the term of one year in the sum of ten thousand pounds and two securities of five thousand each. Nicholas Mercer & Forester Mercer went his securities.

Elisha Nelson, case at last court—the court orders the plantff to be discharged. (My fee paid.)

The Court adjourned till Court in course.

February 1782

25th February.

Present the Worshipful Thomas Houghton, Charles Robertson, William McNabb, Jesse Walton, and William Cobb, Esqs.

Ord. that an orphan child named Betsy Williams, the daughter of Mary Williams now Mary Newberry be bound unto Edward Higgons until sd. orphan comes to the age of eighteen. Bound and payed the fees.

Court adjourned.

Thursday 26th. William Cocke produced a license and taken the usual oaths and is permitted to plead and practice in this court.

John Holmes to Robert Carver 160 acres of land, proven by the oath of John Woods and the same recorded.

Pursuant to a return and directions from James Glasgow, esq., Secretary of State we the Justices do hereby order and direct the clerk to issue his orders for the tryal of the undermentioned disputed Lands the titles of which have been suspended by the Honorable Alexander Martin, Esq., Governor for the time being between the following parties to-wit:

John Robertson vs. Peter McName. For 300 acres of land on the waters of Big Limestone.

John Long vs. William Cobb, Pharoah Cobb, Benjamin Cobb. For a certain tract of land on the waters of Knob Creek in the Watagua settlement.

John English vs. William Walker. For 200 acres of land on the Falling Branch of Horse Creek, and on both sides of Christy Ware's Path.

Thomas Hardeman 4 vs. William Been, Sr. For part of tract of land on Sinking Creek included in Timothy Peningtons improvements.

Andrew English 5 vs. George Martin. For 300 acres of land on Lick Creek.

Joseph Young 6 vs. William Gray. For 640 acres of land on Brush Creek joining Jonas Little's line and William Gray's claim.

George Vincent 7 vs. John Chinn, John Hill. For 150 acres on waters of Boon's Creek Entry and warrant No. 759.

Thomas Brandon 8 vs. William Magbee. For 400 acres on Lick Creek.

Thomas Hardeman 9 vs. Jacob Lyte. For part of tract of land on Sinking Creek purchased of Timothy Penington.

Thomas Hughes 10 vs. William Thomas. For part of a tract in the forks of the Watagua & Holston rivers the west side of Lick Creek.

William Parker vs. John Carter. For the tract of land called Watagua Old Field.

John English vs. William Magbee. For 200 acres of land on Falling Branch of Horse Creek and on both sides of Christy's War Path.

John Blair McMahon vs Aron Lewis. For part of tract of land lying on the head & including the spring of S. E. Fork of Boon's creek.

Robert Young vs. Benjamin Cobb. For tract of land on Knob Creek.

John McMahon vs. Benjam. Cobb. For entry made by Mr. Cobb in the case of Benj. A. Cobb joining a survey made by Cobb on branch of Nob Creek including the Blue Spring.

George Russell vs. Richard Caswell, Esq. For a part of a tract of land on the east fork of Big Limestone.

John Gilliland vs. John Shirley. For a tract of land on Cherokee Creek improved by J. Gilliland 1773.

George Barkley vs. John Fair. For 200 acres of land on the waters of little Limestone joining land of Col. Campbell and James Stephenson running up to the land of Samuel Fain and James Miller.

John Talley in behalf of the orphans of Martha Haire decd. vs. Robert Lucas. For 300 acres on the south side of the Holston river at Jones fall.

John Nolan vs. Abner Green. For 250 acres of land in the Fork of Watagua and Holston rivers. We do therefore direct that the same be admitted to tryal by court.

The court appointed Cap Samuel Williams guardian to the orphans of John Basset decd.

On motion of Wm. Cocke that three negroes now in the possession of the Sheriff who by the information of Colonel Williamson belongs to a certain Isaac Perry of the State of Georgia and that on the aforesaid Williamson proving said negroes to be said Perry's that, they be given up to Colonel Williamson who is to return them to their proper owner. The court considering the same therefore direct the Sheriff to deliver to the said Col. Williamson the aforesaid negroes on his paying the cost.

The State vs. William Magbee. Record for stealing a horse, the property of James Dunham. Joseph Dunbar, Robert Been witness for the State (sworn). The court on considering the matter Dismiss the Defendant with him paying the cost.

An inventory of the estate of John Carter deceased is returned by Susan Carter adm. and the same is ordered to be filed.

A bill of sale for a mare from John Butler to Joseph Bullard, same record.

The court appointed Thomas Houghton and William McNabb to settle with the Sheriff, and make returns to court.

Ord. that a deds potestatem issue to take the Depo. of Ezekiel Smith, Joh'n Drake, Richard Fields, Benjam. Drake, Henry Hickky on behalf of Wm. Parker on a Caveat vs. John Carter on a tract of land disputed with Wm. Parker called Wattauga Old Fields.

Ord. that a deds potestatem issue to take Depo. of Robert Cooper, Samuel Wilson, and Emanl. Carter in behalf of Landon Carter admr. of the estate of John Carter Decd. in a disputed claim of land with Wm. Parker called Watagua Old Field.

An indenture from George King and Margaret King, Binding an orphan child named Robert Maccashlin to James Allison is to be recorded.

A deposition of McCajah Williamson proving a certain negro wench now in possession of Mark Mitchell was made lawful prize &c by the legislature of Georgia was proven by Jesse Walton Esq. and is ordered to be recorded.

John Woods, Michael Woods, & Jacob Brown assessors for the year of 1781.

An inventory of the estate of John Lyles decd is received and recorded.

Joseph McPeters, prin. ....50 pounds

Asael Rawlings, William Snoddy securities in the sum of 25 pounds.

James Boilstone being brought before the Court for being inimical to the United States, &cc.

The Court considering the matter and hearing the evidence against him order the said Boilstone be confined in Goal until next court, and that the Sheriff take sufficient care of the prisoner. Jordon Roach and James Ragin in the sum of one thousand pounds each they appear the next superior Court at Salisbury to give testimony vs. James Boilstone.

Court adjourned till tomorrow 8 o'clock.

February Term, 1782

At a court begun and held at the Court' House, on Monday the 26th of February 1782. Present the Worshipful Charles Robertson, Thos. Houghton, Jno. McNabb Jos. Wilson, George Russell & Rob. Allison, Esq.

Ord. by the Court that all those who gave and entered into recognizance last Court be recognized until next Court.

Thomas Hardeman, William Cox, and Thomas Jonachin have made their return of the assessments within their Districts for the year of 1781, and is recd. by the court.

Court order the Sheriff to take John Odull into his charge, and him safely keep until he give sufficient security to the Court for his appearance in the next term of court.

The court have permitted John Sevier to render to the assessors of the District wherein he lives the Inventory of his taxable property for the years of 1780 & 1781.

The State vs. John Chambers. Misdemeanor. Witness for the State Elez. Bennett, Rebecca Wyal, John Reeves, Thos. Brumit, Wm. Meeks.

The Court on considering the facts alleged vs the defendt order he be bound in Recognizance to appear at next Court. John Chambers, Prin. in 100 lb. specia. George Barkly, Sandifer Goziah Securities each 50 lb. specia. On condition the Principal appear at the next term of Court.

A deed of gift from Jacob Brown to Ann Henderson for certain premises and other property as therein mentioned was proven by the oath of Zachariah Isbell, Esq., and the same is ord. recorded.

Thomas Gillaspy vs. Samuel Hill. Debt, dismissed by plaintiff. Thomas Robertson Prin. in sum of 100 lb. specia. John Gilliland, Samuel Williams securities for 50 lb. specia each. On condition apear next Court. Memo. Thomas Talbot to pay my fees for ....

The State vs. John Holly. Misdemeanor. Defdt. to appear next court. Jas. Alluott, Jas. Anderson, Wm. Fain, Nath. Evans witness for the State—Sworn.

A power of Attorney from Benjamin Johnstone to Colo. Charles Robertson investigating him with certain powers &cc was proven by the oath of John Burrows and the same is ordered to be recorded.

John Sevier and Charles Robertson, Esq. have leave of Administration on the Estate of Robert Sevier decd. (He was John Sevier's brother and killed in King's Mountain battle.)

John Holly, Prin in sum of 100 specia. Joseph Bullard security of 50 lb. specia. On condition that Prin. appear in next court.

John Sevier and Charles Robertson have entered Maj. John McNabb and Wm. Cobb, Esq. their securities in the sum of eight hundred pounds specia for their performance of the administration on the estate of Robert Sevier according to law.

The Court appointed Charles Robertson Guardian to the orphans of Robert Sevier decd.

John Odull Prin. in sum of 100 lb. specia.

Jonathan Tipton, Joseph Bullard, Jas. Denton and Jas Ray securities each 25 lb. specia. On condition the Prin. appear in next term of court.

On motion of William Cocke, Esq., that a negro wench and two children in the custody of Mrs. Hannah Clark that was brought from the State of Georgia formerly the property of Henry Williams now confiscated be taken by the Sheriff and kept in his custody until regularly called for according to law.

James Stuart vs. George Pointer. In case on inquiry. Thos. Gillaspy, Robert Gentry, High Stinson, Jas. Ray, Hosea Roan, Samuel Williams, Jonathan Tipton, Thomas Brumit, John Waddell, George Been, Abner Green and Joseph Bullard, jurymen, passed on the aforesaid tryal of inquiry. The Jury find nine hundred pounds damages.   Thomas Gillaspy, Foreman

John Holly security for Frances Holly case vs. John Medlock.

The court have appointed Jesse Gentry and Samuel Lyles constables.

The court adjourned till tomorrow at Nine o'clock.

Thursday morning met according to adjournment.

Francis Holly vs. John Medlock. Writ of inquiry. John Waddle, Jonathan Tipton, James Anderson, John Allison, Julis Robertson, John Gilliland, James Allison, Hosea Roan, Jas. Millican, James Denton, Wm. Robertson and George Been jurymen passed on the aforesaid inquiry. Jury found a fine for the plaintiff of five hundred pounds damages.   John Gilliland, Foreman.

Charles Robertson vs. James Crawford. In case of inquiry. John Waddle, Jon'n Tipton, Jas. Anderson, John Allison, Jno. Gilliland, Jas. Allison, Hosea Roan, Jas. Millican, Jas. Denton, Geo. Been, Jas. Henry and Thos. Gillaspy passed on the aforesaid inquiry and same find twenty thousand pounds damages. John Gililand, Foreman.

John Sevier has leave to build a grist mill on his land whereon Thomas Fowler lives, and that he be entitled to take and receive the same toll and same rights and immunities as other public grist mills are entitled to.

Ordered that the Sheriff summon Mary Choate and the widow or wife of John McGuff to appear at our next court to show cause if any she have why their children may not be bound out according to law.

The Court resd. the Inventory made by Robert Irwin, Robert Wier, and Anthony Moore assessors for the year of 1781.

Ordered that the Tavern keepers for the present year be entitled to take and receive the following allowances and prices and no more:

West I Best Rum 2 lb., 2 s. pr. gallon.
Continent or taffy do. 1 p., 12 s. pr. gallon.
Peach brandy 1 p., 4 s. pr. gallon.
Good whisky 10 s. pr. gallon.
Beer, 2 s. per gallon.
Hott Dinner, 1 s.
Breakfast or supper with tea or coffee 1 s.
Corn or oats pr. quart, 2 s.
Pasture, stabledge with fodder, &c., 8 d. pr night.

The court have appointed William Cox, George Russell & Joseph Dunham to review and mark a road from .... of Watagua to the Court House and make return by next court.

Court adjourned till court in course.

Thos. Houghton
James Stuart
John Newman
Danl. Kennedy
Jno. McNabb
Andw. Greer
Jno. McMaihen

May Term, 1782
Present the Worshipful Andrew Greer, Chairman

Jno. McNabb, Jos. Willson, Rich. White, William Clark, Charles Robertson, Valentine Sevier, Wm. McNabb.

Grand Jurymen to-wit: Jesse Bounds,, John Nave, Joseph Posey, Hosea Roan, Thomas Jonchin, Samuel Hill, Jacob Brown, James Stinson, Joseph Young, Jesse Been, absent Thos. Brummit, Jonas Little, George Been, absent John Terry, Wm. Cox, Davis Willson absent and Henry Massingale. The Grand Jury sworn, William Meeks appointed to attend the Grand Jury.

On Complaint of Hosea Roan by his attorney Epheaim Dunlap, esq. that the said Hosia Roan had just reasons to believe that Captain Jacob Brown intended to do him some bodily injury and damage and that the complainant may have leave to produce his witness &c which was accordingly done and the Court have ordered that the said Captain Jacob Brown give security for his good behavior &cc for a year and one day himself in the sum of 100 pounds, and two securities 50 pounds each. Charles Robertson and Jonathan Tipton went his security.

The Last Will and Testament of John Pavely decd. was duly proven by Charles Dobson and Lewis Pavely the same recorded.

The Last Will and Testament of William Been decd. was duly proved by Thomas Hardeman and the same recorded.

Ord. that Deds protestatem issue to three Justices in .... District, to take the deposition of Vardara Magbee, George Underwood, William Cooper, James Denard, on behalf of William Saffold in a suit between the sd. Saffold vs. Matthew Gale.

Jonathan Tipton, Joseph Bullard, Jas. Denton and Jas. Ray securities for the appearance of John Odull surrender him to the court. The court discharged John Odull.

Agnes Hays leave of administration of the estate of David Hay Decd She give bond and Pharoah Cobb and William Ward the securities, 5,000 p.

Thomas Ritchie appointed constable in room of William Moore.

Thomas Mitchell appointed constable in room of Abraham Hill.

The last will and testament of Aaron Burlison decd. was proven by Thomas Williams. The same recorded.

Ord. that Jermiah Terrell give bond in 100 pounds and two securities for his good behavior for twelve months especially towards Mildred Bond. William Meek and Thomas Brummit went his bond.

Tuesday morning.

William Cocke, Andrew Taylor, and James Henry assessors for 1781.

Order that George Bond 13 years of age be bound to John Clark blacksmith until he reaches the age of twenty one years, John Clark to give bond. William Clark and James Hubbard went the bond in the sum of five hundred pounds each.

John Clark, John Gillaland and Joseph Tipton added to the Grand Jury.

William Philips summoned to court and fined five pounds for assaulting and ill treating Jesse Been of the Grand Jury.

Michael Woods, Alexander Moore and Samuel Sherrell, Jr., to appraise the estate of Adam Broils, Decd.

On the motion of Mary Handly by her attorney, Luke Bowyer, Esq., that she the sd Mary should be released and set free from an indenture suggested to be fraudulently obtained by a certain William White against her the sd Mary Handly, and that the sd William White had restrained the sd Mary Handly from her liberty, made sale and disposed of her property contrary to law to her great damage. The court takes the same under consideration and are of the opinion that the sd Mary Handly have been illegally dealt with by the sd William White, by him confined and disposed of contrary to law therefore order sd Mary Handly be set at her liberty and she be permitted to go about her lawful occasions.

Ord that Ed Maguff an orphan boy of the age of seven years be bound to Gedeon Morriss and sd Morriss agrees with Court that he will give said child two years schooling and a common good suit of clothes at the close of his apprenticeship.

Ord that Joseph Whitson serve Constable in room of Isaac Taylor.

Ord the sheriff to take John Grimes to next court to answer the complaint of Elizabeth Ireland.

The State vs. John Holly. Misdemeanor. William Fain witness for the State. The court are of the opinion that the defdt guilty and fine him fifty shillings.

The Grand Jury present Thomas Carder for stealing a small piece of steel. Edmund Williams, William Brimer, Augusta Carter, Richard Brasil.

On motion of Wm. Cocke, Esq. that two negroes now in the possession of Cleaver Barksdale, Sheriff and by him taken from Jordon Roatch on suspicion that the sd negroes were plundered from some citizen of South Carilina. But no proof of the same, and ordered into the custody of Jordan Roatch, he to give bond for keeping the said negroes in this county six months from date, and deliver them if any owner can legally prove the same.

On motion that Joshua Baulding be admitted in this county on proviso that he comply with the laws provided for persons being inimical to the State and have rendered service that will expiate any crime that he has been guilty of inimical to the State and United States.

The Court considering the same grant the sd leave (copy issued to his wife)

William Barry have deposited to the clerk three thousand dollars in order to satisfy a Bond on which John Jameson brought with sd William Barry.

William Hopkins discharged by proclamation, &cc.

The State vs. William Carder. Stealing a piece of steel. A jury towit: John Long, Joseph Notion, Joseph Ballard, Isaac Denton, Anderson Smith, Edward Mercer, Forester Mercer, Walton Carr, James Wray, Jesse Coalmen, James McAdams and Isaac Choat. We of the jury do find the Defdt not guilty.

John Long, Foreman.

Court adjourned.

Court met.

I James Roddy, Cornelius Bowman & Jos. Foard, is appointed assessors for the first District 7 Richard White, Esq. Justice, and Andrew Willson constable.

2 Thomas Houghton, Esq.
   Landon Carter
   Val. Sevier
   And. Greer, Assessor
   Jos. Whitson, Constable
3 Geo. Russell, Esq.
   Mark Mitchell
   Pharoah Cobb
   Jesse Been, Assessor
   Wm. Grissom, Constable
4 Charles Robertson, Esq.
   Jesse Bounds
   Isaac Mayfield
   William Murphy, Assessor
   William Meeks, Constable
5 Daniel Kennedy
   Peter Keikendall

William Ritchey
Samuel Wear, Assessor
Jesse Gentry, Constable

John Sevier, William Cocke and Val. Sevier is appointed commissioners of confiscated property, &cc for the year of 1782 given bond and security in the sum of fifteen thousand pounds. Andrew Greer, William McNabb, and Samuel Williams went the security.

John Sevier commissioner for 1781 made return that he sold two slaves that was confiscated from of the estate of Thomas Barker at the price of thirty four hundred pounds and that he has the money to render unto the court.

The State vs. Ezekial Able. Indicmt for stealing a horse. John Odull witness for State sworn. Mary Hopkins, Charles Hughes, & Jesse Coalmen witness for Defdt. sworn. The indictment quashed for insufficiency.

The last Will and Testament of Adam Broils proved by John Waddle, Conad Willhite and Mathias Broils, the same ordered recorded.

On motion that John Clark be bound to good behavior for fear he may do John Nave some damage either in person or property. John Clark bound, Val. Sevier and Wm. Clark his securities.

John Gillaland vs. John Shurly. On Cavit. The sheriff returned into court that the Jury have found for defendant.

Joseph Young vs. William Gray. On Cavit. The sheriff returned into Court that the jury found for the Pltff.

The court allows the clerk to take and receive for issuing orders for each tryal of Cavited land, 20 shillings in specie and for witness as in other cases according to the former laws prescribed in Davis justice of peace.

Ordered the grist mill now building by ———— Allison be a public grist mill and be entitled to the same rights as other Grist Mills have within this county.

Alex McFarlin have leave to build a grist mill on Pigeon Creek on his own land and have the same rights as other grist mills in this county.

The court allows Cleavers Barksdale sheriff in specie fifty pounds for his ex officio service in 1781.

Sarah Bybee have chosen Isaac Mayfield her guardian and is appointed as such by the court and have entered himself with Charles Robertson and Zachariah Isbell, Esq. in the sum of one hundred thousand pounds for the faithful performance as such.

III

GENERAL JOHN SEVIER

The Seviers are of French origin, and the French spelling of the name is said to have been Xavier. Valentine was born in London and settled in the Shenandoah Valley of Virginia, where his son was born in 1740. The first wife of John was a Miss Hawkins, by whom he had six children.

With a party of explorers and land prospectors, John came to the Holston about 1769. He built the first fort on the Watauga, and here he settled together with his father, his brother Valentine, and other immigrants.

The second marriage of John Sevier had a romantic background. While he and James Robertson were defending the Watauga fort, he saw a tall young lady fleeing toward the fort, closely pursued by the red men, and her approach to the gate cut off. Turning suddenly, she leaped the palisade at another point and fell into the arms of Captain John Sevier. She was Catharine Sherrill, who became his devoted wife and the mother of ten children. The first wife of Sevier was delicate and never left Virginia.

While on a visit to his family in 1774, Sevier was commissioned captain and took part in the Point Pleasant campaign.

The settlers on the Holston being beyond the influence of the North Carolina government, adopted the form known in American history as the Watauga Convention, and Sevier was one of its four delegates to the Assembly of North Carolina. He was instrumental in securing the establishment of the District of Washington. For five years the people had been getting along very well under the rudimentary government of the Association, and by sundry laws its acts were validated by the state.

In June, 1776, the Cherokees attacked the Watauga fort, and as we have seen they were indirectly the means of providing Sevier with another wife. The marriage took place about 1779. It was said of the bride that "she could outrun, outjump, walk more erect, and ride more gracefully than any other female in all the mountains around, or on the continent at large."

The American Revolution was now on, and Sevier had much to do in contending with the Indians and tories. In 1777 he became a lieutenant colonel. In 1779 he made a damaging foray into the Cherokee domain. The battle of Boyd's Creek would doubtless have been a complete victory, had his orders been duly executed. The failure led to a feud between Sevier and another conspicuous settler of East Tennessee. A few days later, Sevier was joined by Isaac Shelby and Arthur Campbell with reenforcements, and the command being now harmonious, they chastised the Cherokees and returned home with a better feeling of security.

A critical year was 1780. The British were overrunning Georgia and South Carolina, Gates had been completely defeated, money, clothing, and ammunition were scarce, the tories were daring and savage, and the Indians, instigated by emissaries, were harrying the frontier. Many became despondent, and took refuge under the protection certificates of the British, these, however, not proving dependable. The sun of Independence seemed about to hide behind accumulating clouds.

Sevier is entitled to a full share of the glory won October 7, 1780. The sword and vote of thanks from the state of North Carolina were well earned and were creditable to the state. But the deeds of Sevier deserve to be commemmorated in a cenotaph, hewn out of the beautiful marble of the county named for him. People of East Tennessee, consult, contribute, construct a cenotaph worthy of him and worthy of yourselves.

In the fall of 1780 an infamous tory of the name of Dykes plotted a cruel and ignominious death for Sevier, and would have accomplished his object had not his wife informed Mrs. Sevier.

The preceding June, Sevier had marched into South Carolina to aid McDowell against the Cherokees and Creeks. During this absence the battle of Musgrove's Mill took place.

In February, 1781, Washington District had become Washington County, and Sevier was commissioned as its colonel. A few days later General Greene appointed him a commissioner to treat with the Cherokees and other tribes.

In one of his expeditions against the red men Sevier took back to the settlements about thirty of the Indian women and children. Ten of them remained three years at his own home, working not at all, or not enough to "pay for their salt." But the kind treatment of these Indians was one of his best victories, although neither the state nor the general government ever gave him any remuneration.

The same year, Sevier and Shelby were complimented in a resolution by the Assembly of North Carolina. They were urged to defend the frontier—upon their own hook. Other compliments came to hand, and in some of them Sevier is addressed as "Your Excellency."

In September, 1781, Sevier marched with 200 men to the aid of General Greene, and joined himself to Marion, as did also Shelby. After the surrender of Cornwallis, Sevier and Shelby wished to attack the Hessians at Monk's Corner, near Charleston, but had to be under the command of Colonel Mayhew of South Carolina. Sevier remained till the end of the year, but Shelby returned to attend the legislature. Sevier conducted other expeditions into the Indian country, for the peace with England did not end the warfare on the border.

In 1784 came the episode of the state of Franklin, with its stirring scenes and its medley of strife; and very much of the trouble was directed at the very men who had done more than any others to promote the peace and prosperity of the over-mountain settlements. Sevier was tendered a commission as brigadier general by the government of North Carolina, and not a few held that it was to withdraw him from any active participation in the movement for a new state. In the strife of that day, each party was ambitious for his friendship and desired him as a leader. He had to contend with active and vigilant opponents, but he feared not, faltered not, failed not. To him the coonskin money of the state of Franklin was of more esteem than the two hundred thousand dollars of North Carolina currency in his log cabin. This paper was "not worth a continental." In the several treaties he negotiated with the Indians while he was governor of Franklin, the pipe of peace was lighted with North Carolina notes.

In 1786 the Cherokees disregarded the treaty of Hopewell, and Sevier had to punish them in their towns on the Hiwassee.

In 1787-88 the anxiety of North Carolina to be relieved of the many and urgent demands upon her treasury by the western counties induced Sevier and his friends to accede to measures of adjustment. The transmontane region was ceded to the United States and was organized as the Territory South of the Ohio. The state of Franklin gently passed out of existence, and in 1796 the state of Tennessee was admitted to the Union. General Sevier was the first governor, and until the end of his days he was much in public life. The settlers of East Tennessee regarded him as father, friend, and protector and his word and will were law and gospel. So often was he engaged in negotiations with the Indians that he was known as the "Treaty-Maker." But his more familiar soubriquet was "Chunky Jack."

After Wayne's victory in 1794 the Southern Indians became less warlike, yet neither they nor their white neighbors always kept the peace.

Sevier's second term as governor closed in 1801, but he was called back to succeed Archibald Roane in 1803, serving until 1811, when he was chosen as one of Tenessee's three Congressmen. In 1813 he was reelected, and during the war of 1812 was a member of the military committee, a very important post, and his opinions, especially in regard to Western affairs were earnestly sought and highly respected.

On retiring from Congress in 1815, he was persuaded by the president to become a commissioner to adjust difficulties with the Creek Indians. In accepting this position he went against the advice of friends, who took into account his age and his impaired health. While on this official duty he died near Fort Decatur on the east side of the Tallapoosa, September 24, 1815, and was buried with the honors of war. General Gaines, was in command, and although himself quite sick, paid the last tribute of respect to a brave fellow soldier.

General Sevier was in every instance elected to the governorship and to Congress with practically no opposition.

In this brief summary there has been no mention of the battle of Hightower, or of the other military enterprises for which no compensation was received. Sevier was nearly ruined thereby, and while absent on military service, personal and political enemies seized his fifteen slaves and took them off.

The life of Sevier was a busy life. He never became a retired man or private citizen. No stone marked the first resting place, and near the grave is that of the good captain who fired the last volley over the dust of the patriotic hero. And the gazing, thoughtful Indian raised the question: "Is this the goal of ambition?" Is it enough to pass resolutions and wear crape a few days—and then forget?

IV.

LETTER BY DRAPER TO MARTIN

The following letter to William Martin is of special interest. It contains information Dr. Draper was intending to use in a second volume, but he died before he could prepare his manuscript. William Martin was a son of General Joseph Martin, who was born in Albemarle county, Virginia, in 1740. At the age of sixteen he ran away from home to become a trapper and trader. He traveled with Boone and Walker and visited Powell's Valley as early as 1769. In 1774 he was commandant of a frontier fort. Patrick Henry, governor of Virginia, appointing him an Indian agent in 1776, he built a block-house on Long Island near where now is Kingsport. General Martin was very tall, handsome, robust, and fearless, and was liked by all. His married life was irregular. His first wife was of a prominent Virginia family. After she died he married another Virginia lady, yet was already living with an Indian wife, and spending most of his time with her. She was Betsy, the handsome daughter of Nancy Ward, the Pocahontas of Tennessee. Both wives approved of his marital conduct, and would not allow their children to criticize their father, although it is now known they had bitter feelings on the matter. General Martin excused his bigamy by saying it was the only way by which he could secure favorable treaties from the Indians.

William Martin was living at Dixon's Springs, Smith County, Tennessee.

Buffalo, N. Y., February 18th, 1843.

My Dear & Aged Friend:—

I need hardly tell you that while your eight sheet packet of the 1st January afforded me great pleasure in view of the Pioneer store of information it contained, yet I was & still am, greatly grieved and alarmed in consequence of the announcement at the close of your communication—that it is the last, probably, I may ever receive from you. I am pained that you are so afflicted & I say this not merely from selfish considerations. I cannot bear the thought of having it so; & still if necessity, or your comfort even requires it, I will try & be submissive. I trust and pray that you may be restored again to enjoy yet many more happy years in your old age, that I may be permitted often to hear from you, &, withal, that Deo Volente I may yet see you face to face. I still flatter myself the pleasure of a trip to Southwestern Virginia and Tennessee this coming autumn.

My intention is to strike for your brothers in Henry county—those old manuscripts, & those young girls, you know are powerful to one of my age and composition. But as I am not just now in a joking mood, I will dismiss that part of the allusion. Of course I must visit Gov. Campbell; and I hope in time to get track of General Andrew Lewis' descendants & make them a call— there I must suppose are old documents. Governor Jas. Preston of Montgomery county I presume had those of his father, Col. Wm. Preston. Once through with So. W. Virginia, I should push for the neighborhood of Blountsville, the Long Island Flat battle ground, thence down to Jonesborough and to Knoxville, & since I last wrote you I have a long communication from Col. George Christian—he, it seems, was with your father on the Lookout Mountain campaign, but does not give any particulars, save that his father was aide to General Martin—that the army consisted of about 500 men, had "a smart brush" at Lookout mountain—had three men killed & five wounded, while the loss of the Indians was some 9 or ten. I must ask Col. Christian for a detailed account; which, with yours, our brother Tobey's in anticipation, my old man Job's and Haywood's will enable me to draw up a pretty full and interesting history of that campaign. I am the more anxious to do this from the fact that your father's name is more intimately associated with this noted military transaction than with any other. It is due to his memory and services—it is due to the great subject in the prosecution of which I am engaged—the Pioneer history of the great Western Valley.

And while speaking of Col. Christian let me add, that he has given me some particulars of the Flat battle from an aged neighbor of his—one Cornelius Carmack, who was in the battle. I have fortunately ascertained that one person at least of all those engaged in that affair, yet survives. This is an additional incentive for me to hurry my intended tour to the South West. I am pretty sure Mr. Carmack's memory in some particulars is defective—he enumerates James Thompson, James Shelby, William Cocke, Robert Edmondson, & a Mr. Buchanan as having commanded companies—& Mr. Buchanan, he

thinks, remained to defend the Station, while the others
went forth to battle.   Robert Edmondson I know for a
certainty was there, but I feel confident he did not command a Company—I have often conversed with Capt. A.
J. Edmondson of Pontotoc, a son of Robt. Edmondson, &
had his father commanded a company I should have had
the fact from his son.   I never before heard of a Captain
Buchanan being there at the head of a company and
must think it is an error.   Gov. Campbell's father, Captain John Campbell, commanded a company in the battle & it seems probable that John Morrison (afterwards
Col. John Morrison of Kentucky) and William Russell,
afterwards Gen. Russell, also commanded companies.
Gov. Campbell says he is sure Morrision was at the head
of a company & Russell was certainly in the action &
was then a captain—as indeed he was at Pt. Pleasant
in '74; but while I think he commanded a company at
the Flats, I do not yet feel positive of it.   The Hon. William B. Campbell inclines to the same opinion, & thinks
he can ascertain for a certainty.   I cannot but think that
Captain James Shelby was at the Station, not in the battle.   Even Haywood speaks of John Morrison & Robert
Edmondson as making "conspicuous exertions," "they advanced some places towards the enemy & began the bat
tle by shooting down the foremost of them;" but the
Judge is careful to class them among "the men" as con-
tradistinguished from "the officers."   I have said this
much about the Captains who commanded companies in
the Flat battle, in the hope that you may be able to recall to your recollection something definite about the
doubtful matters.   As there was no official account of
that engagement, I must keep Digging at the subject until I get it as near accurate as may be at this late day.
And here let me say, I am gratified not a little with what
you tell me of "Big Elleck Moore."   Have you any idea
to whose company he was attached?—& what finally became of him?   Haywood speaks of "Heaton's Station"
—in yours of 1st of Dec. you speak of the same.   Now
Gov. Campbell assures me it was "Eaton's" not Heaton's,
& Col. Geo. Christian says so, too, & adds that at all
events the old man after whom it was named, was always known as "Amos Eaton."   The peculiar mode of
pronunciation as practiced in England with the rough
breathing, would make "Eaton" "Heaton."   May not
this have occurred in some such way as this?
      Now a word as to the origin of the name of the
Frankland government. You and some others are impres-

sed with the idea that the name was originally Franklin in honor of Dr. Ben. Franklin. I had a long conversation with Gen. Stephen Cocke, a son of old Colonel William Cocke and this matter was brought upon the tapis. You know full well that Col. Cocke figured conspicuously in the Frankland affair. His son told me his father had often informed him that as the friends of the new government aimed to form a sovereign State, free of North Carolina, they hit upon the name Frankland as peculiarly appropriate—for Frankland is equivalent to Freeland. I dare say Judge Haywood adopted the name Frankland with this impression as to its origin and meaning. I will shortly write to Maj. James Sevier of Jonesboro, asking his recollection about it. I do not doubt that the idea was pretty generally prevalent, that the short lived republic was named in honor of Dr. Franklin. I feel curious to know which was the true original name. I dare say Dr. Ramsey would know something about the matter; but, as I said to you in a former letter, I cannot draw him into a correspondence with me. I regret this for many reasons.

KING'S MOUNTAIN—You have certainly given some new views with regard to this great campaign and battle. I already have the official account signed by "Wm. Campbell, Isaac Shelby, Benj. Cleveland." I clipped it from a newspaper some years ago copied from the "Columbia S. C. Telescope" & that is the residence of the Hon. Wm. C. Preston & I doubt not this document was obtained from him. I may here add this original report was published in the Virginia Gazette in November 1780; at least I have the authority of Chief Justice Marshall for it. You spoke of nine Tories being sentenced to be hung after the action & one broke and escaped. From the several statements I have, I must suppose nine were executed, & one escaped. The present venerable Maj. Benj. Sharp of Missouri, avers that nine were hung —& he was in the battle; & Silas McBee of Pontotoc county Miss., who was under Col. Williams has told me the same, & that the tenth effected his escape. I would be glad if further reflection would lead you to coincide with them—It is, I am aware, not very important whether eight or nine were hung; still I would like to be positive. This Silas McBee was a Tugalo resident, afterwards settled in the Cumberland country about '90 or '92, then in Kentucky aided in capturing and killing Big Harper. I took full notes of his recollection of all these early trans-

actions—Spent several days with him He is a wealthy
& hospitable old planter just about your own age, the
father-in-law of Gov. T. M. Tucker of Miss., and of the
Hon. Thos. H. Williams, late U. S. Senator from that
State—One word more with regard to King's Mountain.
I have written Gov. Campbell about the Shelby & Preston correspondence, to which you alluded in a former letter & of which I had an imperfect knowledge from my
friend Capt. A. J. Edmondson and others. If the Governor nor Mrs. Gen. Francis Preston possess not a copy
then I will apply direct to Wm. C. Preston. I doubt not
it would throw some light upon the battle and its distinguished actors, & that without prejudicing my exalted
opinion of General William Campbell and Governor Isaac
Shelby.

COL. BENJAMIN CLEVELAND—I have been de-
lighted with your sketch of this great & daring borderer.
It confirmed me in my opinion of the man & corroborates
many incidents I had heard of him from aged Tugalo
residents. Maj. Meredith Thurmond, Mr. Portman, Silas
McBee, Dr. John Miller (son-in-law of Gen. Pickens) &
his estimable lady, Mr. McCord and others. I am chiefly
indebted to Maj. Thurmond for what I know prior to the
reception of your last packet. The Major told me in substance, 'tis not so minutely, his origin from the Cromwell
stock—from Orange or Albemarle, Va.,—about his early
trip to Kentucky—his being taken by the Tories and finally rescued, & I had visited a daughter of Gen. Ben.
Cleveland's (of Georgia, the son of "Devil John")—this
lady, and she is a lady, gave me some account, or I should
say a very particular account of the descendants of Col.
Ben. Cleveland and promised to prevail upon her father
to write me what he knew. Gen. Cleveland visited his
daughter near Pontotoc in the spring of '41, but I was un-
luckily absent from Pontotoc & missed seeing him. I
however wrote him at length—& not long since he sent
me quite a large packet by private hand to Pontotoc & a
friend of mine there took the liberty to enclose it to
Senator Walker—and it has somehow or other miscar-
ried. I do not exactly despair altogether, but it being
seven weeks ago, I confess I have my doubts. I had
submitted some doubtful points to General Cleveland—
one I recollect was a romantic story told me by a Mr.
Portman, who knew Col. Cleveland on Tugalo. It was
in substance this: A gentlemanly person had, near the
close of the Revolution, put in for the night with Col.

Cleveland. On the leave taking the next morning the Col. affected to suspect him a Tory, took from him a noble horse & tagged him Andy. As the story goes—the man, who resided somewhere in the Eastern part of the State, was a good Whig, a man of some note and prominence & of course took umbrage at the treatment he received at the hands of Col. Cleveland—but there was then no help for it. When the Col. settled on Tugalo, which I should suppose was in 1786 (and I judge from the fact that Hawkins, Pickens and your father made three several treaties in Nov. 1785 & Jan. 1786) this ill treated stranger paid him a visit incognito, professed a desire to purchase some wild land belonging to the Colonel some 3 or 4 miles off. The Col. not recognizing the man, went on horseback to show it to him. When there the stranger unmasked his real character, drew a pair of pistols, ordered the affrighted Colonel, unarmed as he was, to "Say his prayers" before entering eternity—the Colonel all the while begging for his life, yet the man thus kept tantalizing him for some time—until finally he made the old Colonel lay flat upon his back & fastened his limbs to convenient saplings, & thus left him—taking good care, however, to take with him his identical horse filched from him by Colonel Cleveland, & which the Colonel had ridden on this occasion. This occurrence said my informant, took place in sultry summer weather, & for three days the Colonel was exposed to the scorching rays of the sun by day & to the chilling damp by night, before his alarmed friends and neighbors found and relieved him. The fact that Col. Cleveland acquired, as you and others have told me, much of his property by the system of plunder so prevalent at that day has led me to suspect that there might be some truth in this story. The other old Tugalo men with whom I conversed about it thought the same, & yet none of them had ever heard of it before. And Dr. Miller and his lady were pretty strongly of this opinion. As a matter of course Cleveland himself would not care to tell a story of that kind, certainly not very creditable to him. I speak of it to you and ask you to comment upon it.

One other matter—& perhaps more than one before I get through with Col. Cleveland. You spoke of his boys hanging a Tory—this reminds me of a story I read some three or four years ago in a newspaper, purporting to be an anecdote related by a Mr. Jones of Rowan Co., North Carolina, in the Legislature of that State. I will here give it you from memory—I have the clipped newspaper account so snugly laid away that I can't just now lay my hands upon it.   A Colonel John Cleveland, a King's Mountain man, had captured a notorious Tory & with the aid of a servant or two, took him to a sapling by a neighboring hillside, fastened the culprit to it, and attempted to give the word to the negroes to swing him off—but being afflicted with stammering, was some time before he got it out, & at last broke out with an oath "to give it to him," or something to that effect, for the precise language I cannot just now recall.   Could this have referred to Col. Ben. Cleveland—or "Devil John?"—were either of them habitually or occasionally afflicted with stammering?   This Mr. Jones who told the story in debate in the North Carolina Legislature—perhaps the celebrated Jo. Seawell Jones—conveyed the idea, at least inferentially, that the Cleveland in question was of King's Mountain.   I am aware, however, that the old Colonel had some of his brothers with him—perhaps the reverend John—& perhaps, too, Young John was there.   Can you throw any light upon this affair?   Another matter.   You remark that Colonel C. did not take much part in the Revolution until the fall of 1780, except perhaps "an Indian campaign or so."   About this "Indian campaign or so" I would right well like to know something.

Per adventure he went out with General Rutherford, who raised a large force in the neighborhood of Salisbury, N. C., and penetrated the Cherokee country in 1776.   See Haywood, page 54.   And if he went with Rutherford, then the question follows, in what capacity? And the varied dates I have had from different persons as to the time of Colonel Cleveland's death I had placed the most reliance on what Major Thurmond told me— that it was in the autumn of 1806.

I forgot in the proper place to ask of you a description of Eaton's or Heaton's station as you saw it three or four years after the Island Flat battle.   Such a description will prove both interesting and useful to me, and while the thought is in my mind, I will add, that when I visit you, we will try and make a rough map of the position of the old forts, stations, and settlements, as they were during the old Cherokee wars.

POINT PLEASANT BATTLE, 1774.   I feel pretty confident you have some wrong impressions respecting this battle.   You seem to think that after Gen. Andrew Lewis and his brother Col. Charles Lewis, who was killed in an action, there were no officers engaged of higher grade than captains. Col. John Field was killed at the head of his volunteer regiment, and Col. William Fleming was sadly wounded at the head of his. I have two lengthy and minute letters written just after the battle— one by Isaac Shelby, the other by Col. William Preston (the latter was not in the action, but obtained his information from Col. Christian and others on the expedition) and both warned me in making this statement. I am aware that Col. Christian did not reach the battleground till the midnight succeeding the battle. Another view of yours has puzzled me somewhat—that Gen. Lewis was blamed for keeping a large portion of his men in camp—and only three hundred were permitted to go forth to battle, and no reinforcements save five who disobeyed orders. I feel safe in saying that Col. John Fields and his whole regiment, of nine companies and near three hundred men, reinforced Col. Charles Lewis, who had one hundred and fifty men, and Col. Wm. Fleming, who had one hundred and fifty more—so there could not, by any calculation I can make from all the lights before me, have been less than six hundred men in the engagement, and probably near seven hundred, for I find some three captain's companies engaged with (out) being enumerated or belonging to either of the three regiments in the action. In round numbers General Lewis' army consisted of 1100 men, and probably 400 were fortifying the camp and certainly not over 500; but I do not feel altogether certain that he was justified in keeping so many men in camp as four hundred even, while so fierce and doubtful a battle was raging around them. One other matter. Shelby's old letter distinctly states, that two of Captain Russell's company first discovered the enemy. One was killed, and in a few minutes two of Evan Shelby's company, James Robertson & Valentine Sevier, came running in and corroberated what Russell's man had stated. Does this tally with Dr. Felix Robertson's recollection of his father's version? I have another proof that Val. Sevier was the person with Robertson, other than Shelby's old letter; and certain it is, that Sevier was not killed on that occasion. You must make a desperate effort to coincide in this view of the matter—so much for Point Pleasant.

YOUR FATHER'S SERVICE IN 1774. At my request your brother has sent me a couple of brief letters from Wm. Preston, dated respectively 12th Oct. 1774, &

4th. Nov. following, and directed to "Captain Joseph Martin," at Culberson's. I herewith send you copies. I am puzzled with them—Preston, I dare say, had the military jurisdiction—County Lieutenant most likely—writes your father as Captain Martin and his commission as such was dated the preceding August, yet these letters show that your father was under the command of Captain Penn. I am thinking Penn's company was in "the fort" alluded to—that your father was mostly out with the scouting party—not an entire company, and probably not any part of Penn's company, but a District squad or party of his own; and yet towards the close of the campaign in October—Preston orders the Scouts, who had evidently until then, been under the orders of their respective leaders, to be "under the Direction of Penn." And what strengthens me in this opinion is the decisive wording of the second paragraph of Preston's letter of 12th Oct., 1774—in which Preston speaks gratifyingly of the "several long fatiguing" scouts with your men. Let me have your views of these matters. Who was this Capt. Penn—What was the name of the fort spoken of? What "pass" was alluded to?

COL. ARTHUR CAMPBELL. I could wish your opinion of Col. Campbell's private character was different from what it is—you seem impressed with the idea he was mercenary-swindling-dishonorable. I am fully aware that Col. C. had one great defect—a slackness in paying his debts. This very naturally made him not a few enemies. His character, you know, was of the severe, haughty, austere cast—little disposed to make compromises with any one—not only exercising great severity towards the Tories in the Revolution, but also towards the Whigs who were disposed to plunder. This course made him vindictive enemies on both sides who were untiring in traducing him. Besides, he was unhappily very passionate—often got involved in trifling quarrels (I have one in my mind's view just now, with Col. John Floyd, a distinguished Ky. Pioneer, which occurred at Williamsburg, in '76) & in these quarrels these traducing whisperings would be dropped in the ear of his adversary and thus these unfortunate little slanders would be borne on the wings of the wind. I cannot but think that I ought, from these causes, to make great allowance for these traditionary impressions—& I heard of them long before I ever received your first letter even. Sixty years have now passed away since their occurrence & I beg you will not think me doing wrong if I throw the mantle of charity over these errors and defects of Arthur Campbell's character. Though his services were not so brilliant as William Campbell's yet I cannot but place quite a high estimate upon them, commencing, as they did, in the old French war of '56, & extending to the close of the Revolution. These old frontiersmen had many obstacles to encounter, unnumbered toils and sufferings to endure, & if I must err "the milk of human kindness" will prompt me rather to add than pluck one solitary laurel from their brows and will you blame me?

Now for a perfect medley of inquiries—& I make them, as I have all the preceding ones in this hurried communication, with the hope and supposition that you recover from the affliction of your eyes—otherwise you must let them all pass unnoticed. You have done so much for me, it would be unkind in me to ask more, except your health and love for these matters, prompt you irresistibly to volunteer—

1. Did Col. William Campbell, or Col. Arthur Campbell—or both remain on Long Island of Holston 3 months after the campaign of '81, as intimated by Haywood on page 98?

2. Was the Col. Hord mentioned on the 159th. page of the same work your father's old friend of that name?

3. What was the character of William Cocke's Judicial malfeasance, to which you made allusion?

4. Was the Jesse Walton who was with Cleveland in his trip to Kentucky, the same person of that name who was a major under Sevier in some of his Indian campaigns?

5. Have (you) any knowledge of Col. John Carter, the brother of Col. Landon Carter? The son of the latter, the Hon. Wm. B. Carter, promised me near three years ago some sketches of these two brothers, but for some reason has never done so, though more than once kindly reminded of it. Do you know anything of Major Jonathan Tipton & Major James Hubbard, who served in the Indian wars under Sevier? or Col. Jacob Brown, or Major Jacob Womack, or Col. Charles Robinson? Well I think this must do this time—as I made some singular inquiries in my last.

If your health will not permit you to write me at length, I shall nevertheless be anxious to hear from you and beg neither you nor my friend Wilson will forget me. As you have suggested so pleasantly the idea of your yet being my uncle-in-law, you must not get out of patience with me even should I Uncle you half to death. Never mind I'll try and be generous. The goodness of your heart that prompted so happy a suggestion, calls for my unbounded gratitude,—a Virginia Companion—a baked yam and a glorious cup of coffee for supper (I'm Anti-tea anyway you can fix it) is certainly the height of my ambition the inmost limit of my worldly wishes. I must say, my aged brother, that as much of a recluse as I am, & aside from all pleasantry, I should be more than half disposed to wed, IF SOME KIND HEARTED BEING WOULD ONLY CLAIM ME AS HER OWN. But ah me, the sight of a girl even well nigh affrights me out of my senses & with much timidity (& the secret I apprehend, of all this timidity is, I never had any sisters) pray tell me, how can I possibly avoid the bachelor's fate?

With my prayers for your restoration to health & that true happiness may ever be yours, I close by sub-scribing myself.

Your obliged friend & Christian brother,
LYMAN C. DRAPER

V.

LETTERS BY CHRISTIAN TO DRAPER

The following letters were written to Lyman C. Draper, the historian, by George Christian, son of Colonel Gilbert Christian. They throw an interesting light on the settlement and early history of East Tennessee.

Livingston 24th, June 1842.

Lyman C. Draper, Esqr.

D. Sir, your letter of the 24th ult. was rec'd through the Hon. William B. Campbell, asking of me such information as I may possess in relation to my father, Col. Gilbert Christian who died at Knoxville on his return from Hightower Campaign in 1793, (which is the true date.)

My father Gilbert Christian was a native of the State of Virginia, born and raised in Augusta county about the year of 1723-4, and was the son of Robert Christian, there were two other brothers, John and William. All three settled on Christian creek, which took its name from the three brothers. They were the first settlers of that country. Each one of the old men had a son Gilbert, which was the name of my great grand father. Uncle William Christian was the youngest of the three old men, and I always understood one of the most successful Indian fighters of his day in that part of the country. Under him, my father got his training for Indian warfare, and to give a detailed account of the many adventures of those men of the early days of our back settlements, would require more space than could be comprised in a letter.

Suffice to say that when mischief was done old Capt. Christian was uniformly called on.

My father moved from the place of his nativity in Virginia, to the western country in 1774 and settled permanently at the Long Island of Holston. The Cherokees at this time were at peace tho the Shawnees on the settlement on Clinch which lay north of us were very troublesome. My father from his acquaintance with Indian fighting was almost continually kept from home. At this time the settlement where we lived were very weak, and few men trained to war, and here I will mention some of the most distinguished characters, the Shelby family. The old General had four sons, Isaac, James, Evan and Moses. Tho they were all brave men yet Isaac the eldest of the four, afterwards Governor of Kentucky and perhaps was one of the most popular men of his day. Anthony and Isaac Bledsoe were brothers. John Anderson, several of the Looney family. Those were the most prominent men of the first pioneers of our country in that quarter, and who stood the brunt of all the wars.

The two Bledsoe brothers removed to Sumner county at Bledsoe Lick where they both were killed by Indians near the latter part of the war; likewise two of the Shelbys, James and Evan lost their lives by the Indians, and altho we were in a very exposed situation in our first settling, no block house, no fort, or anything sufficient to secure us from attack, and although the Indians on several occasions passed us, murdered families further in the settlement, it was our good fortune to escape. But at the breaking of the Cherokees in 1775-6 the frontier settlement broke up and either returned to the old settlement or else went into Forts. My father, after conveying the family out of danger and leaving them, returned to join the little army which had been collected at Eatons Station, consisting of three or four companies commanded by Capt. Campbell, Shelby and Cock, the others not recollected, but on the day before my father reached the Station, certain information was brought stating the Indians had concentrated all their forces and was marching directly on the station, on which a council was held by the Officers, and it was agreed there being a great many children and women in the fort, that the men with the exception of a few to guard the fort should sally forth and meet the enemy outside. After proceeding some four or five miles, the Indians were seen advancing in great force. Our men, a great many of them not being used to Indians, took fright at first and ran, and by something that occured and not being shot, took up heart, rallied and engaged the Indians so effectually that they soon put them to flight, leaving a great number of their warriors dead on the ground, gaining a complete victory. This happened in July. In the Autumn of the same year, Col. Wm. Christian was ordered to take the command of an army and proceed to the Cherokee country and lay waste to their towns. My father joined this army under Col. Wm. Christian and proceeded to the Cherokee Towns on the Tennessee which they destroyed, and not finding any Indians to fight, returned home leaving a Garrison at

Long Island. Shortly afterwards the Cherokees sued for peace, and the treaty was held on the Island near the fort. This was in 1777-8. This peace was of short duration, and the British at this time were making advances through Carolina, and it was feared they would attempt to cross the mountain, upon which Col. Campbell, Col. Shelby and Col. Sevier collected what of the militia could be spared, proceeded without delay across the mountain and through Carolina to King Mountain, where they found Maj. Ferguson who had taken advantageous position on top of the Mountain with a band of British Regulars, aided by some hundreds of Tories—whom they encountered and defeated, killing and taking prisoners nearly every man. In this battle my father commanded a company under Col. Sevier. It will be remembered that in those days captains wore no apperlettes, carried rifles, and knew how to use them. But to give any kind of a detailed account of the many incidents and campaigns my father and others, which I named, were engaged would fill a volume—suffice to say, within the recollections there has been no less than five campaigns carried against Cherokees in all in which my father acted a conspicuous part.

About the year 1787 or 88, an occurence happened which very much disturbed the peace of the inhabitants, which was occasioned by an act of the Legislature of North Carolina in which this country was seceded to Congress for the benefit of the General Government, but Congress not liking the terms did not accept it. Whereupon the people being left without a Government, the leading men, or the people through them proceeded to call a convention, form a constitution, and organized a Government accordingly, elected Representatives and met in General Assembly. But some discontented men who thought they had been overlooked, prayed to be taken again under the old Government. This occasioned considerable disturbances—all the discontented joining the old State party, while those in office under the new State not willing to yield, the contest for a time was hot, and some blood shed in the strife. North Carolina in the meantime repealed the cession act—finally the new State party had to yield. This new State was named Franklin, in honor of Benjamin Franklin.

In all this strife father and Sevier took an active part with the new State party. Sevier was elected Governor, my father was a member of the Convention, I think, and of the General Assembly, but the failure of the new state party reduced them all to the ranks. This state though was of short duration. North Carolina made a cession of the country which was accepted by Congress, and we became a Territorial Government of which the late Governor Sevier was appointed delegate to Congress. My father was made Col. Commandant of the county, and nearly all the offices were filled by the new State party. My father held the rank of Col. until his death. Sevier was elected Governor of Tennessee. (William Blount was appointed Governor over the Territory.)

The settlement commenced in Miro District about 1780. Col. James Robertson, I believe was considered a leader at this time, tho there was a goodly number of others well qualified to form a respectable society. The Donilson family, R. Weakly, Sampson Williams, some of the Shelbies were among the first settlers. Separated by a wide wilderness from the old settlement, required considerable nerve to sustain themselves, but they weathered the storm, notwithstanding so many of the first adventurers lost their lives by the savage foe.

The Cherokees seldom took prisoners, their aim being to exterminate. I shall conclude with little hope that you will have patience to read what I have written. My only aim was to state facts as they occured, and if they are of any interest whatever, you are at liberty to use them as you may think proper.

I am, Sir with

Much respect, Yours,
GEORGE CHRISTIAN

Addressed:

Lyman C. Draper, Esqr., near Pontotoc, Miss.

Endorsed: Col. Gilbert Christian—the Shelbies, etc. From Col. G. Christian, 24 June, 1842. No. I.

At Home, 4th Dec., 1842

Lyman Draper, Esqr.

Dr. Sir, Yours of the 24th September has been rec'd through the politeness of the Hon. William B. Campbell and is now before me.

It would give me great pleasure indeed could I have it in my power to furnish anything in addition to what has become matter of history, particularly as relative to the early settlement of our State.

But believing your object to be more with a view to obtain matters of fact than anything else, and hoping at the same time your good sense will excuse my inaccuracy, as doubtless you will find many, I shall proceed to furnish you with all the information in my power on the subject in question.

Now as respects the adventure of Captain William Christian of Augusta, Virginia, I can state what has come to me by tradition, or at least in part—I suppose the reason that ex-Governor Campbell has referred you to Gilbert Christian, instead of William Christian, may have been because Gilbert was longer in service and more known as a public man than his uncle William. I know no work which would furnish the information required respecting this border warfare, nor have it in my power to furnish dates with any degree of accuracy—though I can vouch for the facts stated as to date. In the latter part of the old French war a party of Indians under the celebrated chief called Cap Dickenson (?) with a party of 12 or 15 warriors fell in upon the Frontiers of Augusta, Va., killed old Mr. Trimble, made prisoners of the daughter, a son of 14 or 15 years old, and a mulatto boy, and having done further outrages in the neighborhood, made off with the booty, upon which Uncle William with a chosen band of young men, on hearing what had happened, repaired to the spot where the scene had been acted, where they took the trail of the Indians pursuing them across the mountains. The Indians had some days start, which was always allowed them purposely as the most certain way of taking them by surprise in order that they might save the prisoners. It was in the afternoon they were overtaken. Our party had proceeded with all possible precaution, so as not to be discovered, so that when they came on them, they were camped on a level spot surrounded with a tolerable thick undergrowth. The Indians had unpacked their horses, for they had several loaded with the spoils they had taken. Except for the few left to guard the prisoners they all had turned out to hunt, which undoubtedly saved the lives of some of them.

But our men acted for the best, which was to surround the encampment with as much secrecy as possible, which they effected undiscovered, but while they were lying in wait for the return of the hunters, an Indian lad, a son of the chief, came riding in with a deer which they had killed, and riding immediately up to where one of the men was posted, on finding he must give the alarm, shot down the boy, upon which our men fired on the guard at the camp, killing or wounding what few of them was there, and so sudden was the surprise that the prisoners were all recovered safe except the mulatto boy who had been mistaken for an Indian by one of the men and shot through the arm—the fray being over, old Christian and his men being at this time hungry and fatigued, concluded to remain at the Indian camp for the night, and having in good time gotten the Indian boy's deer made a plentiful supper—but on the next morning 2 or 3 of the men went out to look at the Indian boy which had been shot off his horse, and while one of the men stooped to look at the boy, an Indian, said to be the father of the boy, had concealed himself for the purpose, fired on the man, whose name was Rutledge, shot him through the body, and ran away out of the sight of his pursuers. Rutledge was carried to the station, where he received timely aid by a skillful physician (Dr. Fleming) and recovered.

I will here relate another adventure of old Cap. Christian for which he was much applauded. It was probably in the year preceding Braddock's campaign—the Indians had become so troublesome on the frontiers that militia companies were kept on duty constantly. At this time Cap. George Moffit of Augusta, Va., (a cousin of father) who commanded a company on duty being informed of a large body of the enemy near at hand marched at the head of his company against them. The two companies met being nearly equal strength, some 65 strong on either side. But after a severe fight and after losing a number of his men, Moffit was completely defeated, himself narrowly escaping by sinking himself in a creek. This victory served to inspire the savages with fresh courage, and while they were disposing of their wounded and collecting their scattered warriors— old Cap. Christian on hearing of the defeat of Moffit lost no time collecting together his company of picked warriors—the Indians had time to retreat after their fight with Moffit, but seemed in no hurry to retreat further than to procure more provisions. But before they were apprized of their danger, old Christian was on them with his warriors. As it was intended, one of the lines discharged their guns upon the enemy, on which they flew to their guns, taking trees on the opposite side, when the men in the rear gave them a deadly fire. This threw them in some confusion, though they fought like tigers, but so completely were they surrounded and so deadly was our fire that in a few minutes they were almost entirely cut down. So complete was their defeat that only two or three reached their home.

Father was an officer under his uncle, Wm., in all these and many more scrapes of a like nature on the frontiers of Augusta.

Uncle Wm. commanded a company at the battle of Little Meadows, where if I am not mistaken Washington commanded—and I think at the battle of the Point, as it was called, under Col. Lewis who was killed at this battle. Father was under Maj. Evan Shelby in that battle.

Uncle Wm. Christian performed his last campaign a Maj. under Col. Wm. Christian against the Cherokees in 1776.

My recollection of the battle of the Point is very imperfect, tho my father and two uncles, Robert Christian, and George Anderson, were in this battle, also Wm. Moffit, a cousin of fathers, who was killed in this battle. This battle I think was in 1774.

With respect to my recollection of the part my father took on the Bird Campaign, my father commanded a company on that campaign. The officers under him were John Sawyers, John or William Anderson, which I do not know, for both were in the company, and as you are informed after the return of the army, built a cabin on Reedy creek about a mile above the junction with the Holston. Those who formed this party were Father, John Sawyers, John and William Anderson, James McNair, Robert Christian, and Nathan Page later joined them at the cabin all winter and to late in the spring, when each made an improvement on Reedy creek. They lost all this by an old title or grant made to Edmund Pendleton by the British crown.

After the attempt to settle on Reedy creek the next fall, Father in company with 7 or 8 others set out from Augusta with a view to exploring Kentucky. In this company were Uncle Robert Christian, George Anderson and one Hayes. I do not remember the names of the others. This party were well furnished for a long trip.

But after penetrating into the wilderness within 40 or 50 miles of the Crab Orchard, it being Sunday, the whole party except one man were lying at camp, when a party of Indians were seen approaching their camp

The Indians 14 in number, altho they made signs of friendship, were viewed with suspicion by our party Father, in particular objected to them being allowed to advance up to the camp and the men instantly took trees determined to defend themselves, on which one of the Indians named Tom Benge, (This was the Tom Benge prominent among the Cherokees, and the one who headed the Cavett Station massacre, when a thousand Indians were on their way to destroy White Station, now Knoxville in the year of ———) who spoke English called to our people, saying they were friends and brothers and that they were Cherokees with whom we were at peace, by which the wily savages obtained an advantage which otherwise might have resulted in his defeat. Our men by the artifice were completely outwitted and proposed the Indians be allowed to advance. Father still objected, but was overruled by the party, and the Indians being allowed to advance showed great friendship. But after smoking and eating for some time, Benge stepped up to Father, (who sat off on a log at some distance with his rifle across his lap) took a seat by him, asking him at the same time to look at his gun, upon which Father cautiously threw out the priming, handing the gun to the Indian, who after examining the gun for some time bounded to his feet, at the same time giving a signal, presented the gun at Fathers breast and snapt her, and the Indians as one man flew at our men with their tomahawks and knives, there being no chance to use the guns, when a struggle for life ensued. There being two Indians to each white man, the scuffle was very unequal, which resulted in the death of only one white man, one Hayes. The others all escaped without any other injury than the loss of everything they had but two of their horses.

Our party were so scattered while disengaging themselves from the Indians that they were several days in getting together which, however, they effected after several days travel. There being snow on the ground and having lost their blankets, and some of them their hunting shirts, pulled off in the scuffle, they suffered incredibly, but with the exception of Hayes all reached home.

At another time, (whether before or after this occurrence I have just related I am unable to state,) Father in company with some 12 or 15 others, set out from Augusta with the intention of exploring the Mississippi country. This party was well furnished with pack horses loaded with flour and other necessaries for such a trip—

the settlement at that time had been extended within 30 or 40 miles of Long Island, which leads me to believe to be before the Bird Campaign. In this party were two or three Andersons, William and George, Robt. Christian, John Sawyers, and perhaps McNair, the others not recollected.

At this time the geography was imperfectly known, so much so, that our party thought by taking the route down the Tennessee they could travel to the Mississippi without any material obstruction, but to their astonishment when they reached the Clinch river, near its junction with the Tennessee, they found themselves entirely disappointed. This was early in the spring time, I know, from the circumstances they had caught two buffaloes, calves, which they had succeeded in taming by feeding them on flour mixed with water and had them to follow like dogs. But this party were doomed to defeat also, for while they were exploring the country between the Clinch and Tennessee, they were met by some 60 Indians on the way to fight the Northern Indians, and altho they offered no other violence to our party they swapt guns for such of our people as suited them, giving them old, useless shot guns. Likewise they took most of the flour and most of the ammunition our people had, and after taking some other exchanges departed, leaving our folks to prosecute their journey (See Geo. Christian's letter Aug. 25, 1853-L C. D.)

In answer to your question respecting my Father's age, his family, etc., I could not be very exact, not having the old family register, tho I believe I can come very near the correct date. Father was married in 62 or 3 to Margaret Anderson, daughter of George Anderson of Middle river, Augusta Co., Va. There were four brothers of the Andersons (John, James, George, and William.) These were among the first settlers in Augusta—they were from Pennsylvania, their native State. My grandfather and Uncles lived to be old men, leaving behind them a numerous posterity, some of whom I presume are in Augusta to this day. The Christian family lived in Augusta about the same time on Christian creek of which I have spoken before. My Father's brothers were John, Robert, Israel, and Jacob, the two latter died young, and were never married. Father had two sisters, Margaret and Mary, the former married Uncle William Anderson, the latter married Robert Patterson. My two uncles and aunts above mentioned all lived to a good old age in Augusta, leaving behind a numerous posterity.

With respects to the relationship between Col. Wm. Christian who commanded the Campaign in '76 against the Cherokees I could not speak with any degree of certainty than it is always understood they were from the same ancestry.

I think from what I can find out since I wrote you, Father must have moved to Holston in 72 or 3, made a temporary settlement on the waters of Reedy Creek, seven or eight miles from Holston river from whence he removed in the Autumn of '75 to Holston river, at the mouth of Reedy creek opposite the Long Island, where we remained until the next summer at the breaking out of the Cherokees. At this time they were five children of us, one daughter the oldest of us. The first intimation we had of the approach of the Indians was given to us by a trader named, I think, Ellis Harlan. At this time the settlement had extended some distance below the Long Island, and here it may be proper to observe that since I rec'd your letter I have conversed with an old man in my neighborhood who I know was in the Island battle, (Cornelius Carmack). Mr. Carmack has convinced me that I was mistaken in the time of the battle. He says that it was in '76. From this time I have some recollection of what was doing in this country. On the first intimation of the hostile movements of the Cherokees, the frontiersmen left their farms and collected in Stations or in some cases several families banded together for mutual defense as was the case with us. On rec't of the intelligence bro't by Mr. Harlan we were removed some miles to James Clendennin's where they were eight or ten families collected I think with intent to build a fort. But after collecting at this place a second express arrived, more alarming than the first. I think it was brought by Isaac Thomas who had been a trader among the Indians. So urgent was the news that an attack was apprehended for that same evening. It was thought it would begin about three o'clock. At this time Father was home having gone to the farm. Our horses all in the woods, mother had a brother and brother-in-law in company. Her brother in bad health, each of those had a wife and one child. The scene which was now acted was truly interesting, all bustle and confusion, no commander, nobody to give direction, every one seemed intent on saving their own lives. There must have been at this place between 50 and 100 persons altogether, chiefly women and children. But there was no time to be lost, not knowing what the next minute we would be saluted with Savage yells or report of their guns.

But a little before sunset Mother and all her children were all mounted and on the road for the interior. Mother was on a borrowed nag, but as luck would have it, we had not proceeded more than a mile when we were met by an Irishman (one Morrow) mounted on Mother's riding mare. The Irishman quickly dismounted and Mother was safely placed on her favorite filly. We then proceeded at a rapid pace until dark closed in, which checked our progress, but we were flying for our life, so the difficulty was encountered cheerfully. We must have traveled some 15 miles this night. Was joined next day by Father, who conveyed us some forty miles to a relation, Mr. Trimble, where he left us and returned to Eaton. not Heaton, as Haywood has it, any way the old man was always called Amos Eaton.

From Trimble's Mother with her brother John Anderson and her Brother-in-law, Adam Guthery, proceeded to Augusta where we remained until the Autumn of '78, when Father, who had stayed on the Holston, went on with a wagon and brought us home. The journey must have been in June, as it was in time of harvest. With respect to the battle, I have some recollection, but Mr. Carmack was an eye witness, so can still tell more. He says there were five companies collected at the fort, commanded by Cap. Thompson, Edmonston, Shelby and Cock, this was James Shelby, Carmack thinks Buchannan stayed in the Fort when the army marched out to meet the enemy. He says they worked all night preceding the battle setting up pickets.

The word was brot on the evening preceding the Battle by the spies that the Indians were encampt on an upper end of the Island a distance of about six miles from the Fort. Their numbers variously estimated supposed to be somewhere between 500 & 1000. Our little army could not have exceeded much over 300 effective men.

It seems a council of officers were called to determine on the course to be pursued. Some for awaiting the attack of the enemy, others for giving them Battle outside. On this Occasion Capt. Cock was vehement, swore no man but a d———d coward would think of remaining penned up in the Fort. Eventually it seems Cock's council prevailed—early in the morn our little army sallied out & took the road leading to the Island—there was a high ridge to cross before reaching the flats. This road keeps along the main top of the ridge near three miles. After descending on the opposite side from the Fort commences the flats, or as it is called the Island flats. Our men proceeded after reaching the Flats perhaps about two miles when they were met by the whole Indian Army, with their line extended making as much show as possible.

No sooner were our men discovered by the enemy than they raised the savage yell, tomahawk in hand. This sudden charge was too much. Our little army wheeled about and run, but still keeping rank, and after retreating in this manner perhaps a mile & half, some one more courageous than the rest wheeled & fired on the advancing enemy, which induced another to do likewise, which almost instantly brot on a general engagement. Our men extending their lines to the right & left gave the enemy Indian play by taking trees. It seems Capt. Cock at this time at the head of his company aiming as he said to prevent being surrounded, extended his line until when he turned to see what had become of his men, behold they were not to be seen, he having run a little too fast for his men, or what was thought more likely, ran farther than the men chose to go who had taken trees & fought the battle out manfully. In which, however, their captain did not participate, he on finding himself some distance in advance of his men on the retreating side, made for the Fort.

But although Cock used every argument in his power to excuse his unofficer like conduct on this occasion, he was ever after considered a coward, nor did he ever afterwards perform any act in the service of his country calculated to make a different impression.

Immediately after this battle troops were collected & marched from Virginia & North Carolina and placed under the command of Col. William Christian, as you have already learned, who rendezvoused at or opposite the head of the long Island where they built a fort.

This army marched into the Indian country—but of its services or incidents attending it I need say but little—Father commanded a company on this campaign. Under him was John Sawyer & I think John Anderson.

The peace which succeeded this campaign was of but short duration—as I think they commenced hostilities in '80 or '81—but the occurrence to which you have alluded of a meeting at Patterson's (not Patten's as Haywood has it) and Rice's Mills I have some recollection of. Those Mills were the only mills in that part of the country at this time. Patterson's Mill was situated about eight miles below the Island near Holston River on a small creek, and Rice's Mill three miles still lower down on a creek emptying into the river—the former seven miles below the north fork where Ross's bridge crosses the same—Father was unquestionably the Gilbert Christian spoken of on the occasion you mention of meeting at those mills.

In the spring of eighty or eighty one, (it was in '79— L. C. D.) Evan Shelby sign (senior) commanded on a campaign which was marched in canoes down the Holston & Tennessee to the Chicamoga Towns near what is now Chattanooga. I think Col. Arthur Campbell commanded some troops from Va. Col. Charles Roberson commanded a Regiment from Washington & Father those from Sullivan, this time a Major.

This army on coming in view of the Town where they landed, seeing a newly paled garden mistook it for a stockade Fort, and expecting to be repulsed when attempting to land—orders were immediately given by the Commander to the officer in front (which on this day was Col. Roberson) to land his canoes. Campbell at this time was in the rear & Father in the centre.

Roberson though seemed to sheer off from shore, making a contrary move from the Col's. order on which the Col. called out at the top of his voice, "d——n you, Col. Roberson, I say land your canoes." Still the order was not obeyed, on which Shelby called to Father and ordered him to land his men which he did promptly—(I relate this as a matter of fact though it may seem a little like boasting.)

This little army suffered incredible hardships on their return, which had to be performed on foot mostly, though the men picked up a good many Indian ponies, Father one amongst the rest which he rode home.

This Campaign, though they never could bring the Indians to fight, served to show them we were able to make war offensively—and after destroying a quantity of Indian property returned without the loss of a man—

This campaign I think went out in the spring preceding the campaign against the British in Carolina. At this time we had the British on one side & the Indians on the other. I am conscious of being liable to mistakes as respects dates, but this I know to be certain, the British under Cornwallis were making such advances through the Carolinas that it was thought by some they might attempt to cross the mountains which, though we had enough to do to keep off the Indians, yet apprehending some danger from the British and tories should they succeed in crossing the mountains, our hardy backwoods men under those Gallant Chiefs Campbell, Shelby & Sevier, left their homes, though exposed to the attack of our savage foe, to brave the more formidable enemy, the British.

Father commanded a company on this campaign. Under him were George Rutledge & Robt. King—(The former afterwards General Rutledge of Sullivan, the latter the celebrated Bob King known all over Tennessee.)

This little band contributed largely in defeating Maj. Ferguson at King's Mountain.

I think late in the same autumn after returning from the Kings Mountain campaign, another small army was raised of mounted Infantry, but unless this campaign was under the command of Col. Arthur Campbell (as I feel very certain he was along) I cannot say who commanded. Father I think had a Major's command. On this tour James Eliot was killed by an Indian at Tellico—these excursions into the heart of their country served to keep them in check besides gave them some trouble to support their families—which brought about a temporary peace.

This brings me down to the time of the Frankland Government, and you desire to know something about the part my Father took in this matter, but first I will answer some of your enquiries concerning several of the old pioneers, &c.

The Shelby Family except the old Gen. (the father of Isaac and others) had all removed or had been killed by this time. James Shelby was killed on the Kentucky Road and his Brother Evan subsequently was killed on the road somewhere between Kentucky & Cumberland. Moses the youngest settled below Nashville where he liv- many years.

Of the Bledsoes, Anthony & Isaac who had been prominent men in their day, removed to Bledsoe's lick at an early day, at which place they were both killed by Indians—the Looney Family also were amongst the leading characters of this day in Sullivan. J. Rhea of whom you speak was a prominent character in early times, was for many years a member of Congress, had practiced law, and quite old died a Bachelor. Stocklye Donnaldson, I believe the first surveyor that ever stretched a chain in Sullivan, became the greatest land manager (man) in the state but became dissipated and involvent.

Of Cols. Maxwell, Long & Pemberton, I cannot say they were ever distinguished for anything except the part they took with the old state party against the Franklin Government, which served to procure them appointments when the government ceased, but so soon as we became a Territorial Government they were all—I mean the old state party—left out.

The circumstances which led to the setting up the Franklin Government were these—North Carolina made a cession of the country to Congress—the cession Act not being rec'd by Congress we were then without a Government, upon which a meeting was held as you are informed at Jonesborough, where it was determined to call a convention—which they did, of which Father was a member. In short they organized a Government, in which Father took an active part, was a member of the legislature. Some two or three sessions was held at Greenville—John Sevier was appointed Governor, but who were the other state Officers I do not recollect.

But those men I have named above not having gotten any share of the spoils, and North Carolina having rescinded the cession act claimed Jurisdiction over the whole state of Franklin, which brought about an unhappy state of things and proved nigh coming to a civil war. Indeed there was a little brush between a party of Franklinities & Tiptonites as they were called—but although the Franklin Government was undoubtedly popular with the people, yet it was thought most prudent to abandon it, well knowing that we must soon become a Territory at least.

Amongst those in Sullivan in favor of the Franklin schism was Col. John Anderson, Col. W. Craigie, Capt. John Menifee, Col. John Sawyer. . The Looney family I think were rather neutral, at any rate the new state had a Majority of the people—after the authority of the Franklin Government yielded to those of the old state, a new set of Officers both civil & military were appointed by the latter, when those men Scott & others were appointed in Sullivan.

I cannot say precisely in what year the second session act was passed by the legislature of North Carolina, but this I know, we were organized as a Territorial Government in 1791—during the period, I mean to '91, the Cherokees broke out, doing some mischief on our frontiers—when Gen. Joseph Martin was ordered out with an army of about 500 men. This I think was in the autumn of '89 or '90. On this campaign Father went out as Aid to the Gen. I was on this campaign myself for the first time—we penetrated into the Indian country as far as the Lookout Mountain where we had a smart brush with the Indians, had three men killed & five wounded. Of the enemy it was said their loss was some 9 or 10—after this affair the army returned doing little more than destroying some of their towns, &c.

But so soon as we became a Territorial Government the old Franklin Officers were reinstated, Father amongst the rest—when in the autumn of '92 the Indians still harassing the frontiers, there were two Regiments ordered out by Governor Blount for the defense of the frontiers. My Father took command of the Sullivan Regiment, but I have forgotten who commanded the troops from Washington. Those troops were marched to South West point where they erected two block houses. After performing a tour of perhaps three months they returned home.

Those troops were regularly mustered into & out of service by a proper office which being filed in the War Office will shew correctly who the officers were in those two regiments.

The Captain Chistian you mention as having performed a Tour to Miroe Dist. in '92 was Robert Christian an older brother of my own.

Again in the summer of '93 Father was ordered out against the Cherokees at the head of a Regiment from Sullivan. Those troops were partly mounted & part intended to guard the frontier stations—these were marcht on foot.

This little army rendezvoused at Ashes (Ishes) station, some 25 miles below Knoxville—I was myself left at this station with a part of the troops and Captains Beaty, Scott, & Gregg. Also Majors Taylor & Conway. At this time I was Ensign of Capt. Beatie's Company, also had the appointment of adjutant of the Regiment.

Father being mounted took the command of a Regiment & marcht into the Cherokee Country under Genl. John Sevier. This was called the Hightower Campaign spoken of by Mr. Dunlap.

On this campaign Father was attacked with fever which after returning home as far as Knoxville terminated his earthly existence.

This event happened in November, 1793. He was buried in the manner as stated by Mr. Dunlap though I was not present, being still at the Station.

I deem it unnecessary to say more believing I have given you a sufficient task already to read this scrawl— But if I have succeeded in giving you any satisfaction in what I have endeavored to sketch out, I shall consider myself sufficiently compensated.

And now let me express the high sense I have of the honor done me in thus noting what I have been able to furnish.

Yours Truly
GEO. CHRISTIAN

P. S.—What you will find in this communication different from the former are mere corrections, as I have been able in some degree to correct some mistakes. In answer to your inquiry respecting old manuscript papers in Father's possession at the time of his death, I can say there was a quantity. Amongst others there were manuscript copies of the laws of Franklin and all of which old papers fell into other hands after Mother's death in 1812. I presume my youngest sister, Margaret (who married Rev. Thomas Milligan) and removed to White River Indiana, if preserved at all, must have possession of all the old papers.

Father left at his death eight children, five sons and three daughters. Of his sons first Robert, George, William, and John. Israel the youngest died young and never married. Of daughters there were Elizabeth, Isabella, and Margaret. At this time there were upwards of forty grandchildren living—it might be proper to remark that Sullivan county until the running of the State line on '79 was deemed to be in Va. but when that was extended the Campbell family fell into Virginia, though several of them afterwards removed to Tennessee, and took an active part in the affairs of our State, many of them too well known for me to attempt to add anything to their fame in the councils of the nation.

I am with sentiments of high regard,

Yours

GEORGE CHRISTIAN.

VI

FRANKLIN AND THE WHITES

In the following speech by Hugh Lawson White and the expansive pension statement by Benjamin White will be found much of interest relative to the State of Franklin and the battle of King's Mountain.

James, a son of Moses and Mary McConnell White, was born in Iredell county, North Carolina, in 1747, and in 1770 married Mary, daughter of Hugh Lawson and his wife Margaret Barry. He was a captain under Major Chronicle, and located a landgrant at Knoxville, Tennessee, where he died in 1831. The graves of himself and wife are in the yard of the First Presbyterian church. White was the founder of Knoxville, the town being surveyed on his land in the fall of 1791. He was a steadfast and strong supporter of the state of Franklin, a brigadier general of the militia, and when Governor Blount was impeached, he resigned his seat in the Tennessee senate so that Blount might be elected in his place. General White was of commanding presence, being six feet four inches in height. Many of his descendants are to be found in Knox county and in other communities of the South and West. His daughter Margaret married Charles McClung, the first surveyor of Knox.

Below is an extract from a speech delivered by Hugh Lawson White in the senate of the United States, March 24, 1838. He was speaking on the Sub-Treasury plan, but took occasion to answer some disparaging remarks concerning the state of Franklin.

"It will be remembered that the Governor, Chief-Justice, and some other Officers, were to be paid in deer skins, other inferior officers were to be paid in raccoon skins. Now, at that day, we were all good Whigs.

We thought these taxes might safely remain in the hands of the collectors as sub-treasury funds until wanted for disbursement. The Taxes were, therefore fairly collected in skins and peltry pointed out in the law. But the collector as the report says, knew that although raccoon skins were plentiful, opossums were more so, and they could be procured for little or nothing. They, therefore, procured the requisite number of opossum skins, cut the tail from the raccoon skins, sewed them to the opossum skins, paid them to the general or principal treasury, and sold the raccoon skins to the hatters.

The treasurer had been an unlucky appointment, although a worthy man; he was a foreigner, knew nothing of skins or peltry and was, therefore, easily deceived by the sub-treasurer. When this imposition was discovered, the whole system went down, and we never had a great fancy for leaving the taxes in the hands of the sub-treasurer or collectors from that day to this.

But, Sir, these old proceedings more clearly developed the true character of my State than almost anything of the present day. The Territory or state called Frankland was composed of four counties of North Carolina, and separated from the body of the State by the great ledge of Mountains, called at different places by different names, and from what is now west Tennessee, by the Cumberland mountains, and a wilderness of 200 miles.

The Revolutionary war had terminated in 1783; but it continued with the powerful tribes of Indians who had been in alliance with the British. The depredations of these Indians were so severe and serious that aid to arrest their ravages was desired from North Carolina. That State was not in position to furnish protection, and instead thereof, from good motives no doubt, but without due consideration, passed an act ceding us to the United States. When the news was received, the leading men, who were King's Mountain men, Sevier, the companion of the gallant Campbell, and Shelby, at their head, took fire, the discontent ended in a declaration of independence, and the formation of the State called to perpetuate whig principles, Frankland, followed.

North Carolina discovered her error, and before Congress could act on the subject, repealed her act of cession. But it was too late. We had been disposed of without our consent. Though but a handful, with a powerful savage enemy infesting our whole frontier, and without a dollar to begin with, we set up for ourselves. We would not brook the indignity. We had begun the fight for liberty, and liberty or death we would have. We continued the controversy till 1789, when an accommodation with our parent state took place, and with our consent, and upon terms thought just, we, with other portions of the Territory, were ceded, 1789, to the United States.

In 1796, we became the State of Tennessee, and how we since have conducted ourselves, I am willing to leave to the judgment of our sister States. I confess, instead of feeling humble, I feel proud that my ancestor was one of that unyielding band, that I now find myself associated with a Sevier and a Tipton."

The pension statement of Benjamin White and the story of his wife are taken from the papers of Selden Nelson of Knoxville, Tennessee. Mr. Nelson is a son of T. A. R. Nelson, an attorney of national reputation who went to the aid of his personal friend, Andrew Johnson, when the latter was impeached as President of the United States. Many veterans of the Revolution applied to him for help in securing pensions. The historical papers of Selden Nelson are many and valuable.

Martha, wife of Benjamin White, was a daughter of David Jobe, a fighter in the wars with the Indians. Her courage was as undaunted as that of her father and her husband. While the men were standing guard to keep the natives from murdering their families and burning their cabins, we hear more of them than of the women who were meanwhile performing heroic acts. The story of Mrs. White is told by Selden Nelson, a great great grandson of Benjamin White and also a great great grandson of the Robert Sevier killed at King's Mountain.

Following the story of Mrs. White is a letter by her son, Benjamin J. White, written from Texana (Texarkana?), Texas, October 17, 1852. Mr. White was still living at that place in the spring of 1860. The pension application of his father was granted.

I, Benjamin White, of Knox County, Tennessee, do certify that I was in the King Mountain battle, the 7th of October, 1780, in Colonel Campbell's regiment. He was riding a bay horse. I saw Colonel Campbell receive the sword from the British captain, I think his name De-Peyster, and heard Col. Campbell order the flag to be received, and I believe it was Evan Shelby received it. I saw Col. Campbell very frequently during the whole action encouraging his men, and feel confident he was not absent from his men one moment during the whole battle. When I was eighteen years of age, I was at the battle at the mouth of the Big Kenhawa with the Shawnee Indians, 10th of October 1774, in the battle of Princeton 3rd June, 1777, in the battle of Brandywine, 11th Sept., 1777, in the battle of German Town, 4th of October 1777; in the battle with the Shawnee Indians at the Miami towns 9th of April 1779; in the battle of Kings

Mountain, and in a battle in Florida with the Indians 10th of Feb. 1813; and in all those battles I never saw a braver man than Col. Campbell according to my judgement, and to the above statement I am willing to be qualified.

Knoxville, May the 28th, 1823.

I certify that I knew Benjamin White, soldier for upwards of eighteen years. That he maintained the character of a man of honesty and veracity. That I would have great confidence in any statement he would make.

Mr. White served under my command as a volunteer against the Seminole Indians in the winter of 1812-13. He afforded many evidences of undaunted bravery on that campaign, and would be as likely to give a faithful narrative of the events of a battle as any man whatever.

John Williams
July 4th, 1823

It was the warm summer days of the month of June in 1786, when the women and children were outside the blockhouse, watching the lovely scenery across the Holston river, where the wild flowers were blooming among the beans and corn planted on the rich ground across the river. Suddenly they heard the swish of silent moving bodies somewhere back of the forest nearest to them. First it seemed the sound of stealthy animals of the wild, and then one woman caught a glimpse of the gay headdress of an advancing Indian, and with a scream she called ,"Indians, Indians." The women carried and hurried the children to the blockhouse, while the men closed the gates and barred them with stout timber, as the first arrow sped over their heads. The Indians kept up the onslaught until the darkness hid them. The men in the fort kept watch all night, and as soon as the sun arose in the mist of the east, the Indian rifles sounded out in the renewed attack on the Fort. All that day the men in the blockhouse were put to their strength in keeping the Indians from coming close enough to fire the place. The third day was the same, only the food was found almost gone, and the terrible fear that they could not long resist the Indians without food, made the fighting force desperate. At the close of the third day the Indians crossed the Holston and disappeared beyond the corn field in the cane rushes and wild grape vines out of the sight of those watching from the Fort. Were they gone for good, was the question of each face. The men thought they were waiting to see if any one would come out to shoot them;

else were they going to stay in order to starve them out? The question of food was intense, and their corn and beans were in sight, between them and where the Indians disappeared. Finally it was decided by lot who should be the one to go across and gather the corn and beans. Mrs. Benjamin White, who was a beautiful woman with a glorious crown of golden red hair, and who was often lovingly called "Red-headed Squaw" by her family, arose and said, "I am the one to go. The Indians are less apt to molest a woman than a man." Every man protested against it, but who can change the mind of a brave and courageous woman? They had to let her have her way. A young girl, Emily Hunt, was very devoted to Mrs. White for the many kindnesses she had shown her, so she, too, insisted she would go where Mrs. White went. The two slipped out and went down the bank to where a canoe was safely hidden. The sun burst out in its brilliancy as the two women softly paddled across the river. Now and again they thought they could see the rushes move, and their hearts beat fast as they nervily went on. On landing, they tied the canoe, stood for a moment looking back to the Fort discerning from the portholes the muzzles of guns pointed their way. Not an Indian was in sight. They quickly gathered the corn and beans, and yet, when Mrs. White went a little closer to the rushes she thought she heard supressed breathing, and unmistakably the rushes did stir. She and Emily Hunt moved away hurriedly with their sacks, made for the canoe, and were across much quicker than they came. What a relief was their return to those inside the Fort. Now they all felt they could resist for days until help could be procured. The Indians did not return. Some months afterwards, Mrs. White, and her handmaids were busy spinning and putting up the summer herbs, that Mrs. White knew the use of so well that she was considered the Doctor of the settlement. They did not notice the shadows of two Indians, until they appeared in the doorway. It was a time of peace, and the Indians were friendly. Mrs. White invited them to enter. They did so and stood solemnly watching the mixing of herbs. The first Indians turned and asked Mrs. White if she remembered him. After looking closely she said she could not. Then he held out his hand and pointed to a scar on his finger. Then she remembered that two years before a neighbor brought this Indian to her house to be cured of a large felon on the first finger. She had poulticed it with lime and hog's lard until it ripened and broke. Then she took horehound and honey and cured it after several days treatment, and forgot all about it, for every day she was called on for help of some kind. She smiled, and told the Indian he looked better than the last time she saw him. Then he told her, he was the chief who attacked the Fort on that day, and that they were all in the rushes when she came across to get the corn and beans. When the sun shone on her red hair he recognized her. A hundred arrows and guns were raised to shoot, but he restrained his men. That was why they did not come back, and that was why they made peace.

In a letter written from Texana, Texas, Oct. 17, 1852, Mr. White says:

"With regard to my fathers services I do not know if they can be reached at this late date. Unfortunately in 1836 at the time of our runaway scrape (that is the families of Texas) in packing our effects at my son-in-law's I had about ½ bushel of old papers of my father's and mine, among which was my father's discharge. In looking over them Mr. Williams and Mary persuaded me to burn them as they never could do me or any other person any good. I refused and they commenced throwing them into the fire, so I had to yield. But I recollect the regiment he belonged to, from the fuss picked up in Kentucky, between Gen'l Adair and Col. Shelby, one party accusing the other with cowardice and Col. William P. Anderson of Nashville, Tenn., taking sides with——I think Adair came all the way to Knoxville to procure my father's certificate which was taken before James Park, Esq., which proved that Col. Campbell and not Shelby made the main attack and defeat at King's Mountain, and as well as I recollect, Col. Shelby did not go into action until about the close. My father was also in the battle of the Cowpens——these things I have heard him and others talk about often. I do not recollect the date but can testify I once had it in my possession and that was burnt in the home of Robert H. Williams, the brother of Hon. C. H. Williams. You can mention these things to 'Squire Park, and see if he has any recollection of the certificate——maybe so. Judge Thomas L. Williams may recollect, as my father and him used to talk together a great deal about old times. Have you obtained the bounty warrant for his services in the Seminole War? I have got mine, and I want my dear old sister to have his. You can prove it up by Thos. L. Williams, who was along with us and Mat Mynatt, if he is still alive."

VII

MILITIA ROSTERS

The first roster is that of Captain Shelby's company in the Chickamauga campaign of 1779. The second is that of Captain Bledsoe in 1777. Most of the men enumerated were at King's Mountain. The lists were copied from the Draper manuscripts in the Lawson McGhee Free Library of Knoxville, Tennessee.

In the Shelby list, the successive columns of figures are (a) blankets, (b) leggings, (c) moccasins, (d) arms, (e) tomahawks, (f) gunsacks. In the second column "11" means 2.

	(a)	(b)	(c)	(d)	(e)	(f)
Catel Litton	1	11	1		1	1
William Linn	1	1	1		1	1
Hans Ireland	1	1	1		1	1
David Hendricks						
Andrew Linn	1	1	1		1	1
Benj. Sweet	1	11	1		1	1
Tho. Maner	1	1	1		1	1
John Mouer	1	11	11		1	1
William Clem	1	11	11		1	1
William Harwood	1	1	1		1	1
Evan Shelby, Jun.	1	11	1		1	1
Garrett Pendergrass						
Alexander Carwell	1	1	11		1	1
Joseph Wells	1	11	11		1	1
John Harmison						
John Fleming	1	1	1			
Elias Dawson		11			1	1
Anthony Millon	1	1	1			
Robert Chambers	1	1	1			
John Brown	1	11	1	1	1	1
Tho. Applegate	1	11	1		1	1
Geo. Parker						
John Shelby	1	1	1		1	
Charles Prather	1	11	1		1	1
Elisha Perkins	1	1	1		1	1
John Higgins						
Robert Friggs						
E. Bruster	1	1				
Joseph Latman						
Buk Nealley	1	11	1		1	

Joseph Pierce					
Daniel Linn 1	1	1	1	1	1
Barnett Johnson 1	1	1	1	1	1
David Jennings 1	1	1		1	1
Richard Long					
Samuel Price					
Robert Blackburn 1	11	1		1	1
William Tom 1	1	1			
Tho. Cheney 1	1	1	1	1	1
John Detgaoorett 1	1	1		1	1
J. C. Friggs					
William McSpaden 1	11	1		1	1
Isaac Morgan					

Andrew Folson, his own blanket

LIST OF SOLDIERS

Isaac Bledsoe, Capt.	John Barton
James Douglass, Sergt.	John Bennedict
W. M. Broom, Private	Robt. Dobson
Joseph Cartwright	Joseph Dobson
David Cash	John Givens
Peter Waldrin	James Givens
John Miller	Hugh Henry
Andrew Avender	Jno. McNelly
Philip Williams	James Mason
Wm. Inglis	Marcum Marshall
Sam Axer	Richard Perry
John Tucker	Jacob Stephens
John Sufferet	Moses Sweeney
Thomas Brooks	Alexander Sloan
Jas. Freeland	William Sloan
Wm. Patterson	John Sloan
Robt. King	Tho. Shannan
James Dunlop	Robt. Limonton
Jas. Donald	Isaac Shelby
John Rice	David Warres
Tho. Blyth	Charles Williams
Jas. Williams	John Withers
Jn. Francis Budvine	Edward Douglas
John Patterson	John Carter
John Robertson	Charles Bakly
John Bentley	John Besall

VIII

INCIDENT IN THE LIFE OF ALEXANDER MOORE

The following is without the name of either addressee or writer, but appears to belong in the Draper collection. Alexander Moore is spoken of in Section Two of this book. The letter tells of an incident in his career, and there is mention of persons and occurrences in early Tennessee history.

I have been personally acquainted with Alexander Moore of whom you speak—Robt. King & others who knew all about the affair of Moores killing the Indian called Big Sawga, but never heard of Moore having had any assistance and to use a common phrase Moore was called at that time much of a man was a tall finely formed man of undaunted courage & withal proud of his muscular powers. For when the Indian was seen after the firing was over in a large sink hole Moore proposed to some of those about him to have a single combat with the Indian & seeing that he was a large fellow he thought there would be some honor in a victory of that sort altho the Indian was wounded in the knee & in one hand held a tomahawk in the other his scalping knife— as Moore advanced upon him with no other weapon but his knife the Indian standing on one knee placing himself in the best position he could to receive his adversary & before Moore got within reach threw his tomahawk but Moore being appraised of his intention dodged it & closed with the fellow when a deadly scuffle ensued and as Moore said the unhandiest chap he had had anything to do with for the Indian by holding to Moore was often on his feet and being naked would slip from his grasp in such a way as to make it difficult for Moore to keep on his feet but after a hard scuffle Moore succeeded in plunging his knife into the Indian's body several times which ended the battle but I never heard of any one assisting Moore at all but Samuel Young came up just when the battle was ended and shot the Indian in the head— as respects the affair with the party going from Parson Cumminges I have no recollection sufficient at least to give you any satisfaction neither do I know any thing about the party of from 20 to 40 Indians you speak of though it might all be so but when this should have happened our family were all safe in Augusta, Va. my recollection of what occurred on the frontiers after the Island Battle is quite vague—I never learnt of Mr. Carmack that he was on any other campaigns & at the stations I think pretty much until the end of the war—and here I will take the liberty of joining you in congratulating each other of the happy result of the late Presidential Election I join with you in toto on that subject. But how you became acquainted with my political views I am at a loss to know but at any rate you have made a good guess. But I will add more that there is no man in the union more gratified than myself at the success of the Democratic party in the late contest and I am further gratified that James K. Polk should be the man to beat Henry Clay and I am not gratified because I expect office or anything in the gift of the President I neither ask or expect anything of the kind.

You ask to be informed about Major Jonathan Tipton I have known a good many of the Tipton family but I never knew any of the name of any distinction in this County & if there is or has been he must be quite obscure.

Capt. Haynes defeat happened in this wise, a party of some 15 or 20 or perhaps more undertook one day to cross the Tennessee & load themselves with apples at the Indian town of Citico there being no such a thing as apples on our side I am not quite certain the party went from Craigs Station or not but I think that was the station. So little were our people expecting danger that but a few of them were armed the distance was such they expected to make the trip in a day & return with every man his bag of apples how the Indians came to be so well prepared was not known but so it was whilst all hands were busied in filling their bags the Indians fell on them killing the number which I have forgotten & taking most of their horses & chasing those that escaped several miles—

GREER AND McELWEE DATA

Joseph Greer was the messenger who carried to the Continental Congress at Philadelphia the news of the victory of King's Mountain. He walked barefoot all the way. For his services he acquired a grant in Lincoln county, Tennessee twelve (?) miles square. Here he settled, and the town of Petersburg grew up on his land. Two of his twelve children were twins, and like their father they were about six feet eight inches in height. They lived until about 1813. On the monument marking the grave of Joseph Greer is an interesting tablet, placed there by the Daughters of the American Revolution.

James McElwee, who died 1820, aged sixty-eight, served under Shelby at Chickamauga, and under Campbell at King's Mountain. A family tradition has it that McElwee and William White were fellow soldiers, and that White was slightly wounded at King's Mountain. McElwee took White to his home, which was near by, where he was nursed by a sister, whom he afterward married. White was one of the original justices of Roane.

McElwee was one of the five first settlers at Knoxville. In his account book he noted some local events, one of which was the massacre of the Cavitt family. This account does not altogether agree with the one given by Ramsay. He says the incident took place at a little town called Steckee, where now is Lenoir. An Indian carried the little Cavitt boy on his back, but at night the child cried so much that the warrior thought it might be heard and accordingly killed it by hitting its head against a tree. Another entry states that Elizabeth McElwee, born February 22, 1791, was the second child born at White's Station (Knoxville), Richard Dunlap being the first.

DIARY OF CAPTAIN ALEXANDER CHESNEY

The manuscript of this diary is in the British Museum, where it was copied by Samuel G. Williams, who used it in his article, "King's Mountain Battle, as Seen by a British Officer." This was published in the Tennessee Historical Magazine for April, 1921.

When Cornwallis sent Ferguson on detached service, Chesney was second among the captains, DePuyster being first. Gates was defeated by Cornwallis August 16, 1780, and two days later, Sumter was defeated by Tarleton. Elsewhere as well, the American arms were unsuccessful. Ferguson was sent to dispose of the hornet's nest of whigs west of the Wateree, and make the British victory complete.

Nearly all the engagements mentioned by DePuyster and Chesney are referred to in the pension declarations by the King's Mountain veterans. Chesney gives more details than his comrade. He was born in Ireland and settled in South Carolina about 1772. He early entered the British army and fought to the end, honestly believing he was on the right side. For a short time after his capture at King's Mountain he took part with the Americans against the Indians. His two sons attained high rank in the British army.

"On 9th of August I was appointed Capt. and Assistant Adjutant General to the different batallions under Col. Ferguson; and same day we attacked the enemy at the Iron works, (Wofford's Iron works) and defeated them with little trouble to ourselves and with a good deal of loss to the Americans in whose hands I found some of our men prisoners whom I released.

12th. Our next route was down towards the Fishing Ford on the Broad river, where there was a fight near the mouth of Brown's creek with Neale's Militia (This was Capt. Wm. Neale in the King's Mountain battle) where we made many prisoners, among the rest Ensaw Smith who had so recently taken me. After this we crossed that river, and formed a junction with the troops under command of Colonel Turnbull and the Militia under Colonel Philips, and having received authentic accounts that Sumpter had cut off our retreat to Lord Cornwallis Army at Camden, we had in contemplation to cross Broad river and retreat to Charleston. At this time the half-way-men, (as those not hearty in the cause were called) left us.

Augst. 16. We then marched to Col. Winns, a Rebel, and encamped there waiting for more authentic accounts. On the 16th we heard heavy firing towards Camden which kept us in the utmost anxiety until the 18th, when a letter was received from Capt. Ross, Aid-de camp of Lord Cornwallis, informing us that his Lordship had attacked and defeated General Gates Army; had taken or killed 220 men, 18 ammunition wagons, and 350 wagons with provisions and other stores. This news made us as happy as we could possibly be, until the next night (19) when we received an express that the Rebels had defeated Col. Ennis at Enoree. This occasioned a march that way. The main body having crossed the Enoree, I was left behind in command of the rear guard, and being attacked in that situation (Aug. 20) we retained the rear guard until the main body recrossed to our support. The Americans retreated after some loss.

We encamped for some time in the neighborhood of Enoree and then marched up to Fair Forest. Some particular business having called Colonel Ferguson to Camden, Captain Depeyster who succeeded him in Command marched us to the Iron Works, and Sep. 1, I received leave to see my home and family, whither I went for about two hours, and sent orders to those who so shamefully abandoned us some time ago to join us at the Iron Works, in order to do three months duty in or on the border of North Carolina, and returned to the camp that night.

We continued some time at the Iron Works and whilst there a party of loyalists with whom I was, defeated Colonel Brandon, destroyed some of his party and scattered the rest. I was present also at a small affair at Fair Forest, the particulars of which as well as the numerous other skirmishes having escaped my memory; scarcely a day passed without some fighting.

Colonel Ferguson having resumed his command and finding himself pretty strong he marched us to North Carolina line and encamped.

A dissatisfaction prevailed at this moment among the Militia founded on Gen. Clinton's hand bill which required every man having but three children, and every single man to do six months duty out of their own province when required. This appeared like compulsion, instead of acting voluntarily as they conceived doing; consequently they were ready to give up the cause; but owing to the exertions of the Officers, a great part which I attribute to myself, the tumult was happily appeased, and the same night in Sep. we marched with all the horses and some foot past Gilbert town towards Col. Grimes, who was raising a body of rebels to oppose us, whom we succeeded in dispersing, taking many prisoners; and the foot at Gilbert's town and encamped there for some time; sending away the old men to their houses, and several officers to raise men to supply their places and strengthen us. Col. Ferguson soon afterwards got intelligence that Col. McDole was encamped on Cane and Silver Creeks, on which we marched towards the enemy, crossed the winding creek 23 times found the rebels strongly posted toward the head of it toward the mountain. We attacked them instantly, and after a determined resistance defeated them, and made many prisoners. The rest fled towards Turkey Cove in order to cross the mountains and get to Holston settlements.

On this occasion I commanded a division and took the person prisoner, who was the keeper of the records of the county which I sent to my fathers as a place of safety. We then fortified Col. Walker's house as a protection to the wounded, and proceeded in pursuit of the rebels to the mountains on Cataba river, sending out detachments to search the country and caves. (This was the time Col. Ferguson sent Col. Shelby's nephew, Samuel Philips, one of the prisoners taken in this raid, over the mountain to tell them if they did not come over and join him, he would come and hang them.)

A fight happened in the neighborhood between a detachment of ours and the Americans who were posted on a broken hill not accessible to horses, which obliged us to dismount, and leave our horses behind. Whilst employed in dislodging the Americans, another party of them got around and took all the horses, mine among the rest; but it was returned by the person who was my prisoner in the last affairs; about a week before he was released, as was usual at this time with prisoners.

Octr. At this period the North Carolina men joined us fast. Our spies returned from beyond the mountains with intelligence that the rebels were embodying rapidly. Other spies brought us word that Col. Clarke had taken Fort Augusta with its stores, etc., on which we marched towards White Oak and Green River to intercept him on his return from Georgia. Col. Ferguson detached the horse in three divisions, one under my command to proceed along the Indian line until I could make out Clarke's route, and join Captain Taylor at Bailey Earle Fort. I proceeded as far as Tyger river and there learning that Clarke had gone up the banks of bushy fork of Seluda river, I took six of the best mounted men and got on his track until I overtook the main body and one of the enemy prisoners in view of it, whom I carried to Col. Ferguson who thus obtained the information wanted.

Oct. 4th. Our spies from Holston, as well as some left at the Gap of the mountain brought us word that the rebel force amounted to 3,000 men; on which we retreated along the north side of the Broad river, and sent the wagons along the south side as far as the Cherokee ford, where they joined us. We marched to King's Mountain and there camped with a view of approaching Lord Cornwallis army and receiving support. By Col. Ferguson's orders I sent express to the Militia officers to join us here, but we were attacked (Oct. 7th) before any support arrived by 1500 picked men from Gilbert town under command of Cols. Cleveland, Shelby and Campbell, all of whom were armed with rifles, well mounted, and of course could move with the utmost celerity. So rapid was the attack that I was in the act of dismounting to report that all was quiet and the pickets on the alert when we heard their firing about a half mile off. I immediately paraded the men and posted the officers. Duringt his short interval I received a wound which however did not prevent me from doing my duty; and going towards my horse I found he had been killed by the first discharge.

King's Mountain from its height would have enabled us to oppose a superior force with advantage had it not been covered with wood which sheltered the Americans and enabled them to fight in their favorite manner. In fact after driving in our pickets, they were able to advance in three divisions under separate leaders to the crest of the hill in perfect safety until they took post and opened an irregular but destructive fie from behind trees and other cover. Col. Cleveland was first perceived and repulsed by a charge led by Col. Ferguson. Col. Shelby next, and met a similar fate, being driven down the hill, last by Col. Campbell, and by desire of Col. Ferguson I presented a different front which opposed it with success. By this time the Americans who had been re-

pulsed regained their position, and sheltered by the trees
poured in a destructive fire. In this manner the engagement was maintained an hour, the mountaineers flying
when in danger from a bayonet charge, and returned as
soon as the British faced about to repel another of their
party. Col. Ferguson was at last recognized by his gal-
lantry, although wearing a hunting shirt and fell pierced
by seven balls, at the moment he had killed the American Col. Williams with his left hand. (The right being
useless.)

I had just rallied the troops a second time by Ferguson's orders when Captain Depeyster succeeded to command and after gave up and sent out a flag of truce, but
as the Americans resumed firing, afterwards ours renewed under the supposition that they would not give quarter. And a dreadful havoc took place until the flag was
sent out the second time when the work of destruction
ceased. The Americans surrounded us with double line,
and we grounded arms, with the loss of one third of our
numbers. I was wounded in the first fire, but was so
much occupied that I scarcely noticed until the action
was over. We passed the night where we surrendered
amidst the dead and the groans of dying, who had not
surgical aid or water to quench their thirst. Early next
morning we marched at rapid pace towards Gilbert town
between double lines of Americans, the officers in the rear
and obliged to carry two rifles each, which was my fate
although wounded and stripped of my shoes and buckles
in an inclement weather without cover or provision until
Monday night when each was served with an ear of corn.
At Gilbert town a mock tryal was held and 24 sentenced
to death, 10 of whom suffered before the approach of
Tarleton's force obliged them to move towards the Yadkin, cutting and striking us by the road in a savage manner. Col. Cleveland then (Oct. 11th) offered to enlarge
me on condition that I would teach his regiment one
month the exercise practiced by Col. Ferguson, which I
refused, although he swore I would suffer death at the
Moravian town. Luckily his threat was not put to the
test as I had the good fortune to make my escape one
evening when close to that place."

The rest of Captain Chesney's story deals with his
hardships until he finally reached Charleston, where his
British officers saw that he had a home of comfort for his
wife and child, while he continued in service under Lord
Rawdon in and about South Carolina. After the surrender of Cornwallis he sailed for England.

SUNDRY PENSION DECLARATIONS

In this chapter are given the application papers of John Adair, Richard Allen, Andrew Carson, Elizabeth Carter, William Lenoir, Hezekiah Love, and James Sevier. In seeking the benefit of the pension law of 1832 the declarant was required to specify his, or her husband's services in the Revolution, and to mention the officers under whom the service took place. This was to enable the Pension Office to tell whether the information in the statement was authentic. Some of the narratives of this period, relating events of fifty or more years earlier, are interesting and important.

JOHN ADAIR'S SERVICE

State of Kentucky
County of Wayne
s. s.

On the 2...th of September, 1832, personally appeared in open court (It being Court of Record) before the Justices of the Court of the county of Wayne, and State of Kentucky, now sitting, John Adair, a resident of United States of America, in the county of Wayne, State of Kentucky, aged seventy eight years, who being first duly sworn according to law doth on his oath, make the following Declaration in order to obtain the benefits of Act of Congress passed June 7th, 1832.

That he entered the service of the United States under the following named officers, and service as herein stated. He was born in Ireland in the county of Antrim in the year of 1754. His father with him and family came to America and landed at Baltimore, the year he cannot state with certainty, but it was when he was a youth, perhaps not quite 18 years old. His father lived in Maryland a little upwards of a year. He then moved to Pennsylvania and stayed there something like 12 months. His father then moved with the family to Sullivan county, North Carolina (where the applicant lived) but now Tennessee. When the war of the Revolution commenced he lived in Sullivan county aforesaid, until sometime in the year of 1791, when he moved from said county to the place now called Knox County, State of Tennessee. He lived about 14 years in Tennessee. Then he moved to Wayne county Kentucky about 27 or 28 years ago, where he has since, and now lives. He lived in Sullivan county, North Carolina, when he entered the service of the United States as a volunteer private soldier with a number of men in the Militia to go against the Indians. He states that it was usual in the part of the country he lived for the men to volunteer in small companys without any commissioned officers, to range or scour the country and march against the Indians. He states that the Captain or supreme officer, who commanded them in their expeditions was by the name of Campbell. He states he volunteered at different times. He cannot state the number of times or length of each, that he was out, at least three months. They marched about the head of Clinch river, a place called Elk Garden, and Blackmore's Fort. It was against the Indians they marched. It was the latter part of 1776. The Indians were, as he was informed, of the Shawnee tribe, and commanded by a Chief called Logan. He states in the year of 1777 or 1778, as well as now he recollects, he was drafted as a private in the Militia for the term of six months. He lived then in Sullivan county, North Carolina. Captain George Brooks commanded the company when raised. They ranged and marched over the country about the head of Clinch river, and sometimes on the waters of Big Sandy. He states that during the six months tour they had no important engagement. They marched against the Indians, and frequent skirmishes, one he recollects above the place of Elk Garden. He states he served the six months. He was discharged, and returned home to Sullivan county. He states he received a written discharge, had lost, or mislaid it, so he can't find it. He states, in the spring following, he volunteered as a private in the Militia of Sullivan County, to watch the Indians as a spy, in a company commanded by James Elliott. He states, he sped at the head waters of Clinch river, also on the old Kentucky road, and frequently at a place called Flat Rock. He states, he was to receive $1.50 a day for service, but never received anything. He states, he served three months as a spy in that company, and was then discharged. He received a written discharge, but from the great length of time, and not viewing it as of much importance to him has lost it. He states that the next year, in the spring, probably about the first of March, his father was drafted as a private in the Militia, to be marched and to be forted at the mouth of the north neck of the Holston, to defend the frontier from the depredation of the Indians. He states, he marched, and went in place of his father. That they forted at the mouth of the Holston. He states, that the Captain who commanded the company was Samuel Brashear. Brashear lived in Sullivan county, N. C. He states, he served three months and was discharged, but received no written discharge. They were no important engagements during the three months.

Sworn and subscribed, the day, and the year aforesaid, in open Court.

JOHN ADAIR

COL. RICHARD ALLEN, SR.

(Extract from the declaration for pension (dated Sept. 4, 1832, of Col. Richard Allen, a resident of Wilkes County, North Carolina.)

That he was born on the 26th day of November, 1741, in Baltimore County, the State of Maryland, the record of which is made in his old family Bible; that he continued to reside in the said County until he was twenty-one years of age when he removed to Frederick County, in the State of Virginia, where he lived about seven years, and then removed to Rowan County (now Wilkes), in N. Carolina which was in the month of September, 1770. In the month of October or November, 1775, he entered the service of the United States as a volunteer for six months in Capt. Jesse Walton's Company of minute men (it being the first company ever raised in the county of Wilkes), of which company he was appointed first Sergeant. Immediately after the company was raised and organized they marched to Salisbury, where they remained about sixteen days engaged in training and exercising the men, after which they were discharged and returned home, where they arrived a few days before Christmas.

On the 13th day of February, following they set out upon their march for Cross Creek or Fayetteville, having understood that the Scotch Tories were committing depredations in the country around about that place. On their way they were joined by Col. Martin Armstrong with the Surry militia at a place called Old Richmond. After joining Col. Armstrong they continued their march until they reached Randolph County, where they were joined by Col. Alexr. Martin of the Continental line with a small body of troops under his command. From thence they pursued their march direct to Cross Creek or Fayetteville. The day before they arrived at that place a battle had been fought between the Tories under Gen'l McDonald and the Whig militia under Gen'l Moore in which the former were defeated with considerable loss and a great number taken prisoners. The prisoners taken in this engagement were delivered over to Capt. Jesse Walton and his company who were ordered as a guard to convey them to Hillsboro. They immediately set out with the prisoners for that place but before they reached it they were met by two companies of Light Horse under the command of Captains Mebane and Shepard who took charge of the prisoners, when Capt. Walton and his company were discharged and returned home, where they arrived the 29th March, having been gone near two months.

After their arrival at home they met twice every week and continued to train and exercise themselves until their term of six months had expired. Not long after the expiration of his first term this deponent was chosen an ensign in the company of militia commanded by Capt. Benj. Cleveland, and very soon afterwards they received orders from Col. Armstrong to go against the Indians who were committing great depredations upon the frontier of the Western part of N. Carolina. In this expedition they served about two weeks principally in scouring the frontier settlements. Soon after their return orders were received by Captain Cleveland fom Col. Armstrong to take his company and go in pursuit of Col. Roberts (a Tory Col.) who had embodied a number of Tories on the Northwest side of the Blue Ridge. They immediately set out in pursuit of Col. Roberts and continued to pursue him and his company without being able to overtake them until they advanced considerably into the State of Virginia, when they learned that Roberts had disbanded his men and that they had dispersed. Upon receiving this information they returned home, having been gone about three weeks.

Early in the year 1778, Captain Benjamin Cleveland was appointed a Lieutenant Colonel and this deponent was appointed to succeed him as Captain of the company which commission he held until the close of the war. In the latter part of the year 1779, a call was made for troops to march to the defense of Charleston. A draft was made from the militia in Wilkes for the company and a draft also made from the Captains of Companies for a Captain to command that company. The lot fell upon this deponent and he accordingly repaired with his company to Hamblin's old store, where they rendezvoused on the 13th of January, 1780. As soon as they could organize and make the necessary preparations they marched direct to Charleston, S. C., where they joined the third regiment of North Carolina militia, commanded by Col. Andrew Hampton. After joining the regiment they were stationed about two miles from the city at the smoke camps where they remained a considerable time and until a report obtained currency that the Tories intended to set fire to the town and thereby enable the British to effect a landing.

Upon hearing of this report Gen. Lincoln ordered all the troops into the city where they remained until the term of service of this deponent and his men expired, when they were discharged and returned home, where they arrived sometime in the month of April, 1780, having been gone between three and four months. From the month of April, to September, 1780, this deponent, with small detachments of the men under his command, served three short tours, the precise length of each not particularly recollected, one of which was against a body of Tories assembled near the head of the Catawba river, another against Col. Bryan (a Tory Col.) who had embodied a band of Tories in the Southern part of the State, and the other against some Tories on the north-west side of the Blue Ridge. In these three tours this deponent believes he served about two months. In the month of September, 1780, information was received by Col. Benjamin Cleveland that Maj. Ferguson of the British army was advancing from South Carolina with a large body of British and Tories, upon which Col. Cleveland immediately issued orders for all the troops within the County of Wilkes to rendezvous at the Court House. This deponent with what men he could collect repaired thither immediately and after the troops were organized they all set out on their march to meet Maj. Ferguson. Upon the way they were joined by Cols. Sevier, Shelby, and McDowell, with troops from North Carolina. After a junction of the troops was formed, as most of them had horses it was proposed that all those who had horses or could procure them should advance immediately upon Ferguson. This deponent had a horse and was anxious to proceed with the main army but as a great many were on

foot and would necessarily be left behind, it became
necessary that the charge of those should be committed
to some officer. The command of the foot men was first
offered to Col. Herndon but he positively refused to accept it unless this deponent who he said had more exper-
ience than himself, could be detailed to stay with him.
In this state of affairs Col. Cleveland thought proper to
order this deponent to remain in charge of the foot men
and he according done so. They continued their march,
however, with all possible speed in the direction of King's
Mountain but was not able to reach it in time to engage
in the battle, it having been fought and the Americans
with their prisoners being on their return some short distance before they met with them. When they rejoined
the army they continued with them and assisted in guarding the prisoners until they proceeded as far as the Moravian towns in the County of Stokes, and after remaining there a considerable time they were relieved by Col.
Winston with a detachment of fresh troops, and Col.
Cleveland and his men returned home, which place they
reached some time in November—the precise time not
recollected—but they were in service in this expedition
about two months.

About the latter part of January, 1781, an express
arrived at Capt. Benjamin Herndon's, in Wilkes, from
Gen. Davidson, informing that Lord Cornwallis was approaching the State from South Carolina and requesting
that as many troops as possible should be collected immediately to oppose him. This deponent collected all the
men under his command that he could get and set out
with the other troops from the County in order to rendezvous at Salisbury; but when within about fourteen miles
of Salisbury they heard that Lord Cornwallis had crossed the Catawba and was then in Salisbury. Upon receiving this information they changed the direction of their
route and marched towards Salem in order to join Gen.
Green who was at that time supposed to be on Dan river
or near the borders of Virginia. When they had advanced as far as Person County, North Carolina, they received
orders from Gen. Green to return and endeavor to form
a junction with Gen. Pickens, who was expected to be
advancing from South Carolina through what is now East
Tennessee and to inform him of the situation of affairs as
also to conduct him through the country so that he might
be within a convenient distance of Gen. Green's army and
to co-operate with him if necessary. They did return and

this deponent met with Gen. Pickens at Mitchell's river in the County of Surry, and conducted him to Salem where they joined Col. Locke with his regiment. When they left Salem Gen. Pickens and Col. Locke with the respective troops under their command separated, the former taking the direct road to Hillsboro and the latter taking a route leading higher up the country. This deponent was attached to the troops under Col. Locke and when they had proceeded as far as Stony Creek in the County of Guilford or Rockingham, information was received from Gen. Pickens that a large number of Tories had embodied themselves with Col. Pyles, and requesting Col. Locke's troops to repair with all possible dispatch to meet him at Trollinger's ford on Haw river. Col. Locke with his troops set out immediately but before they reached Trollinger's Ford Gen. Pickens had engaged with the Tories and defeated them. As soon as they heard of the defeat of the Tories they turned their course and marched directly for Gen. Green's army which they met with near the High Rock. After remaining with Gen. Green a few days Col. Locke's regiment was discharged and returned home together with some others of the troops. In this expedition this deponent served a month to five weeks.

In addition to the service above enumerated this deponent performed a number of short tours (amounting perhaps to twenty), against the Tories in various parts of the Country, and disarming and arresting suspected persons and bringing them to trial, but it would be impossible for him to specify the particular periods of these services.

This deponent further states that he was duly commissioned as an Ensign and Captain as stated in the foregoing declaration. He cannot now recollect by whom the Ensign's commission was signed, but he believes the Captain's commission was signed by Governor Caswell—both of which are lost or mislaid so that they cannot now be produced.

RICHARD ALLEN, SEN'R.

Sworn to and subscribed, the day and year aforesaid, R. ALLEN, J. P.

STATE OF NORTH CAROLINA, IREDELL COUNTY

On this day 22d day of August, 1832 Personally appeared in open court now sitting for said county, Andrew Carson, a resident of said county and state, aged 76 years, who being duly sworn, doth on his oath make the following declaration in order to obtain the benefit of the act of June 7th, 1832. The first campaign he served under Captain Joseph Dixon, Lt. Carr or Kerr, Ensign Ewin.

He does not recollect the year—but it was in the fall, recollect the snow was plenty—it was cold—went out to Ninety-Six, South Carolina, under command of General Rutherford—his son James Rutherford was aid to his father. Wm. Lee Davidson was adjutant, was gone three months, and discharged at Sherrell's ford, by Captain Dixon, which discharge is lost.

Next campaign was against the Cherokee Indians under the command of Captain David Caldwell, defeated them on the Tennessee river, and destroyed their towns. Do not remember the names. Next campaign was under General Rutherford on the Savannah river. He was four months in the fall of 1778-9 under General Rutherford and General Lincoln and was discharged by these two Generals. From this time until Shadow Ford battle, he was in several tours of days and weeks at a time not recollected. He was one month under Wade Hampton, and in another tour under Cap. D. Caldwell after Tories. He was under four weeks tour with General Davidson, 31 days under Captain John Graham,—he was always on the alert, and considered a good minute man, with a good horse and gun.

He was born in Rowan county, North Carolina, March 1st, 1756, and when in the service he was on the Catawba in that part of Rowan, now Iredell county, and now lives there. He was mostly in what is called the partisan warfare, and very little with the regulars as the Tories of North Carolina were sufficient to keep the Whigs engaged. He had a family record as kept by his father; it is lost.

This is to certify that Andrew Carson hath served fifty-two days in my company in actual service by general order. Given under my hand March ye 23, 1781.

D. CALDWELL, Captain.

Several other officers certified to his service in the Revolution.

Inscription on tombstone in the family burying ground near Houstonville, Iredell County, N. C.

CAPTAIN ANDREW CARSON
Born 1st March, 1756
Died 29th January, 1841
He was a soldier of the Revolutionary War.

State of Tennessee)
Carter County)

On this 8th. day of December, 1838 personally appeared before me David Nelson, a Justice of the Peace for the County of Carter in the State of Tennessee, Elizabeth Carter a resident of Elizabethton in the County aforesaid, aged seventy three years on the ninth day of July last, who being first duly sworn according to law, doth on her oath make the following declaration in order to obtain the benefit of the provision made by the Act of Congress passed July 7th, 1838, entitled an act granting half pay and pensions to certain widows. That she is the widow of Landon Carter who was a Captain of the militia in the army of the Revolution, as she is informed, and believes that said Carter as a Captain raised a company of soldiers, principally volunteers and served a tour of duty of four months or nearly so under Col. John Sevier and Col. Arthur Campbell, in the years seventeen hundred and eighty and eighty one, in an expedition against the Cherokee Indians. The said Landon Carter as she believes set out with his company in the month of November in the year seventeen hundred and eighty and marched from the upper part of East Tennessee, his then residence supposed to be Washington County, to the Blue Springs supposed to be situated in what is now Blount County, Tennessee, when, where Col. John Sevier met & fought the Cherokees, in which battle the Indians loss was estimated at about thirty, and in which my husband commanded as a Captain. After said battle the said troops marched back, as she believes, to Buckingham Island near the mouth of Boyd's Creek, where they were reinforced by Col. Arthur Campbell who took the command and marched the troops to the Cherokee Nation & took several towns to wit: Chota, Chilhowee, Tellico, Highnaupte (Highwassee?—L. C. D.) and returned after an absence of near four months. She further declared that said Carter as she believes served another tour of duty in the Fall of seventeen hundred and eighty, one as a Captain. The particulars of which she is not now able to state, but believes he set out with his Company to join Gen. Marion in the south, and was in service about four months. She further declares that she was married to the said Landon Carter on the twenty-sixth day of February seventeen hundred and eighty four. That her husband the aforesaid Landon Carter died on the fifth day of June in the year eighteen hundred. That she was not married to him previous to his leaving the service but the marriage took place previous to the first of January seventeen hundred and ninety four, viz, at the time above stated. She further declares that she has no documentary evidence to her knowledge by which she can establish the services aforesaid. She further declares that she is now a single woman and has been so ever sinc the death of her said husband Landon Carter, never having married.

Her
ELIZABETH X CARTER
Mark

State of Tennessee)
Carter County   )

Personally appeared before me David Nelson, a Justice of the Peace for Carter County, Jeremiah Campbell, Esq., aged seventy-six years this day, who being first duly sworn according to law doth upon his oath say that in the month of September seventeen hundred and eighty one, he set out as a private in the company of Captain Landon Carter from the County of Washington, State of Tennessee to join Gen. Greene or Marion in the south. That Capt. Carter's company was delayed in starting and did not get to start with Col. Sevier. Sevier crossed the Yellow Mountain, as it was said Carter crossed the Stam (Stone—L. C. D.) Mountain, and went by the way of John's River and joined Sevier at the Tuckaseege Forge (Ford—L. C. D.) on the Catawba River in the North Carolina, from thence they went on by the way of Charlotte in North Carolina and joined Gen. Green at the high hills of Santee, but Gen. Green having gone into Winter quarters, Col. Sevier staid but a few hours with Greene. But passed on immediately to join Gen. Marion and did join him in the swamps of Santee River near the British encampment which was then at Marks (Monks—L. C. D.) Corner. This junction of Sevier and Marion he thinks took place about the latter part of October. They remained under his command until they started home, he cannot state the precise day on which they got home but believes it was in the latter part of February having been in service near five months, the exact time he cannot now state. He further states that during all the time mentioned the aforesaid Landon Carter commanded as his Captain and was considered a good officer. He further states that he was well acquainted with Capt. Carter, afterwards Gen. Carter, 'till his death. That said Carter he believes died in June eighteen hundred. That he has been acquainted with his widow Mrs. Elizabeth Carter the applicant for a pension ever since. That she is now a single woman and has been so ever since the death of her husband the aforesaid Landon Carter.

Sworn to 15th December, 1838.

JEREMIAH CAMPBELL

State of Tennessee)
Carter County)

Personally came before me David Nelson, an acting Justice of the Peace for the county aforesaid, Doctor Isaac Taylor and after being sworn duly, saith that he was personally acquainted with Landon Carter Sr. (the reputed father of Hon. Wm. B. Carter) and Isaac saith on oath that in the year of eighty, he thinks sometime in November that he went out with Landon Carter against the Cherokee Indians and said Carter acted as Capt. that they served nearly four months tour against the said Cherokee Indians in the company of said Carter, who had raised a company of nearly all volunteers. That during the campaign Carter and his company were in one battle in which there were about thirty Indians killed. The battle was fought at a place called Blue Springs between French Broad and Little River. Doctor Taylor thinks that place is now in Blount county in this State. Gov. John Sevier was commander in chief and marched back to Buckingham Island near the mouth of Boyd's creek on French Broad. There they met a reinforcement under the command of Col. Arthur Campbell. The said Arthur Campbell then took the command; they then marched to the Cherokee Nation and took five principal towns, to-wit—Choto, Chilkowe, Tellico, Hiwassa, Chischewe, and then they returned home and during the said time the said Landon Carter acted the part of a brave gentleman and a soldier and a good officer.

Sworn to Nov. 1838.

ISAAC TAYLOR

State of Tennessee)
Washington County)

This day appeared before me W. K. Blair, a Justice of peace for the said county, Darling Jones aged seventy-five years and being duly sworn according to law of deposeth and saith that he during the war of independence served in one tour of duty in the year of 1781 in the company of Captain Landon Carter to South Carolina to the high hills of Santee, in the regiment commanded by Col. John Sevier, that we marched through Charlotte town, North Carolina and Camden, South Carolina to the high hills of Santee where General Green's army lay after the battle of Eutaw Springs, from there down the Santee river to where General Marion lay with his militia and joined him. We had no battle while there, but took on a British garrison without fighting. We were in service about four months and was then discharged and returned home in the winter. We went from Washington County, North Carolina, Colonel Isaac Shelby and his regiment was along from Sullivan County.

DARLING JONES

Sworn to 8th of December, 1838.

State of Tennessee   )
Washington County)

This day appeared before me Henderson Clark, a justice of the peace for said county, John Clark aged eighty, and being duly sworn to law disposeth and saith that he served a tour of duty of the year of 1780 in the summer and during the war of Independance, that he was in the company of Captain Samuel Williams commanded by Colonel Charles Robertson. That he well recollects that Captain Landon Carter commanded a company at the time in said regiment, and that Colonel Isaac Shelby was along in command from Sullivan county, that Colonel William Cocke was along. We marched from Washington County, North Carolina. We passed a place called Gilbert Town, North Carolina, went to Cherokee Ford on Broad river, staid about two weeks, then went and took an enemy Fort on a creek called Thicketty, and then returned to the main army at the Cherokee Ford. From the Ford we marched about from place to place until we thought proper to return home, all being volunteers, I suppose the tour was between two and three weeks.

Sworn to 5th December, 1838.

JOHN CLARK

LENOIR.   Pension Statement of William

In May, 1833, he was residing in Wilkes County, N. C., and states he was born May 8th, 1751, in Brunswick County, Va., and lived, during his service in the war of the Revolution, in Surry (now Wilkes) County and he has resided there since. He was a volunteer in the service and that his commission as Lieutenant was signed by Governor Caswell, as he believes, but by whom his commission as Captain was signed he cannot say, as both are lost. After the said war he was promoted to higher rank in the Militia and gave no attention to the preservation of his former commission.

In the year 1776, a requisition was made by the government, to raise a certain number of Militia, as minute men, and he volunteered as a private (although he was Lieutenant in the Militia Company of Capt. Joseph Herndon) under Capt. Jesse Walton, which was soon ordered to the eastern or lower part of N. C., to suppress an insurrection of the Scotch Tories. After he had proceeded about fifty miles assisted in the capture of the Tory, Colonel Gideon Wright, whose house was surrounded in the night, and conveyed him to the little town of Richmond, where he was disposed of in some manner not now recollected. After this event Lenoir was taken sick on the road rendering him unable to travel and Capt. Walton discharged him. He made his way home with much difficulty. The calls for Militia, from Surry County to suppress insurrection were repeated in quick succession and as soon as he was able to travel he volunteered as a Lieutenant of Militia Co., to which he belonged, commanded by Capt. Herndon, which marched to Shallow Ford on the Yadkin, distant 60 or 70 miles, from the place of rendezvous, when orders were received to return home. A very short time after the Company was ordered to the same point of destination as before and after marching the same distance, they were again directed to return home. In these two expeditions Lenoir was absent five weeks.

As Surry was a frontier county the inhabitants were much annoyed and alarmed by the frequent depredations of the Indians, it was necessary for the public safety and security that active measures should be adopted to effect that object and Lenoir was selected, by the Colonel of the County, to raise a Company of Rangers to patrol the frontier settlement and protect them from the incursions of the Indians. In obedience to this order he organized a Company which was stationed at a convenient point on the headwaters of the Yadkin River, from whence they ranged the country on the Blue Ridge for a considerable distance as well as west of it, between the water of the Yadkin and New River, the inhabitants of which localities, from depredations and the great danger of their exposure, were compelled to abandon their homes to seek security in the interior settlements. In this service, he believes, he was engaged as Captain of the Company for 6 weeks or upwards in the summer of 1776.

In August 1776 he volunteered as Lieutenant with Capt. Benjamin Cleveland in an expedition against the Cherokee Indians. His Company of Rangers having just returned from the expeditions above mentioned, were not all prepared to join another, he accepted the position under Capt. Cleveland, who had a very large Company that required two Lieutenants, of which he was the first. He set out on the march under Colonel Martin Armstrong, the Colonel of the County, direct to the Pleasant Garden, in the County of Burke, where they joined General Griffith Rutherford to make the necessary organizations and other arrangements. From thence they went to the Cherokee Nation, the towns which were generally abandoned, except by straggling Indians, women and children. Capt. Cleveland was stationed with a few men at the middle towns, while Lenoir was appointed to the command of the remainder of the Company, and marched, under Colonel Armstrong, to the Hiawassee towns, which they destroyed and killing some Indians. The S. C. Militia was to have met General Rutherford at the Middle Towns, but upon his arrival no intelligence could be obtained from them and he set out for the Hiawassee towns as before stated. After the departure of General Rutherford from the Middle Towns, the S. C. Troops arrived there and immediately started for Hiawassee with expectation of joining him at that place, but taking a different route they were attacked on the way by a party of Indians who had formed an ambuscade, but by the skillful and prudent conduct of their officers they were dislodged with a considerable number killed whom it is believed they carried off. The S. C. troops lost about 15 men who were buried in a swamp and upon whom they constructed a pole causeway, over which the Militia marched as they returned from the Hiawassee to the Middle Towns. Lenoir served 20 days as Captain on this occasion. After having destroyed the Indian towns, with all their stock, corn, and other property that could be found, the troops returned to N. C., and their respective homes. Although but few were killed in this expedition, yet from the fatigue, exposure and privation, a great number died after they arrived home much of which Lenoir suffered. He believed he served 70 days as Lieutenant, making with the twenty days as Captain, three months. After his return home he was appointed Captain of the Company in the District where he resided, which rank he held until the close of the war. In 1777 Surry County was divided by an Act of the Legislature and Lenoir was included in that portion which is now Wilkes County, but his Company District was the same. Shortly after the division he was ordered by Colonel Benjamin Cleveland who was Colonel of the County, to march his Company down Hunting Creek to detect some outlying Tories and other suspicious characters. He was unsuccessfully employed for some weeks in the Spring of 1778. In the Fall of 1778 he, with his Company, accompanied Colonel Cleveland over the Blue Ridge and down New River to Virginia to detect and subdue some Tories who infested that section of the country and captured some of them and thus restoring tranquility and apparent security to the settlements, recrossed the mountains for their homes. The Tories taken, after an examination, were permitted to go at large by promising future loyalty to the cause of independence. In some instances Colonel Cleveland administered the oath of allegiance. He was gone about 26 days. He was again ordered out with his Company to march across Brush Mountain together with other troops under Colonel Cleveland, to subdue some Tories on Cowe's Creek and its waters, who kept that neighborhood in a state of alarm. A Tory by the name of Williams was captured, from whom they endeavored to obtain information relative to suspected persons, but he refused to give any until Col. Cleveland adopted the expedient of hanging him to the limb of a tree, or a bent down sapling, which, however, did not produce the desired effect. This was repeated a second time with more severity, then only to give encouragement to the Whigs and alarm to the Tories. The result of the expedition was to restore a tolerable state of security in that part of the country. He was absent 20 days.

In May or June, 1779 information was received that the Tory Captain Whitson with a Company was committing great depredations on the waters of the Catawba, and Lenoir was ordered with his Company and some others to march under Col. Cleveland up the Yadkin River, and across the Catawba, in quest of Whitson. On the march down the Catawba, Colonel Larkin Cleveland, a brother of Colonel Benjamin, was badly wounded by a shot from a high cliff of rocks, supposed from a Tory, who made his escape. Capt. Lenoir, with a detachment of forty men, well mounted, was ordered to patrol the country between the Catawba River and the South Fork after Whitson, which they did all night without success. On their return Colonel Cleveland returned home, after an absence of about one month. A short time after this last service Colonel Cleveland received (late in the afternoon) intelligence that the Tories were embodying, towards the head of the Yadkin, whereupon he repaired immediately to Wilkes, C. H., distant fourteen miles from his residence, where Lenoir with what men he could collect immediately joined in and by their united exertion succeeded in raising about 200 men, and at daybreak on the following morning had marched to the place where the Tories were said to be, a distance estimated at 21 miles, but the Tories had fled with great precipitation towards the south. They promptly pursued them with all possible speed as far as Lincolnton, but did not arrive until after the celebrated battle at Ramsour's Mills, in which the Tories were triumphantly defeated (June 20th, 1780). Upon hearing of this event they returned home, absent about one month.

In August or September 1780 he was ordered by Colonel Cleveland to march with his Company southwardly against the British and Tories who were harassing the people to great extremities in Burke County, and Colonel Cleveland receiving information of the encampment of about 100 Tories at Little John's Meeting House, a few miles in advance of his troops, directed him to select 25 men, well mounted, to approach the Tory camp until they fired upon him, with strict injunction to retreat without returning the fire, in order to lead them into ambuscade, which he, Colonel Cleveland, would form for that purpose. This arrangement was countermanded by an express which was received before the Tory Camp was reached, and all the men ordered to return except five, to be selected by Lenoir, with whom he was to proceed to execute the original arrangement, but he found the camp abandoned. They, however, advanced considerably farther into Burke County, where they joined a regiment from Virginia under Colonel Campbell and some Militia from the Northwestern side of the Blue Ridge under Colonels Sevier and Shelby, together with the Militia of Burke County under Col. Charles McDowell. With these reinforcements the march was continued southwardly until reaching Rutherford County, when they were informed of the progress and advance of a large body of British and Tories, commanded by Colonel Ferguson. Upon this intelligence orders were immediately given for every man that had a horse, or could procure a suitable one, to be ready to march at sunrise the next morning to oppose Ferguson. There being no regular officer or even soldier except two belonging to the troops (and they having joined as Militia men) nor no militia officer above the grade of Colonel, it was agreed that Colonel Campbell of Virginia should command the whole detachment. They accordingly took up the line of march at the appointed time (leaving behind all those who had been unable to procure horses) and on the way they were joined by some militia from South Carolina under the command of Colonel Williams, which augmented their number to about 700, according to the best calculation which he (Lenoir) could make (the footmen who were left behind amounting to about 1500). They continued their march all day that day and all night, it being very dark and rainy, and on the next day (being the 7th October 1780) attacked Colonel Ferguson on King's Mountain, near the line between North and South Carolina, and after a hot engagement, which lasted about three-quarters of an hour, achieved the total defeat of Colonel Ferguson and his whole army, every man of whom was in camp at the commencement of the action, being either killed or taken. The killed on the side of the enemy being estimated at 250 and on the side of the Whigs at 32. The remainder of the army amounting to about 937, according to the best estimate which could be made from the papers of the commander, were detained as prisoners of war. In this action he (Lenoir) received two wounds from bullets, one in his side and the other in his arm, and a third bullet passed through his hair above where it was tied.

The next day the American army started on their return with the prisoners (of whom as counted by Capt. Lenior, 725 were embodied men) who, exclusive of officers, wounded, sick, etc., were compelled to carry the guns that had been taken, many taking two guns each, and proceeded on until they met with the footmen who had been left behind. Together they marched to and halted in Rutherford County, where a court martial, composed of field officers, selected about 32 of the most obnoxious of the Tories who had been taken, and ordered them to be hung. After executing three at a time until nine were executed, the remainder were respited. The army then left Rutherford County with the prisoners for the Moravian towns in Stokes County, where they were stationed a considerable time guarding them, until relieved by other troops, then Capt. Lenoir with his Company returned home. Absent three months.

About the time, but before, Lord Cornwallis arrived at Salisbury from S. C., Capt. Lenoir, with his Company volunteered and also six other Captains from Wilkes County with their Companies, marched to join Gen. Greene, as they expected at Salisbury. On the way, there being no Field Officers with the troops, a dispute arose between Lenoir and Capt. Benjamin Herndon respecting their seniority, or who was entitled to assume the command, and being unable to determine it themselves, agreed to leave it to the soldiers to make choice of a commander for that tour, when all but six followed Lenoir, and he assumed command accordingly.

Before reaching Salisbury he was informed Gen. Greene had marched toward Virginia, and Cornwallis was in or near Salisbury and he changed his course towards Salem, crossing the Yadkin at Enoch's Ferry. On the way he succeeded by stratagem in retaking three British officers, who had been captured by General Morgan at the battle of the Cowpens, but had made their escape from the guard. Several outlying Tories were also taken who were in the Company of the British officers. In pursuing his march they camped all night near the old Moravian town, where he learned that the British Army was then in that place. Not knowing where to find Gen. Greene he turned his course up the country to effect a junction with General Pickens, which took place near Mitchell's River in Surry County. Selecting about forty mounted infantry he joined him and leaving the remainder of his troops which were under his command, under the command of Capt. Herndon, immediately set out with General Pickens towards Hillsboro, at which place Cornwallis was. Gen. Pickens having understood that Tarleton with his dragoons and infantry had crossed Haw River, set off immediately in pursuit, after being joined by Colonel Lee with his cavalry. They crossed Haw River at Batler's Ford, but before overtaking Tarleton, fell in with a body of Tories under Doctor Pyles, a Tory Colonel with whom they immediately engaged and literally cut them to pieces. Some, however, made their escape and some were taken prisoners. When the conflict first commenced it was believed that they were a part of Col. Tarleton's infantry, but they were not. Lenoir escaped without a wound himself, but had his horse wounded and his sword broken. General Pickens learning that Tarleton was encamped at Col. O'Neil's Mill detached Capt. Lenoir with a few men to reconnoitre his camp, by which means he learned that Tarleton had decamped about midnight going on the road towards Hillsboro. General Pickens being apprised of this movement, started forthwith in pursuit, but finding that he could not be overtaken before arriving at Hillsboro, it was abandoned and he turned his course up the north side of Haw River. On the following second or third night it was learned that the whole British Army was after General Pickens and near at hand, Colonel Lee, with his dragoons, having left Gen. Pickens. Major Micajah Lewis an American officer went out to reconnoitre, as well as to ascertain the facts, but unfortunately approaching too near to Tarleton's dragoons, believing them to be Lee's, he received several wounds that terminated his life. General Pickens continued his march and joined General Greene near the High Rock Ford on Haw River.

At this time Lenoir being Clerk of the Court of Pleas and Quarter Sessions for Wilkes County, and the session of the Court coming on in a few days, it was necessary for him to return home. He accordingly obtained leave of absence from the service. Absent six weeks. This last expedition terminated his military service during the war, although considerable other service was performed which has not been enumerated herein. He died May 6th, 1839. In a letter dated Fort Defiance May 16th, 1833, he states that he was commissioned Colonel of cavalry of the 5th Division of N. C. Militia, and Major General of said 5th Division in January, 1795.

REVOLUTION PENSION

State of Tennessee, Circuit Court, March Term, 1832 Roan County.

Be it remembered that on the — day of March, 1832 personally appeared in the Circuit Court of the County of Roan in the State of Tennessee, being the court of records Hezekiah Love, aged eighty years the tenth of October, 1832, and made the following declaration in order to obtain the benefit of the act of Congress passed the 18th of March 1818 and the first of May, 1830 for the benefit and the relief of the soldiers of the Revolution

Army. Said Hezekiah Love being duly sworn in open
Court deposeth and saith as follows as to wit: That to
the best of his recollections and belief he enlisted in the
month of March 1776, in the State of South Carolina as a
soldier for eighteen months, in the company of Captain
Eli Cashion who was a captain in the regiment commanded by Lieutenant-Colonel Mason, and the first Colonel to
the best of my recollection was of the name of Thompson,
the Christian name of Colonel Thompson is not now recollected. That he was in the battle of Fort Moultrie,
near to the city of Charleston, which he believed happened in the first year after he enlisted. He also fought
and was engaged in the battle of Hanging Rock, about
thirty miles above the town of Camden, he was also in
the battles of Columbia and Eutaw Springs; but in those
two last engagements he fought in the Militia, he was also
a Militia soldier at Sumpter's defeat and the battle of
Fish Dam Ford on Broad river, and on King Mountain.
At the time of the Acts of Congress were passed authoriz-
ing payment to the Revolutionary soldiers he was poses-
sed of some property and was unwilling to take the oath
required from applicants. But for a time of two years
and a little afterwards he has been destitute of property.
He now is destitute of everything like property except his
wearing apparel.

The discharge which he obtained from the regular
army was placed in the house of his brother James Love
which was attacked and pillaged by a party of Tories.
It is out of his power so far as he knows, for he thinks the
Tories destroyed it, to prove his service as a regular soldier, except so far as that fact may be established by the
affidavit of Edward Eskridge Esq., which accompanies
this declaration.

Sworn to in open Court March 12, 1832.

His
HEZEKIAH X LOVE
Mark

Henry S. Pinus, J. C.

Robert Christian and Milton Center respected citizens and freeholders of Roane County, make oath that
they are acquainted with Hezekiah Love the above applicant for a pension, and that they know he has no property except his wearing apparel, and that is of very common inferior sort of homespun clothing.

Sworn to in open court, March 12th, 1832.
Robert Christian
Milton Center

H. S. Pinus.

And the foregoing declaration and affidavit at the request of the parties, be permitted to be spread on the records.

State of Tennessee

I, William Brown, clerk of the Circuit Court of Roane County by my deputy, Henry S. Pinus do certify that the foregoing declaration and affidavit copied from the records also of the Court ordered and permitted them to be spread on the records. And I certify further that I am satisfied that the facts stated in said declaration and affidavit relative to the value of declarative property is correct.

WILLIAM BROWN, Clerk
By his Deputy, Henry S. Pinus

PENSION STATEMENT

James Sevier, Washington County, Tennessee: Declaration, 11th September 1832; aged 68 years. Served in 1780 in his uncle Robert Sevier's company, in his father Col. John Sevier's regiment in the battle of Kings Mountain; that Capt. Robert Sevier was mortally wounded in that battle and died a few days after: that immediately after, the regiment collected at a place called the Swan Ponds, in now Greene County; Col. John Sevier commanded, Jesse Welton & Jonathan Tipton were the majors: Affiant was in Capt. Landon Carter's company: Left home the last of November, met the Indians in force on the South Side of French Broad, on Boyd's Creek, and had a pretty severe engagement with them in which we were successful, must have been more than two months on this tour.

Shortly after Gen. Greene's battle with the British at the Eutaw Springs, there was a request made for men from this side of the mountains, who were to serve three months after they joined General Greene. My Father, Col. J. Sevier, & Lt. Col. Charles Robertson, commanded the Washington troops; Valentine Sevier and Jonathan Tipton were the Majors; commanded our march for South Carolina in September, 1781, we passed through Morgantown and Charlotte, N. C., and through General Gate's battle ground; joined General Greene, at the High Hills of Santee, where he was recruiting his men after the se-

vere service at Eutaw; we were sent on to join General
Marion in the swamps of Santee; while with General
Marion, declarent was one of a party that took a British
post below Monk's Corner, consisting of about a hundred
men.   They had fortified round a large brick tenement,
belonging to a Mr. Colleton: The officers commanding
the Americans were Colonels Sevier, Mayhew, Oree,
(Horry) or Horre, and Maj. Valentine Sevier.   We made
some attempt to take some of their outposts, but found
them all evacuated.   I suppose called in by the British
General.   Having served out the time, we returned home,
although General Marion expressed a great desire that
we should remain a few weeks longer.   My father, Capt.
Carter, and most of his company, did stay for some considerable time longer, and were then discharged.   Believes he was upwards of four months from home on this
service.

Shortly after his return home from S. C., he thinks
in February, 1782, there was an Indian alarm, and call
for men; that himself and an elder brother who had returned from Virginia that fall; equipt themselves as volunteers and went about fifty miles to the place of rendezvous on Holston river; that shortly after they got there,
and before many men had collected, the weather became
extremely cold, and a deep snow fell, so that it was
thought the Indians would not disturb the frontier people
at that time, and that it would be most advisable to break
up and return home; we did so.   Who was the officer that
ordered out the men at that time I do not recollect, unless it was Col. Charles Robertson, as my father and Captain Carter had not returned at that time from S. C. My
brother and myself joined no company, and think were
not more than two weeks from home.   That through the
summer of 1782, the lower Cherokees near the Lookout
Mountain and on Coosa River were very troublesome.   As
soon as their crops were matured my father raised an
army of men, set out the last of August or first of September, and went and destroyed all the lower towns on the
waters of Tennessee, and two towns on Coosa River, one
call Estanaula, the other called Spring Frog's Town, two
villages on the waters of Coosa.   On this campaign we
had no fighting.   The body of Indians kept out of our
way; we took some seven or eight prisoners, (warriors),
with a number of women and children.   After remaining
some length of time in the Nation, and having destroyed
everything that came within our grasp, on which they

could support.   An Indian countryman by the name of
Rodgers came in with a flag for peace—the Indians were
requested if they wanted peace to go up to Old Chota
town, on Tennessee River, and there a peace talk would
be held with them.   They did so; a peace was made, and
the prisoners restored to their friends.   Major Valentine
Sevier was all the Major that was out at that time, as I
believe.   Declarent served in Capt. Alexander Moore's
company, there was Capt. Samuel Weare and Capt. Robert Bean who commanded companies, the other captains
now forgotten.   I believe we were upwards of two
months on that campaign.

In August, 1780, a campaign was ordered against
the Middle Settlements Indians, the place of meeting was
beyond the limits of the Settlements, one Creek called Indian Creek; that he was one of the men that met to go
on said tour; while at the place of rendezvous, and waiting for others to collect, a man by the name of Hill went
into the mountain to hunt, and was shot at by an Indian
before he discovered him, but being missed, and seeing
the Indian, he fired at and killed him.   This circumstance
caused a mutiny amongst the men.   They were afraid
their families would be killed in their absence, broke for
home, and the campaign fell through.   I mention this to
show, that I was twice called out to go on campaigns that
fell through.   My father, in this latter instance, was to
have commanded; there was no Major that I recollect; I
believe we were not more than ten days or two weeks
from home.

Early in the summer of 1781, the frontier inhabitants
became much alarmed about Indians.   My father, who
was Colonel of the County, ordered out a Company of
Rangers, or what was then called a scouting party; this
declarent was one of that party, and went out, and James
Hubbard was the Captain, as well as he recollects, were
out about two weeks.

Was born in 1764; Col. Richard Campbell, who was
killed at Eutaw Springs was the declarent's uncle.

(Had married the sister of Maj. James Sevier's
mother, Sarah Hawkins.)

SECTION TWO

PERSONAL SKETCHES
OF
KING'S MOUNTAIN SOLDIERS

The paragraphic sketches below are in alphabetic order, the orthography used by Miss White being almost always followed.

Names marked with a star are of persons not clearly known to have been in the battle of King's Mountain, or not explicitly stated as such in the manuscript. Unmarked names are those of bona fide soldiers present in the battle or of persons closely associated therewith.

Dates in brackets are those of birth and death.

When Washington is mentioned without qualification, Washington county in Virginia is meant. When Lincoln is similiarly mentioned, Lincoln county in North Carolina is referred to.

In several of the sketches there is mention of Fincastle and Tryon counties, neither of which now exists. Each was named in honor of a royal governor, and as each governor sided with Britain in the war for American independence, the names at once became obnoxious to the whigs and were abolished by the simple expedient of subdividing the two counties. Fincastle, named for the British home of Governor Dunmore of Virginia was divided in 1776 into the counties of Montgomery, Washington, and Kentucky. Tryon, named for Governor Tryon of North Carolina was divided into Lincoln and Rutherford.

When "the battle" is spoken of without special explanation, the battle of King's Mountain is meant, this being the express subject of the present volume. If a soldier was "also" in one or more other specified engagements, it is to be understood that he was present at King's Mountain.

If a given soldier was "under Campbell" he was presumably a resident of Virginia, the same as Campbell himself. And as James Williams was a South Carolina officer, a soldier "under Williams" was most probably a South Carolinian.

When "Shelby", "Sevier", and "Campbell", are mentioned without front names, Isaac Shelby, John Sevier, and William Campbell are alluded to, these being the most conspicuous officers under the three respective names.

Reference is repeatedly made to Draper's "King's Mountain and Its Heroes," to Eckenrode's "Virginia Militia in the Revolution," and to Summers' "History of Southwest Virginia," the last named book containing a list of King's Mountain men from Washington County, Virginia. By "Draper manuscripts" is meant the typewritten copy of Draper's King's Mountain Papers, in two large volumes, placed in the Calvin McClung Historical Collections of the Lawson McGhee Free Library, Knoxville, Tennessee.

Abernathy. The record of Robert is found in the North Carolina D. A. R. Booklet, Volume IX. In 1776 he was a delegate from Tryon county, the legislature then sitting at Halifax. He was granted a pension by North Carolina in 1833.

Adair. John* was born 1732 and died at Grassy Valley, four miles north of Knoxville, Tennessee, February 24, 1827. The report that he died the next April was because his will was probated in that month. He was entry-taker for Sullivan county (now Tennessee), and had collected $12,000 from the sale of North Carolina lands. Colonels Sevier and Shelby begged the aid of this money in meeting Ferguson's threat to exterminate the Watauga people. Adair thus replied: "Colonel Sevier, I have no authority by law to make this disposition of the money. It belongs to the impoverished treasury of North Carolina, and I dare not appropriate a cent of it to any purpose; but, if the country is overrun by the British, our liberty is gone. Let the money go, too. Take it. If the enemy, by its use, is driven from the country, I can trust that country to justify and vindicate my conduct. So take it." The fund was turned over to Sevier and Shelby and used in the purchase of ammunition and military equipment. The two colonels agreed to refund the money unless Adair's act were legalized by the legislature of North Carolina. That body paid the claim in full in 1782 (see Ramsay's Annals.) In 1791 Adair settled four miles north of White Station, Knox county, Tennessee, and under North Carolina was a commissary to furnish provisions to the Cumberland Guards, this duty calling him to the extreme frontier. He and his wife were buried at Adair Station, now the "old John Smith farm" on Broadway Street near Knoxville. John Smith was a son-in-law.

A son or near relative of the foregoing was the John Adair who made a pension declaration in Sullivan county. In many of the pension statements by the soldiers who fought at King's Mountain nothing is said of that battle, because it was fought by self-constituted volunteers and was not for a long while officially recognized by the Federal government. So the applicant named the service that was more certain to entitle him to a pension. The statement is found in Chapter XI.

Adams. John lived in Washington county, Tennessee, and many descendants are still in the east of that state. In 1796 he was a commissioner for Jonesboro. He married Winnie Russell, August 15, 1768, and had a son John.

William was born in Ireland in 1733, served in the Fifth South Carolina regiment, and died in York county of that state in 1799. His powderhorn used at King's Mountain is still in the family. His wife was Margaret Ewart, and a son, Rev. James S., married Erexon McEwen.

Alexander. Daniel was in the Mecklenburg militia 1778-1781. When granted a pension he was on the invalid list. His statement includes the following: "I also volunteered under Captain Martin Fifer on the same day and at the Moravian Town near the Yadkin River, and also in Guilford Courthouse (battle) under Captain Alexander. We were called out, and in the command of Major William R. Davie—an attorney and officer, later Minister to France, I believe—to join General Gates at Camden. Major Davie was a tall sallow-complexioned man with blue eyes. On getting as far as Gaston's, which is near the South Carolina line, we met the American army retreating. General Gates and Major Davie had some conversation. We advanced some distance, when on meeting some French officer flying we also joined in the retreat. General Gates had on a pale blue coat with epaulettes, velvet breeches, and was riding a bay horse. We retreated as far as Charlotte very much fatigued and worn down."

An account of Elias Alexander is in a foot-note in Schenck's History of North Carolina. He was born in Rutherford county and carried to his grave twenty-seven British and tory balls. Major Green of the same county was at King's Mountain on the tory side. After the war Green was several times elected to the state senate from

Rutherford. In 1823 Alexander resolved to have Green beaten and brought out his son as an opposing candidate. To gain votes Green joined the Baptist Church. Alexander went to see Green baptized in Broad River. When the major rose out of the water, wet as a rat and gasping for breath, Alexander drew himself to his full height of six feet three inches, and towering over the people sang the following stanza:

There stands old Major Green, now neat and clean,
     Though formerly a Tory,
The damndest rascal that ever was seen,
     Now on his way to glory.

The verse became a campaign song and was Green's defeat.

There is a tradition that James Alexander was at King's Mountain. He received a pension for service in the North Carolina militia.

Jeremiah was under Colonel William Campbell, and received a pension for service in the Virginia militia.

John was born in Rowan county, North Carolina, married Rachel, a sister to William and Samuel Davidson, and moved to Lincoln county. His son James, also born in Rowan, was at King's Mountain and also at the surrender of Cornwallis, where he is said to have captured the camp chest of the British general. In 1782 he married Rhoda Cunningham (born 1763) and in 1793 moved to Bee Tree Creek in Buncombe county, where he died. His own son, James married Nancy, daughter of Thomas Foster, in 1814.

Oliver served under Colonel William Campbell. He was one of the magistrates that formed the first court of Blount county, the opening session being held in the house of Abraham Weaver. He was appointed by Governor Blount.

William, Jeremiah, and Oliver are all listed in Summer's History of Southwest Virginia. Eckenrode has seven William Alexanders in his list of soldiers of the Revolution, and the pension list of North Carolina has five. Much history of the Alexanders is in Hunter's Sketches of North Carolina.

Allen. Moses was in several battles with the Indians and tories before going to King's Mountain under Colonel Shelby. He received a pension in Washington county, Virginia.

Richard was born in Baltimore, Maryland, moved to Wilkes county, North Carolina, about 1770, served in many battles both before and after King's Mountain, and led a company for the relief of Charleston in 1780. He chased Bryan's tories out of North Carolina, and was in Greene's army in 1781. He became a colonel of militia, was the first sheriff of Wilkes county, and a member of the legislature in 1793. He died in Wilkes county, October 10, 1833, being then in his ninety-first year. The extract in Chapter XI is taken from his pension declaration, dated September 4, 1832.

Vincent Allen was from Lincoln county, where he afterward received a pension.

Allison. John, who was under Colonel Shelby, was wounded at King's Mountain and went with a stiff knee the rest of his life. He is supposed to have been there a captain, as he was ever afterward known as Captain Jack Allison. His sons, Robert and David were prominent in the episode of the state of Franklin and in Tennessee. John Allison the immigrant came from Ireland and settled in Pennsylvania. His sons John and Finly settled in Sullivan County, Tennessee, about 1773. John Jr. married a Miss Hodge, whose father was from Wales. Their sons were Isaac, Francis, Joseph, Robert, John, George W., and Jesse. Their daughters were Mary, Elizabeth, Susan, and Martha. Francis, Joseph, George, and Martha died single. The one child of Isaac was Robert. The first wife of Robert Sr., was a Hodge, the second was Mary Chester Gammon. His son John also married a Miss Hodge, a sister to Robert's first wife and afterward a Miss Pritchett, leaving children by both unions. Jesse married a Miss Shell of Sullivan county and had issue. Mary married James Scott, also of Sullivan and a captain in the war of 1812. The home of John, the veteran of King's Mountain, was on the site of the Presbyterian Fork Church in Sullivan county. His son Robert (1795-1861) had a handsome residence on the Stage Road, a mile north of Jonesboro, and a plantation and flour mill on Boone's Creek. His wife died 1887, aged seventy-seven. John, the historian, married Sadie Thomas Vaughn of Nashville, 1887, was many years chancellor of the court of the Seventh Division, and lived in the colonial home of the Vaughns. His book, "The Dropped Stitches of Tennessee" is now very rare but valuable for the light it throws on early Tennessee history.

Alston. William was born in Warren county, North Carolina, was a member of the Provincial Congress of

1776, and was appointed by that body lieutenant colonel of the Third Regiment. He was in the battles of Camden and Eutaw Springs, and after the abduction of Governor Burke fought the tories until the close of the Revolution. He died in Elbert county, Georgia, where live descendants of his daughter, Mary, who married James Clark. Her mother's first name was Charity.

Anderson. George was a captain in the South Carolina contingent, according to the Lineage Book, Volume XIX, D. A. R. Waddell's Annals of Augusta relates that George Anderson with his wife and their children, William, Margaret, John, and Francis, proved importation from Britain, March 24, 1741.

Jacob was living in Washington county, Virginia, in 1777, and joined Campbell's regiment. He received a pension in Berkely county, Virginia, 1835.

John* had land in Augusta county in 1738, where he proved importation for himself, his wife Jane, and his children John, Esther, Mary, and Margaret March 24, 1741. John Jr., was justice in Washington in 1777, and also a lieutenant, serving at King's Mountain under Colonel Campbell.

When Colonel William Byrd was at Long Island on Holston River in 1760, he was accompanied by William Anderson and Gilbert Christian, both of whom were at King's Mountain. Summers' History of Southwest Virginia tells of the two men wandering on the Holston, and Ramsay's Annals of Tennessee mentions their trip hither in 1769. Draper places Anderson in Campbell's regiment.

Arbuckle. Thomas was one of the soldiers sent to Fincastle county to protect it from the Indians, and was in other battles.

Matthew, supposed to be a brother to Thomas, was a captain of the Virginia militia, a justice of Botetourt in 1774, and fought at Point Pleasant. It is said that he was at King's Mountain.

Armstrong. The Lookout Magazine places Robert at King's Mountain. He received a pension. Ramsay's Annals says that in 1787 he grew a crop of corn on Holston a little above Swan Pond. He settled here the next year. Colonel Sevier also lived here at one time, and many of his King's Mountain soldiers located in the vicinity.

Matthew was given a pension by North Carolina in 1833.

William, according to the History of North Carolina by Davis, was in several other battles, including that of Guilford Courthouse.

Baker. John was under Colonel Cleveland, and when his commander was ambushed by the Riddle gang of tories, shortly after the battle, he was one of the men who went to rescue him. He received a pension (North Carolina Records, Volume 22). Ramsay's Annals says there was a John Baker in the Watauga settlement in 1770, and that he was one of the Long Hunters, going as far as Miro in Davidson county.

Balch. Amos was born in Baltimore, 1758, and died in Bedford county, Tennessee, 1835. He was a sergeant at Camden as well as King's Mountain, and Tennessee gave him a pension in 1832. In 1793 he was a justice in Jefferson county. His wife was Ann Patton. His son James who married Elizabeth Hazlett, has descendants in Middle Tennessee. The manuscripts of the Historical Society of Nashville contain a receipt by Amos Balch to John Gordon for rations and forage for the militia of Davidson county.

The service of John Balch is given in Volume 3, D. A. R. Lineage.

Ballew. Richard was a private in the Burke county troops under Colonel Cleveland, and was granted a pension in Harlin county, Kentucky, February 14, 1831, when seventy-one years old.

Banning. Benoni, mentioned by Draper, was in Captain William Edmondson's company of Campbell's regiment, and was wounded. Eckenrode mentions three other Bannings as soldiers of the Revolution from Virginia.

Barker. Charles, Edmund, Edward, Enoch, Joel, and Henry were all from Washington county, Virginia, and are mentioned both by Summers and Eckenrode. Edmund received a pension in Washington, 1835.

Bartlett. William was a lieutenant under Captain William Edmundson, and is listed by Eckenrode and Saffell. He was also in the battle at Musgrove's mill and received a pension in Washington county, Virginia.

Barnes. Alexander was a captain under Colonel William Campbell from 1777 to 1780, and was in many skirmishes before going to King's Mountain.

Benjamin* and Shadrach* were on the pension roll of Virginia from Culpeper.

Barnett. Alexander was under Colonel Campbell and received a pension.

Barry. Andrew (1744-1811) was a magistrate before 1775 and enlisted at the beginning of the Revolution. As a captain of South Carolina Rangers he was in many engagements, including those of Ramseur's mill, Musgrove's mill, and Cowpens. His wife was Margaret Katharine Moore, and their daughter Katie married Major Jesse Crook of the Revolutionary army. Andrew was buried at Walnut Grove on the Moore plantation. See Lineage Book 2, Habersham Chapter, D. A. R.

Barton. Benjamin was a private under Colonel Roebuck of South Carolina, and died in that state in 1818. His widow received a pension in Pickens district, 1845, when eighty-one years old.

John, an early settler in Wilkes county, North Carolina, was there a magistrate several years. He moved to South Carolina 1785, and died on the Tugalo in 1827 aged seventy years. His grave is on the eastern slope of Chauga Creek about two miles above the burial place of Colonel John Cleveland.

Bean (also spelled **Been.**) George, Jesse, John, and Robert were all Watauga riflemen under Colonel Sevier. Jesse was a captain. Draper calls them the "sharpshooters from Watauga." Jesse and Robert had a grant of 640 acres in Hawkins county, the grant being signed by Alexander Martin, governor of North Carolina. George settled at Been's Station in Grainger county, 1792. Next year he advertised in the Knoxville Gazette that he had opened a goldsmith's and jeweler's shop, and was also prepared to make and repair guns. George and Jesse were sons.

William is mentioned by Ramsay as captain of a company that routed the tories from Watauga in 1778. Circumstantial evidence indicates that he was at King's Mountain, since most of his men were there. Their names were John, George, and Edmund Been, John Condly, Joseph Duncan, Thomas Hardeman, Aquilla and Isaac Lane, Michael Massingale, James Roddy, William Stone, Robert and Samuel Tate. One of the tories they routed was the notorious Captain Grymes, who was hanged the day after the battle of King's Mountain.

Bearden. Jeremiah and John were under Colonel Sevier. Jeremiah located a landgrant at Bearden Station in Knox county, Tennessee. John received a pension in the same county in 1833.

Beattie. David, John, Francis, and William are listed by Summers and Draper. The first was a captain, the second, an ensign, was killed. David (1752-1814) married Mary Beattie, a cousin, and settled in Washington county, Virginia, before the Revolution. He had four sons and one daughter. His brother William died 1860 at the age of one hundred years. Three brothers came from Ireland and settled first in Frederick county, Virginia. Two of them, John and Henry, were in the Indian wars, the former moving to Rockbridge. He was the father of David.

Henry* was a captain in the Revolution but I do not find him listed as a King's Mountain soldier.

Beeler. Jacob and Joseph were under Colonel Shelby and received a pension in Sullivan county, 1832. Joseph moved to Grainger county. His son Jacob married Nancy, a daughter of Martin Cleveland, brother to Robert and Colonel Benjamin of Revolutionary fame. Joseph, son of Jacob went to Jefferson county and married Addie Hickle. Descendants are in Grainger and Jefferson.

Bell. Samuel, a pioneer settler of Tennessee, married Margaret, daughter of Samuel Edmondson, and was in Shelby's regiment. The sword which Edmondson had at King's Mountain is in the rooms of the Tennessee Historical Society.

Thomas, born 1760, was in the North Carolina militia and in many skirmishes before King's Mountain. He received a pension in Montgomery county, Tennessee, December, 1833.

William (1750-1845) was a private in the North Carolina troops, and moved to Gallatin, Tennessee. He married Sarah McGuire. His son, Robert, married Margaret McCready, and their descendants are in Texas. (Lineage Book, D. A. R.)

Berry. Bradley*, James, and Thomas* were brothers or near relatives of Washington county, Virginia, and all were in the Revolution, at least James being at King's Mountain. Thomas was wounded by Indians in 1776. Bradley was in the Charlotte regiment in 1778, and died in the service of the Fourth Virginia.

Robert* received a pension from North Carolina, 1833. See North Carolina Booklet, G. A. R. for further information.

Beverly. John was a captain under Colonel Cleveland. According to Draper a pilfering soldier was taken to Cleveland by William Lenoir, and ordered to have his thumbs fastened in the notch of a tree while fifteen lashes were applied. This was called "thumbing the notch." Beverly, ordered to carry out the sentence, gave the fifteen lashes, and then kept on striking the wincing culprit without mercy. Colonel Herndon drew his sword, not being able to endure this cruelty, and tapped Beverly. The latter drew his own sword, and the resulting tilt might have had a fatal result but for the interference of mutual friends.

Bickley. Summers relates that in 1776 Charles Bickley helped build a mill for Henry Hamblin, one of the first settlers in Washington county. During the next four years Bickley was in many battles with the tories and Indians, and afterwards in Lee county, where he located his military land grant. Descendants still live on the homestead. Others are G. B. and W. E. Bickley of the Bickley Clothing Company of Knoxville, Tennessee.

Bicknell. James, John, and Thomas were at King's Mountain. The last was a Wilkes county man under Cleveland. He was killed early in the battle.

Bishop. Levi, an ensign, is listed by Summers.

Black. Joseph served under Campbell. The city of Abingdon is on the site of Black Station. After the Revolution he located another Black Station in Blount county.

Blackburn. William, killed at King's Mountain, was a lieutenant under Campbell.

Arthur was also in the battle of Point Pleasant.

Ramsay says that in 1789, while John Blackburn was standing by a creek near Buchanan's Station in Davidson county, he was killed by Indians, scalped, and a spear left sticking in his body.

William and George* were directed by the court of Fincastle county, 1773, to clear a road from Samuel Briggs on Eighteen Mile Creek to James Bryan's on Eleven Mile Creek. In 1777 William was appointed a lieutenant for the militia of Washington county, Virginia. He married 1747, and his widow Elizabeth lived until 1825.

Joseph was still another Blackburn.

Blackmore. John and William, an ensign, were under Campbell, and were also in active service against the tories and Indians. William, who received a pension in Shelby county, Kentucky, was with Colonel Sevier in the Etowah campaign of 1793.

Blacock. Samuel, a major, is mentioned by Draper. Zarach* was a Virginia soldier but may not have been at King's Mountain.

Blassingham. John of Sugar Creek, South Carolina, was a whig who suffered persecution. He married a Westfield and had a son John, who was in the war of 1812 and married Elizabeth Easley. (Lineage Book, D. A. R., Volume 31.)

Blevin. Henry and Daniel were under Colonel Sevier. The first, when seventy-five years old, received a pension in Hawkins county, Tennessee, June 13, 1811(?) Daniel received his pension in Morgan county, Teniessee, 1834, when eighty-one years old.

Blair. James was under Colonel McDowell. On the way to King's Mountain, he was sent ahead to hasten the march of Colonel Cleveland with the men of Wilkes and Surry. He went thirty miles to Fort Defiance before he met Cleveland and his men advancing.

John, a strict Presbyterian, married Martha Laird in Ireland and eight children were born to them. John, their second son, moved from Pennsylvania to Washington county, Virginia, and entered the Continental army. Tradition holds that he was a captain at King's Mountain. He settled on the Big Limestone Branch of Nolachucky, married Susannah Kelsey, and had eight children. His own son John, was a Congressman before 1860. This John married Mary Chester in 1812 and they had eleven children. The descendants of the first John are among the prominent citizens of nearly every county in East Tennessee and beyond. Below is a letter by John the Congressman, who had much to do in procuring pensions for the veterans of the Revolution in Carter county.

Washington City, Dec. 10, 1832.

Dear Sir:

I have the pleasure to inform you that our pension

claims are now under a course of examination upon principles which I feel willing to acquiesce in. All the cases which had been decided upon adversely had been handed in by me, and will be examined on the grounds upon which Congress intended to place the applicants, and of their own statement if sustained by character and reputation, provided their accounts of the matter as to time and circumstances agreed with the history of the events to which they refer. My Carter County cases have been all allowed so far as yet they have been examined, and I mean to let no one finally be rejected that I think just. I have taken the test of all the claims from my district, and directed Mr. Edwards to give me each, investigated separately, and I will take such course therewith as I think it may need. Give A. W. Taylor this information, and tell him both his uncles' claims are allowed.

Yours respectfully,

John Blair

The Blairs of East Tennessee are all descendants of John, a soldier of King's Mountain who came from South Carolina and died in Washington county in 1819. His children were Hugh, John, James, William, Thomas, Samuel, Jane, Mary, Martha, and Rachel. They moved to Loudoun county in 1790 and established the Blair Ferry on the Tennessee River, operated ever since by some member of the Blair family. Hugh was a cripple and never married. James, the second son, married Jane Carmichael of another pioneer family. The Blairs have been a prominent factor in the advancement of Loudoun county.

Boran. Baile was a lieutenant in the militia of Washington county, September, 1780, and it is well known that all well members of this militia marched with Colonel Campbell.

Bowen. Reese, born in Maryland in 1742, was living on the Clinch in what is now Tazewell in 1760. He fought at Point Pleasant and went to the relief of the Kentucky stations in 1778. During the illness of his brother, Captain William, he succeeded, as lieutenant, to the command at King's Mountain, and was shot dead by a tory boy from behind a baggage wagon. He was noted for his strength and activity. He left a family, his son Colonel Henry living in Tazewell to old age. When Charles heard this his brother Reese was killed, he went wild in his anxiety to find him. Colonel Cleveland thought him a tory because of his distracted manner, and commanded the countersign, which Charles could not recall. Cleveland took aim, but his gun missing fire, Bowen drew his tomahawk to cleave the colonel's head. In the nick of time, one Buchanan, who knew both men, gave Bowen's arm a vigorous push and told each who the other was. The story relates that the colonel caught the young soldier in his arms, rejoicing that he had not sacrificed his life. Charles received a pension in Blount county, Tennessee in 1832. John, a son of Reese, was also in the battle, as were Arthur, Robert, and Henry, brothers to Reese. All three were officers, the first being a captain.

Bowyer. Thomas of the Eighth Virginia is supposed to have been killed (Waddell). In the same regiment were William, a colonel, and John. Draper states that John, a colonel commanding a rifle corps from Rockbridge, was wounded and captured, and that his troop was the part of Campbell's regiment present in the battle near Jamestown.

Boyce. John was from Newbury, South Carolina, and was under Colonel Williams. He was also at Blackstock, Cowpens, and Eutaw. Under his brother Alexander he was shot down in the attempt to storm Savannah in 1779. His property was destroyed, but he escaped death, a faithful slave cutting the cords with which he was bound when the tories were going to hang him. His wife was Elizabeth Miller, and his son, Hon. Kerr Boyce, married Amanda Johnston.

Bradley. William, who was wounded was under Major Chronicle of Lincoln county. He was given a pension in that county in 1835. Some of his descendants are in Alabama.

Richard, also from Lincoln, received a pension and died in 1827. A tradition in the family states that he was at King's Mountain.

Brandon. Matthew (1752-1819) was a son of Richard and his wife Margaret Locke, and was born in Roane county, North Carolina. He served under Colonel Joseph Graham in 1780, and is supposed to have been at King's Mountain, Musgrove's Mill, and Ramseur's mill. He married Jean Armstrong and had two daughters, Elizabeth and Elvira. The former married General Paul

Barringer of Cabarrus, and her four sons were prominent in North Carolina history. Elvira married James Davidson Hall, pastor of Thyatira church, but had no family. Colonel John was a brother to Matthew, but the record does not say he was at King's Mountain.

Thomas was born in Pennsylvania in 1741, married Elizabeth McCool before the Revolution, and joined a Scotch-Irish colony in Union county, South Carolina. He entered the war in 1775 as a captain in the Spartanburg regiment, but became colonel of the Second before the fall of Charleston. He was at Musgrove mill, King's Mountain, and Cowpens, killing in the last named battle three British dragoons. After the war he was a magistrate, county ordinary, General of militia, and frequently a member of the legislature. He was a good soldier, but, like Cleveland, a bitter enemy of the tories, who received little mercy from him. He died at his home, Fair Forest, February 5, 1802.

Brashear. Samuel commanded a company from Sullivan county, Tennessee.

Brazleton. William located his military land grant in what is now Jefferson county, Tennessee. His son, William, who inherited this homestead, married first Martha Gillespie, by whom he had a son, John Fain Brazleton, and second Mary P. Reese of Mossy Creek.

Breckenridge. Summers names Captain Alexander and his sons George and John as in the battle. Captain Robert fought against the Indians in 1757, and in 1773 was a justice of Fincastle. Alexander lived on Wolf Creek Hill in Fincastle in 1773. Waddell partially works out the family lineage.

Brooks. The service and lineage of George, John, and Moses are in Lineage Book, D. A. R., Volume 9. The family settled at Boyd's Bridge, four miles above Knoxville, and the three soldiers are buried in the Brooks burying ground on the high hill above the river, but the headstones were carried away for doorsteps. George was also at Point Pleasant.

Brown. Draper mentions Gabriel as captain under Colonel Williams.

James was in the North Carolina militia. He received a pension and was on his way to Chattanooga to locate his military land grant when he and others of his party were massacred by Indians.

Jacob was a captain under Colonel Sevier, having settled on Watauga and Nollichucky in 1772. He was a merchant bringing his goods on a packhorse. He leased a large tract from the Cherokees, was prominent in the early history of Frankland and Tennessee, and was always a staunch friend to Sevier.

John, a captain under Cleveland, was born in Derry, Ireland, in 1738, went to Pennsylvania about 1762, taught school, and married Jane McDowell. In 1770 he was living on the Yadkin in Wilkes county, and he was three times in Congress. He died 1812 leaving many descendants, Colonel H. A. Brown of Maury county, Tennessee being a grandson.

John, born in South Carolina 1760, died in Mississippi 1847, was with his father Andrew under Colonel Roebuck. He received a pension in 1832.

John of Sevier's regiment was killed early in the battle.

Joseph, also under Sevier, died in South Carolina in 1800 aged forty. Joseph, Jr., married Mary Potter, and his own son Joseph married Jemima Broyles and has descendants in Georgia.

Michael is listed by Summers.

Browning. Enos of Washington county, Virginia, was under Campbell and he obtained a grant of land.

Bruster. B—— is mentioned by Draper in his manuscripts.

Buchanan. The Buchanans were early settlers in Southwest Virginia and were active in the Revolution. John (a lieutenant) and Samuel were at King's Mountain. In 1779-1780 a John* and an Alexander* living at Eaton Station were from South Carolina according to Ramsay. Eaton was on the turnpike leading from Nashville to Lebanon. Samuel was killed here in 1783 by the Cherokees. When fired upon he ran from the field where he was plowing and jumped from a bluff, but was scalped. An Eaton Station in East Tennessee is called Heaton by Ramsay and Haywood, but according to Gilbert Christian's letter Eaton is the correct name. In 1776 Captains William Buchanan and William Cocke fought the Indians at Long Island, called also the Heaton Station affair. Robert was in Fincastle in 1775.

Bullen. William of Campbell's regiment was wounded. There is a tradition that Isaac and Luke, listed by

Eckenrode, were in the battle. They received bounty warrants, but I found no service record.

Burney. William is listed by Summers. Simon was a Virginia soldier in the Revolution.

Burns. William, born in Pittsylvania and died in Clay (?), was under Captain Martin. He was in the battle of Long Island on Holston, 1776, and in other border engagements, and was given a pension for a service of fifteen months.

Caldwell. Samuel was born in Orange county, North Carolina, February 10, 1750, but was living in Lincoln in 1772. He served under Captain Green against the Cherokees in 1776, under Captain Chronicle for nine months in 1779, joined Lincoln's army in 1780, and was with Captain Isaac White at King's Mountain. He served with Captain Montgomery at the Cowpens, was at Guilford Courthouse, and continued in active service till the end of the war, afterward settling at Tuckaseegee Ford, where he reared a large family. He received a pension from North Carolina. He was buried in Goshen Creek graveyard in Gaston county.

Thomas, a lieutenant from Washington county, Virginia, was under Colonel Campbell.

William was a brother to Samuel. It was he who drew out the sword a British officer had driven into Robert Henry's hip and arm, the sufferer saying the taking out was more painful than the thrusting in. William brought home the horse, sword, and spurs of Major Chronicle. The sword and spurs were given to James McKee, his half-brother, and are still in the possession of a son of the latter who emigrated to Tennessee.

Callahan. John was an early settler on the Nollichucky, and was a captain under Sevier, to whom he was a sincere friend. He was conspicuous in the early history of Frankland and Tenessee. His brother John was also at King's Mountain.

Callaway. Elijah is frequently quoted by Draper.

Joseph was a legislator from Ashe in 1804 and 1806. He was under Cleveland at King's Mountain.

Richard*, brother to Joseph, was wounded in the ambuscade at the Old Fields.

William, another brother, went with him to the rescue of Colonel Cleveland when captured by the tory Riddle.

Camp. Thomas and five sons were at King's Mountain, but I could not find the names of the sons.

Thomas and Joshua are in Lineage Book, D. A. R., Volume 50. Thomas, the elder, (1717-1798) was twice married, one wife being Margaret Carney. He was buried at Island Ford, North Carolina. His eleven sons were Edmund (1739), Joseph (1741), John (1743) Thomas (1747), Nathaniel (1748), Starling (1749), Hosea (1751), William (1753), Alfred (1755), Benjamin (1757), Joel (1761). In these eleven belong the five sons.

Stephen (1770-1826) held the horses of the whig officers at King's Mountain and Cowpens, an injury at the latter place crippling him for life.

Campbell. The names under this head are Colonel Arthur, David, Hugh, James, Jeremiah, Patrick, Robert, General William and William, Jr. For service and lineage see Draper, Summers, Waddell, Ramsay, and the Genealogy by Mrs. Pilcher.

David married the fifth daughter of Captain Hugh Montgomery, and established Campbell Station, Tennessee in 1787. The Indians killed two boys named Wells at Hind's Station, and then attacked Campbell Station, where Colonel Campbell and another man were plowing. The Indians were not perceived until they fired. Hearing the reports, Mrs. Campbell barricaded the house door, took the rifles from the rack, and waited at the portholes. She handed out the rifles to the men escaping from the field, and though the Indians were pursued they got away. David received a pension from McNairy county.

James and Jeremiah were pensioned in Carter county and Robert in Hawkins.

Candler. William (1736-1787) was born in Ireland entered the revolution as a captain, and at King's Mountain commanded 30 Georgians under Colonel Williams. He was in other battles, became a colonel and was prominent in the political and social life of Georgia. In 1761 he married Elizabeth Anthony. His son, Henry, was with him at King's Mountain and in other battles.

Cantrell. It is claimed that Stephen was one of the 30 Georgians under William Candler. He was a captain under Sevier in the Etowah campaign, being then a resident of Summers county, Tennessee, which he represented in the legislature of 1796. The Cantrell genealogy says Stephen purchased five hundred acres on the Enoree in Spartansburg county. Many of the descendants of his five sons live in Tennessee.

Carmack. Cornelius and John were in the Fincastle troops under Christian. Both received pensions when over seventy years of age.

Carpenter. John, listed by Summers, was under Captain William Edmondson. In the attack upon Carpenter's fort on Jackson's River, when William Carpenter and others were killed, John was captured by the Indians.

Carr. Patrick came from Ireland before the Revolution, was a captain under Colonel Clark in the attack on Augusta in September, 1780, and was under Sumter at Blackstock. The statement that he killed one hundred tories must be an exaggeration, if to be understood as a personal matter. His murder in 1802, in Jefferson county, Georgia, is said to have been by a son of a tory he had killed. At King's Mountain he was under Major Candler.

Carroll. William was a Lincoln county man under Chronicle. He was pensioned by North Carolina, 1833.

Carson. The descendants of Andrew of Iredell think he was at King's Mountain, but this is not mentioned in the pension statement in Chapter XI.

David Carson was under Colonel Campbell and was pensioned in 1835.

John Carson was a captain at King's Mountain from Burke county. By request he was an active spy to outwit Ferguson's men while they were foraging for cattle. Draper gives an interesting account of this.

The service of William Carson is in Historical Collections, Volume 3, Habersham Chapter, D. A. R.

Carter. The Carters were early settlers and of prominence in the county of their name in Tennessee. It is claimed that Captains John and Landon were at King's Mountain under Sevier. John settled on Boone Creek, 1769, and was in the first Watauga convention. The pension statement by the widow of Landon is given in Chapter XI.

Carswell. Alexander (1727-1803) was a native of Ireland who married Isabella Brown. Both he and his son John were at King's Mountain. The latter, who married Sarah Wright, received a bounty warrant for land and located in Burke county, Georgia. His son Alexander married Mary Palmer.

Andrew is listed by Summers.

Casewell. For service of Zadrach see Lineage Book, D. A. R., Volume 12.

Casey. The brothers Benjamin, Levi, and Randolph were in the Second South Carolina under Colonel Elijah Clark. Randolph, a sergeant, was born in Virginia, was pensioned in Smith county, 1831, married Mary Jane Pennington, and his son Zadoc married Rachel King.

William fought at Point Pleasant under Captain Shelby. Two years later, he with his sister Nancy, Arthur Blackburn, and Arthur Harold were on their way to Rev. Charles Cummings to bring some books and other articles to the fort in the vicinity. They were attacked by Indians, Blackburn was shot and scalped, but his body was recovered. As Casey was running for his life, he saw the Indians in hot pursuit of his sister. He called to Harold to help him, and the latter complied although there were from four to six of the foe. By keeping between them and Nancy, the Indians were beaten off, the men firing alternately.

Castillo. John (1760-1830) served under Captain Benjamin Logan and Lieutenant John Logan, and was buried one-half mile west of Wentzville, Missouri. (D. A. R., 18th Report.)

Chambers. Daniel is mentioned in the Draper manuscripts.

Childers. The brothers John and Mitchell from Wilkes county were at King's Mountain under Cleveland. The former was badly wounded, and was pensioned in 1833 at Knoxville, Tennessee. Mitchell was pensioned at the same place in 1833, when eighty-three years old. The gun and powderhorn he used in the battle are owned by descendants.

Childress. Thomas* of Virginia was pensioned in Lincoln county, Tennessee, in 1833 when eighty-four years old.

William* of the North Carolina militia was also

pensioned in Tennessee. It is not known to revisor whether either man was at King's Mountain.

Chisholm. John, a settler on the Nollichucky, was under Sevier and was a lifelong friend of that colonel, serving in several campaigns. He was prominent in the State of Frankland, and was mixed up in the impeachment of Governor Blount. He was one of the early justices of Washington, and kept the first tavern in Knoxville. He died in London, England.

Chittim. John, a soldier under Captain Samuel Martin, was badly wounded but lived to an old age. He was pensioned in Lincoln county, North Carolina, 1815.

Christian. Gilbert, a son of Robert and nephew of Colonel William, was a major under Colonel Campbell. He was active in the border wars, was a lifelong friend of Colonel Sevier, and died in Knoxville in 1793.

George, son of Gilbert, was with his father in the Indian wars. In a letter to Draper he speaks of the battle of Long Island.

"Father commanded a company at Long Island. Under him was George Rutledge and Robert King, both with him at King's Mountain. They rendezvoused at Patterson Mill. . . . There was no Patten Mill at this time (1779-80) as Haywood has it. There were only two mills in that section of the country. Patterson's Mill was situated eight miles below Long Island near the Holston River, near or rather on a small creek, and Rice Mill was three miles still lower down on a creek that went into the Holston."

The letter in Chapter V, by George Christian to Dr. Draper, will illuminate Gilbert Christian's services.

Clark. Elijah was the colonel who worried Ferguson on his way to take a stand on King's Mountain. He was not himself in the battle, but many of his men were.

George was from Washington county, Virginia and was under Campbell.

James* and Michael* were pensioned in Lincoln county, North Carolina, but their applications do not state whether they were in the battle.

John, a captain from Georgia, received a sword cut in the neck in the skirmish at the Wofford Ironworks, but recovered in time to go to King's Mountain. He was pensioned in Washington county, Tennessee.

William, a soldier under Marion, was with Sevier

at King's Mountain. His record is in Lineage Book 2, D. A. R.

Cleveland. Benjamin was born in Prince William county, Virginia in 1738. While still very young he married Mary Graves of a wealthy and influential family. With others he made a trip to Kentucky to see the country and to hunt. The mountain tories raising the British flag in 1776, Cleveland vanquished them with his company of volunteers. He served throughout the Revolution and is considered one of the ablest colonels, wherever he was placed. At King's Mountain he commanded the men from Surry and Wilkes. Draper, Wheeler, and others give much space to his able services.

Larkin was a brother to Benjamin, and while on his way to King's Mountain encountered a party of tories at Loveday Shoals and was wounded.

Robert, another brother, was a captain of infantry at King's Mountain. He died in Wilkes county in 1812.

John, a son of Colonel Cleveland, was born in Virginia in 1760. He entered the service as a private, but was a lieutenant under Shelby in the attack on Augusta in 1780. He led a company at King's Mountain, and was in the fight at the Raft Swamp in 1781. He died on the Tugalo in 1810. His son Benjamin was a prominent citizen of Habersham county, Georgia.

Ezekiel was in the engagements at Kettle Creek, Wofford's Iron Works, Musgrove's mill, Fishdam Ford,, Lone Cane Creek, and King's Mountain. For his service at Augusta in 1780 he had a grant of land from Georgia. His wife was Elizabeth Harman. Their daughter Nancy married William Henry Hardin, son of a soldier of the Revolution. Descendants are in Georgia.

Clon. William is listed by Draper as in Shelby's command.

Cloud. Joseph was a captain under Cleveland. Carruther speaks of him in his "Sketches of North Carolina."

Clowney. Samuel left Ireland with one companion and settled on the Catawba. He was in many battles of the Revolution, and is thought to have been under Colonel Brandon at King's Mountain. After the war he married and settled in Union district, South Carolina, where he died September 27, 1824, aged eighty-one. Both Draper and the Habersham Collections give much

space to his heroic deeds. After joining Colonel Thomas
at Cedar Springs he obtained a leave of absence to visit
friends and procure a change of clothing. He then set
off for the Irish settlement on Fair Forest, intending to
make a quick return to camp. On reaching Kelso Creek,
about five miles from Cedar Springs, he cut through the
woods with a negro boy named Paul. Five armed tories
making their way to a tory camp in the neighborhood,
came right upon Clowney and Paul, being totally un-
aware of their presence, and were peremptorily ordered
to surrender. "Cock your guns, boys, and fire at the
word," yelled Clowney to imaginary companions. Advancing up the bank of the creek as the tories were passing through it, he demanded: "Who are you?" "Friends
of the king," was the reply. Not having supposed any
enemy was near, the tories hesitated to obey the command to surrender. "Lay down your arms, or every beggar of you will be instantly shot to pieces," returned
Clowney, poising his rifle in readiness for use. Thinking
the whig had a large force in concealment, the tories
surrendered without another word. Paul took charge
of the guns, Clowney giving directions to imaginary soldiers in the rear. He marched his prisoners across the
creek and reached the rest of his party at Mrs. Foster's
washing camp, where they were conducted to the quarters of Colonel Thomas. The prisoners were greatly
chagrined to find their only captors were a jolly Irishman and a negro, and the latter unarmed. "Why Pad-
dy," asked the colonel, "how did you take all these
men?" "I surrounded them," was the response. Draper
says Clowney was a real hero. He was very sarcastic
and full of invective, yet always kind-hearted and generous, and liked by all. His wit and his Irish brogue
made him a fascinating companion. His son, William K.,
a graduate of South Carolina College and lawyer, was
many years in Congress.

Cobb. Arthur, Jerry, William, Sr., and William, Jr.,
were active or assisting troops in Shelby's command. On
the way to King's Mountain the expedition halted at the
plantation of William Sr., a justice of Washington in
1778. Ramsay says the Cobbs and the Beens were the
first to make permanent homes on the Watauga. It
was in Cobb's home that Governor Blount resided in
1790 and held his first court for the Territory South of
the Ohio. Cobb was wealthy, patriotic, and hospitable.
His sons were Pharoah, William, and Jerry. Pharoah

was under Shelby at Musgrove's mill and King's Mountain. Since his pension application states that he was in service from 1776 to 1780, he must have been in still other battles. In 1793 he built a handsome brick house in Poor Valley, Hawkins county. The place, still used as a residence in 1906, is called Cobb's Ford.

Cocke. Charles and James are listed by Summers. James was a Captain in the Committee of Safety, presumably for Washington county.

William was a son of Abraham of Amelia county, Virginia, was born 1747, and died in Columbia, Mississippi, 1828. He was a captain, and was under Shelby at King's Mountain, and when an old man went into the war of 1812. He was instrumental in forming the State of Franklin, was in the legislatures of Virginia, North Carolina, Tennessee, and Mississippi, and was a United States senator from Tennessee. He married Sarah McLinn, and his son John Ellis Cocke married Sarah Stratton.

Cockrell (or Cockrill). In 1789 when John Donaldson made an adventurous trip from the Island in the French Broad to the Cumberland, a companion was John* Cockrell. Eckenrode places a John Cockrell in the Sixth Virginia. See also Lineage Book 39, D. A. R.

Cole. Joseph, Thomas, and William are listed by Summers. Eckenrode has about thirty Coles in his list of Virginia soldiers of the Revolution. Hugh died in the Continental service. The magistrates of Sullivan county, Tennessee, met at the house of Joseph in 1787. Several of the Coles mentioned by Summers were at Point Pleasant.

Colley. Daniel and Thomas were from Mecklenburg county, Virginia. *Asa, *Charles, *Isaac and *William were in the Pittsylvania militia, received pensions, and bounty warrants, but may not have been at King's Mountain.

Collins. James and Samuel were from Lincoln county. A Captain James is buried in Greenfield, Ohio. Samuel was pensioned in 1833.

Colville. Andrew was born in Frederick county, Virginia, 1739, and died in Wythe in 1797. He led a company under Campbell, and was one of the first leaders to attack Ferguson's line at a weak point. It was in this charge that Lieutenant Robert Edmondson and others lost their lives. Captain Colville married Mary Craig, and his son, Joseph, married Kathrine Link.

Samuel died November 20, 1780, of wounds received at King's Mountain.

Condlay. John was in Captain Joel Callahan's company of Sevier's regiment. At another time he was a private under Captain William Been.

Cook. William was in the Surry troops under Cleveland.

Charles, Edward, and Robert were pensioned in North Carolina in 1833, and some of their descendants claim they were at King's Mountain.

The record of Robert is found in Lineage Book 9, D. A. R. and that of Elisha in the papers of the Bonny Kate Chapter, D. A. R., Knoxville, Tennessee.

Cope. John was at King's Mountain. As a substitute for Mathias Harman he was in the Continental service also.

Corry. James, an ensign, served under Captain Edmondson and was killed at almost the same moment as Lieutenant Edmondson.

Costner. Thomas, who received a pension in Lincoln county, 1833, is supposed to have served under Major Chronicle.

Coulter. Martin of Surry county was under Cleveland. He was pensioned in Lincoln county 1833.

Coultrie. Robert, serving under Colonel Williams, was killed. See Lineage Book 16, D. A. R.

Cowan. Andrew and William are listed by Summers and Eckenrode. They were captains in the militia of Washington county, 1777-80, and were under Campbell at King's Mountain. Andrew settled at Knoxville.

David* and James* were on the Holston in 1773.

Samuel and Nathaniel were among the first settlers at Knoxville, Tennessee, coming with James White to settle on his military land grant.

Thomas (1747-1817) fought also at Ramseur's mill and Cowpens. He was born in Rowan county, North Carolina and married Mary Blakely.

Cox. William, who was wounded, was under Shelby.

He was living on Watauga in 1775. In 1793 he was a justice in the first court of Jefferson at the house of Jeremiah Matthews. All the justices were King's Mountain men.

Cozby (or Cosby). James was the regimental surgeon under Sevier. He was bold in taking chances and skilfully treated the horrible wounds of the period. He was a neighbor and friend to Sevier, and headed the rescuing party when North Carolina arrested the colonel for his part in forming the state of Franklin. His son John moved to Rhea county, and his daughter, Mary was the wife of Arthur Trayner, a prominent attorney of Cleveland, Tennessee.

Crabtree. Captain James* and Lieutenant *William lived on the North Branch of Holston. William was one of the Long Hunters with Colonel Knox, who went as far as the Cumberland Mountains in 1770.

Craig. David (1731-1785) was given a grant of Tennessee land for leading a company of Virginia militia at King's Mountain. He took part in forming the state of Franklin. Craig Station was between Ish and Henry stations on the Little Tennessee in Blount county. In 1792 all three were attacked by Indians. When Blount was taken from Knox in 1795, David Craig was one of the first magistrates. He married Eleanor Johnson, and many of their descendants are in Blount and Knox.

James was under Captain Craig. In 1783 he was sheriff of Washington county, Virginia.

John was at King's Mountain as a private, but in 1787-88 was a captain, fighting the Cherokees under Sevier.

Robert was a captain in Christian's Cherokee campaign in the fall of 1776, and was in many border fights both before and after. He was an officer at King's Mountain. Eckenrode lists him as a lieutenant colonel.

Crawford. Charles and John were in the battle. The record of Charles is in Lineage Book 3, D. A. R., and that of John in Volume 2, Historical Collections of Habersham Chapter, D. A. R. A John owned land in Southwest Virginia in 1769, was a constable in 1773, and a lieutenant in the First Virginia in 1788. Eckenrode has six John Crawfords among his Virginia soldiers.

There is a tradition that a second John, from Botetourt county, Virginia, was at King's Mountain. Writing
to Dr. Draper in 1825, George Christian has this to say
of him:

"John Crawford at this time was a major, an active
officer, brave enough, though sometimes indiscreet. (He)
was one of the first settlers of Knox county, stood all
the brunt of the Indian wars in those days. About 1792
the upper towns (were) professing to be at peace, whilst
the lower towns kept up constant war on our border settlement. There was sent for the use of the Indians to
Knoxville a quantity of goods, whilst the frontiers were
kept in continual alarm by the frequent murders and
other aggressions by the Indians, so much so, that a
strong party headed by Major Crawford proceeded to
Knoxville, dragged out the goods designed for the Indians, piled them up on the streets, set fire to them all.
All this was done under the eye of the regular troops
commanded by Captain Ricard. For a while this made
a good deal of notice and noise, but the government suffered it to pass, and among the people Crawford got
great applause, for they elected him to the legislature
several times."

Crock. William, an ensign, was in the troops from
Washington county, Virginia.

Crockett. Joseph was a captain of the militia of
Fincastle county.

Walter was a major of Fincastle.

William was in the Fincastle militia, 1770-77.

Walter was at King's Mountain, and there is no
doubt that the above mentioned went along also. He
and Samuel were in Fincastle as early as 1773, and were
probably the children or near relatives of Joseph and
Esther, who owned 450 acres on the South Fork of Indian River.

John, the father of the celebrated Davy Crockett,
was with the militia from Lincoln county. According
to the son, the father was born in Ireland or on the
sea. His mother, Rebecca Hawkins, was born in Maryland, and was related to the first wife of Colonel Sevier.
After the Revolution John Crockett moved from Lincoln county to Limestone Creek, about twelve miles south
of Jonesboro. Here Davy was born August 17, 1786, the
fifth of nine children. His brother Joseph, who was
deaf and dumb, was captured by the Indians and held

seventeen years, but was then located and redeemed by the father and his eldest brother, William. The grandparents of Davy were killed while living in Rogersville. Davy gives this instance of his life on Limestone:

"My four elder brothers, and a well grown boy of fifteen years by the name of Campbell and myself were playing on the banks of the Nolachucky river when all the rest of them got into my father's canoe and put out to amuse themselves on the water, leaving me on the Shores alone.

"Just a little distance below them there was a fall in the river, which went slap-straight down. My brothers though little fellows were used to paddling the canoe, and could have carried it safely any where about there; but this fellow Campbell would not let them have the paddle, but fool like undertook to manage it himself. I reckon he had never seen a water craft before; and it went any way but the way he wanted it. There he paddled and paddled and paddled—all the while going wrong, until in a short time they were all going straight forward, stern formost right plump to the falls; and if they had only a fair shake they would have gone over straight as a whistle. I was mad because they left me on the shore, and would as soon seen them all go over, but their danger was seen by a man by the name of Kendall, who was working in the field on the bank, and knowing there was no time to lose, he started full tilt, like a canebrake afire, and as he ran he threw off his clothes, when he got in the water he had on nothing but his britches. It was then I screamed and screamed but Kendall reached the canoe when it was within twenty feet of the falls, and so great was the suck, and so swift the current, that Kendall had a hard time to stop them at last, but he hung on to the canoe until he got it out of danger. When they got out I found the boys more scared than I was, and I believed it a punishment for leaving me on the shore."

In 1794 John Crockett opened a tavern in Jefferson county on the present line of the Southern Railway. The marriage license of Davy is in the courthouse of Dandridge county.

Cross. Joseph and Zachrach (?) were under Cleveland. Joseph was pensioned in 1833.

Crow. James was in Campbell's regiment.

John* commanded a company from Fincastle at Point Pleasant.

Summers has a sketch of James* of Washington county, who is a descendant of one of the foregoing.

Crumbless. Thomas was born in Ireland. His grandson, Major H. Crumbless of Roane county, says he was under Sevier. His son James was in the war of 1812, and fought in the battle of New Orleans.

Crunk. William was in Campbell's regiment.

Culbertson. Josiah was one of the best sharpshooters in Shelby's regiment. At King's Mountain he and others were ordered to gain an elevated position hotly contended for by a tory captain. It did not take long for Culbertson and his men to drive them out and kill their leader. At Musgrove's mill his company played an important part.

Curry. James was an ensign under Campbell.

Cusick. John is listed as a soldier from Washington county.

Cutbirth. Adam and Daniel were under Cleveland, and went to his rescue when he was captured by Riddle.

Dameron. George was under Major Chronicle at King's Mountain, and took part in several other engagements. He was pensioned in Lincoln county. Descendants are in North Carolina and East Tennessee.

Darnell. David and Cornelius were under Campbell. The former was wounded.

Lawrence was a surveyor who went to Fincastle in 1774, and is supposed to have been in the battle of Point Pleasant.

Daugherty. George was a captain under Sevier and Shelby. In 1778 George Doherty (so spelled by Ramsay) was active in keeping the Cherokees from joining the British. He was a captain under Sevier at King's Mountain, and when the state of Franklin was in existence he became a colonel. In 1788 he commanded the militia of Knox, Grainger, and Jefferson in a defensive campaign on the Cumberland Mountains, not far from the present site of Kingston. He settled at Dandridge in Jefferson, and when that county was formed he was one of its first magistrates. When the state of Tennessee was formed in 1796 he represented his county in the constitutional convention. Colonel Daugherty was conspicuous in the border wars and in the formation of Franklin and Tennessee. He was a staunch friend of Colonel Sevier in his stormy but brilliant career. His unmarked grave is near the courthouse at Dandridge.

It is claimed that James Daugherty (or Doherty) was at King's Mountain. He was a captain in the later campaigns against the Indians. Ramsay says he drew a captain's salary in 1793 for service with the volunteer troops.

Davidson. Benjamin and William were under Colonel McDowell. Their home was at Davidson's Fort in the extreme west of Burke county.

William was state senator from Mecklenburg, 1815-16. He was still living at Charlotte in 1851.

Samuel is supposed to have been at King's Mountain. His record is in Arthur's History of Watauga County.

Davis. John, Nathaniel, Robert, and Samuel were all in the battle in Campbell's regiment. John was a captain. In 1774 the others owned much land in Fincastle.

In 1748 one James owned 300 acres on the head of Indian. This place—Davis' Fancy—is yet in the family.

William was under Major Joseph McDowell. He was pensioned at Jonesboro, 1833.

Joel* and Nathan* were pensioned by North Carolina. In 1783 Nathan emigrated to Greene county, Tennessee, where his son Jonathan married Sarah Crosby, whose father Uriah fought under Shelby, so it is claimed. This Davis family asserts that Nathan was brother to the grandfather of Jefferson Davis. Descendants are in Loudoun county.

Davison. Lieutenant William and Ensign Daniel were under Campbell. The wife of Daniel was Phoebe and died before 1758 (?).

Dawson. Elias was under Shelby, according to the Draper manuscripts.

Delaney. William was an orderly sergeant under Shelby. He was one of the first settlers near Bristol. The fort built on his land became the first schoolhouse in that valley. He acquired much real estate and slave property, became wealthy, and known as Major Delaney. His son,

John Rhodes Delaney, was sheriff of Sullivan, many years president of the county court of Sullivan, and a general in the Indian wars. He was born 1799, and married Margaret, daughter of Thomas McDowell of Ireland.

Dennison. Robert was under Campbell.

Desha. Robert was in the battle, and in 1792, when living in the Cumberland settlement, his sons, Benjamin and Robert were killed by Indians. See Lineage Book 8, D. A. R.

Detgaoorett (?). John was in the border battles with Shelby in the early months of 1780, and I infer that he went with him to King's Mountain. See Draper manuscripts.

Dickenson. Henry was in Captain Colville's company of Campbell's regiment. His record is given by Draper.

Dickey. Draper also gives the record of Andrew and David, who on the eve of the battle were ordered to go with Colonel Graham on a home call occasioned by serious illness. When they heard the firing they returned.

Dickson. Joseph commanded a company of Lincoln county men. His homestead is two miles northwest of Mount Holly. General Rutherford camped there the night before the attack on the tories at Ramseur's mill. He accompanied the general next day, passing over the then vacant land granted him five years later as proprietor in trust for the citizens of Lincoln. With the rank of major he was one of the officers to lead the South Fork boys up the rugged northeast end of King's Mountain, facing the bullets and bayonets of the enemy above. In 1781, when colonel, he was elected county clerk, holding this office ten years. He was chairman of the committee that selected the site of Lincolnton, and according to the usage of the time he granted the deeds to the original purchasers of lots. He was state senator from Lincoln, 1788-1795, and in 1789 was one of the forty original trustees of the University of North Carolina. He was then a general of militia, and in 1799-1801 a member of Congress. In 1803 he sold his 1200 acres and removed to Rutherford, where he died April 24, 1825, aged eighty. He was buried with military and masonic honors.

Joseph of Rowan county was born 1745 and died

1825 in Rutherford county, Tennessee, whither he had removed in 1806. His wife was Margaret McEwen. He was in service throughout the Revolution, and was a major at King's Mountain.

Dillard. Benjamin and James were in Williams' South Carolina regiment. Colonel James was born in Culpeper county, Virginia, 1755, and in 1772 was living in Laurens district, South Carolina. He was at the siege of Charleston. His service at Cowpens, Hammond's store and elsewhere is given by Draper.

Dixon (Dickson). Joseph was at King's Mountain, according to Lineage Book 9, D. A. R. of N. C. He was pensioned, as were also John and Joel of the North Carolina line.

Doak. On the beginning of the march of the Expedition, the Rev. Samuel Doak, the pioneer clergyman of Watauga, invoked the divine guidance and protection, giving the men some stirring remarks on "the sword of the Lord and Gideon."

Dobson. Dr. Joseph Dobson attended the wounded soldiers, and at one time after the battle had eighteen under his care. See Draper.

Doran. Alexander (ensign), James and Terence were under Campbell. Summers names Alexander and James.

Dorton. Moses and William, Jr., were in the battle, serving under Campbell. The former had a horse killed under him at Whitsell's mill.

Douglas. James and Jonathan were under Campbell. The latter was wounded. An Edward received a pension in Jefferson county, 1832.

Dryden. James, Nathaniel, and William were under Campbell. Nathaniel was killed. James (1739-1832) married Lydia Jester.

Duff. David is mentioned by Draper and Samuel by Summers. Captain William*, also of Washington county, was in the Revolution.

Duncan. Jesse was in Cleveland's regiment and Joseph in Sevier's in Been's company. John, also a Watauga rifleman, was no doubt in the battle, for he had just seen service fighting Indians and tories. See Draper and Ramsay.

Dysart. James was born in Ireland and was a Long Hunter in 1761. He settled on the Holston, marrying Nancy, daughter of David Beattie. As a captain under Campbell he was wounded at King's Mountain. Major Dysart saw active service in the Revolution and was a prominent factor in Washington county, Virginia. He died at Rockcastle, Kentucky, 1831, aged seventy-four.

Earnest (Ernest?). The Rev. Felix was in Samuel Williams' company of Sevier's regiment. He was from Greene county, Tennessee, where many of his descendants live.

Eddlemon. Peter was in the Lincoln County regiment and was pensioned in Lincoln in 1835.

Edmondson. Eight of this name were at King's Mountain. Three were killed and one wounded, all being officers under Campbell. These four were Captain William, Robert Sr., and Andrew, killed, and Lieutenant Robert Jr., wounded. The other four were Major William, and privates John, Samuel and William. Summers names two Williams and one Thomas, while Draper names three Williams and no Thomas. The surname was variously spelled in Revolutionary days. Their ancestors came from Ireland to Rockbridge county, Virginia, whence some of them moved on to the Holston.

Elder. Robert and William were with Campbell. Robert was pensioned in South Carolina.

Elliott. Captain James was under Campbell. He was an early settler on the Holston, and was killed by a concealed Indian at Tellico in 1780, while with Campbell in his Cherokee expedition.

Elmore. William was under Cleveland and was pensioned in North Carolina. Eckenrode mentions nine other Elmores.

Ely. William was under Campbell and was pensioned.

Enlow. Potter (1769-1833) was in the South Carolina regiment at Blackstock, King's Mountain, Cowpens, and Eutaw. He married Mary Chummer (1798-1865). Lineage Book 39, D. A. R.

Estill. Benjamin was one of the first justices of Fincastle. In 1779 he bought 1400 acres in Russell county. His wife was Kitty Moffett and many of his descendants are in the South.

Espey. Samuel was a captain under Chronicle. He was born in Pennsylvania, 1758, and in 1770 was living in Lincoln county. He was in active service from 1776 till the close of the war and was wounded at King's Mountain. See Draper.

Evans. Andrew, David, Evan, and Samuel were at King's Mountain. Evan was also at Guilford. The Evanses were early settlers on the Holston and in 1779 suffered from an Indian massacre.

Philip (1759-1849) was born in Rowan county and was in McDowell's regiment. A fall from his horse made it necessary to leave him behind, but he recovered sufficiently to assist in guarding the prisoners on the return from the battlefield. He was also at Cowpens. He died in Greenville county, South Carolina.

Ewart. James and Robert were in the North Carolina line. See Lineage Book 16, D. A. R.

Ewin. Hugh was under Campbell. See Draper.

Ewing. Alexander, listed by Eckenrode as a lieutenant, was a captain in a Virginia regiment and wounded at Guilford. He died in Tennessee. I have no positive proof that he was at King's Mountain. See Lineage Book 9, D. A. R.

Fagan. John of Shelby's regiment was wounded in an assault on a breastwork of wagons. This is mentioned by Ramsay.

Fapolson. Andrew was in Captain Evan Shelby's company at King's Mountain, and was in many other border engagements. See Ramsay and Draper manuscripts.

Farewell. James was with the Lincoln county men and was pensioned in that county. Booklet 9, D. A. R.

Faris. Thomas was in Campbell's regiment, according to Summers. Eckenrode mentions Isaac, two Johns, Larkin, Martin, and Richard as soldiers of the Revolution.

Farrow. Landon, Samuel, and Thomas were brothers and nephews of Colonel Philemon Waters. They moved from Virginia to the vicinity of Musgrove's mill in South Carolina.   In the same regiment was John Farrow. See Habersham Collection, D. A. R.

Fear.   Edmund was a captain under McDowell and was from Burke county.   Thomas of the North Carolina line was pensioned, but his name does not appear on the battle roll.

Findley.   John, a Long Hunter, was wounded at Long Island on Holston while in Edmondson's company. He was in the same command at King's Mountain.

George was a lieutenant in the Virginia regiment. See Summers and Ramsay.

Fisher.   Frederick, a private in Campbell's regiment, was wounded.   He is listed by Summers and Draper.

Flecnor.   Four brothers of German descent were early settlers on the Holston.   Charles and Joel were in the battle.   John* and Michael* settled in Poor Valley. Michael was in the Virginia militia.

Fletcher.   Thomas is mentioned by Summers.   In 1794 he was living in the Mero district, and with a young son was killed by Indians.

Floyd.   Andrew was under Graham and was pensioned.   His name is not in the Floyd genealogy in the Habersham Collection.

Fork.   William is listed by Summers.   One Peter is mentioned by Eckenrode.

Fowler.   William was killed in the battle.

James,* a noted scout under William Russell, and John* were early immigrants to the Holston.

Fox.   John of Burke county was with Cleveland. His son John settled on Beaver Creek in Knox county, Tennessee, 1819, and married Ann Galbraith.   Austin, another son, married Margaret Walker of Burke and also went to Beaver.   See Goodspeed.

Francis.   One of the 3000 graves of soldiers of the Revolution located by D. A. R. chapters is thus mentioned: "Major Henry Francis.   Died June 28, 18—— (?). Buried in Spring Hill Graveyard, Johnson county, Arkansas."

Thomas is listed by Summers.

Frazier. David and John are in Summers' list. The 18th Report, D. A. R. speaks of the grave of a John Frazier near Danville, Illinois. One John Frazier was pensioned in Fleming county, Kentucky, 1833, when sixty-nine years old.

Frigge. John and Robert were under Major Evan Shelby of Isaac Shelby's regiment. See Draper manuscript.

Frost. Micajah was under Cleveland. He was pensioned in Rockcastle county, Kentucky Aug. 6, 1833, when seventy-two years old. Many of his descendants are in Union and Grainger counties, Tennessee.

Fulkerson. James, a captain, and Richard are listed by Summers.

John* was pensioned in Grayson county, Kentucky, October 18, 1833.

Another John*, also of the Virginia militia, was pensioned in Washington county, Tennessee, in 1833, when seventy-nine years old.

Gaines. James* was living in Sullivan county, Tennessee, in 1796, and died there in 1830. Lineage Book 12, D. A. R. He was a nephew to Edmund Pendleton, the Virginia statesman.

James Sr.* was pensioned in North Carolina, 1833.

There is a tradition that Ambrose of the Virginia militia was in the battle. He was pensioned in Sullivan county, Tennessee, in 1833 when seventy-one years old.

Galbraith. Arthur of Virginia was buried in Hawkins county, and is supposed to have been with Bowen's Fincastle company under Colonel Campbell.

Robert*, also of the Virginia militia, located a land warrant in Greene county, Tennessee.

John* was a delegate from Greene to the Tennessee convention of 1796.

Gallaher. John had a horse killed under him. He moved from Washington county, Virginia, and located on land twenty miles from Knoxville. While away on military duty his house on the Holston was burned by the Indians. Many of his descendants are in Knox and adjoining counties.

Gamble. Robert was at King's Mountain and Guilford. He established Gamble's Station on the Little Tennessee near Maryville about seven miles from Craig's Station. In 1796 it suffered from Indian raids. Many descendants are in Blount county.

Choat and Josiah were early settlers on Watauga.

Gammon. Harris, a soldier under Sevier, was in the militia of Washington county, North Carolina. He was pensioned in Knox county, 1833, when seventy-six years old.

Richard represented Sullivan in the state of Franklin in 1784.

James and John were Virginia soldiers.

Gann. Thomas was a private in the North Carolina cavalry, and was pensioned in Hamilton county in 1833, when seventy-one years old.

Gass. John, of the militia of Washington county, North Carolina, was a sergeant under Sevier. He was pensioned in Greene county, Tennessee, 1833, when seventy-two years old. He and Joseph Callaway represented Greene county in the first Tennessee convention.

Gibson. John, George, and Thomas are listed by Summers.

John, one of Sevier's riflemen, assisted Jesse Green in hanging the notorious Dykes, a tory, in 1779. A John Gibson went with John Donelson to Davidson county in 1780. A John settled in the forks of Holston in 1786 with James White and James Cozby. Later, he and Jesse Green went to rescue Colonel Sevier from the courthouse of Morgan county.

Giles. William, a South Carolina soldier under Colonel Lacy, was wounded but recovered, and was in active service in Union district, South Carolina.

Gilleland. James was a lieutenant in Campbell's regiment, and was pensioned in Washington county in 1835.

John was under Sevier, was wounded, and was pensioned. In 1783 he was living at the mouth of Pigeon. He supported the state of Franklin and was a faithful friend to Colonel Sevier.

Gillespie. Thomas, Jr., was only fourteen when under Campbell at King's Mountain.

Thomas and George settled on Watauga in 1772. In 1786 Captain Thomas settled three miles below the mouth of the French Broad, other King's Mountain soldiers locating their land grants in the vicinity. He was active in border service. His fort at Watauga was raided in 1774, and his blockhouse on the Holston was many times threatened.

William, a captain, was with Sevier in much of his border warfare.

George must have been a brother to Captain Thomas, since he came with him to the Watauga, was a partner in his land deals, and was living in 1777 near Sevier at the mouth of Big Limestone.

All the above must have gone with Sevier to King's Mountain, but though I have no proof to this effect, there is ample proof of their participation in the border warfare.

The ruins of Thomas Gillespie's cabin on the north bank of the Holston could be seen a few years ago near the residence of James Huffacre. In 1787 a party of Indians crossed the river and suddenly appeared before the door. They knew the captain was twelve miles away on Dumplin Creek. The Indians entered and made a motion to scalp a sleeping baby. Mrs. Gillespie rushed to the door and called loudly for help. Thinking men were near the Indians fled to the canebrake. Mrs. Gillespie then caught up her baby, and fled along the path by which her husband would come, all the while thinking she was pursued. After going several miles she met the captain, who took the wife and child to Manifold Station, and then went home with some companions. He found the Indians firing the house, but they were driven away.

Gilliam. Devereux was in the border wars, and there is a tradition that he was at King's Mountain. He was an early settler in the fork at the mouth of the French Broad. His cabin was called Gilliam Station and stood between Lebanon Church and the stone house of the Ramsays. After the building of the stone house, the station was called Mecklenburg. Here the Rev. Samuel Garrick organized the first Presbyterian church in Knox.

Gilliham. Jacob was with Colonel Williams. After the war he moved from South Carolina to Maury county, Tennessee, where he was pensioned in 1833, when eighty-seven years of age.

Gilmer. Enoch and William were brothers from

Lincoln county. William was wounded. Enoch was recommended by Major Chronicle as a good spy to locate Ferguson's army. Others thought differently, because he was a stranger to the section which they supposed Ferguson was marching through. But the major insisted he was capable of finding his way through any country, that he was shrewd, a stranger to fear, could laugh and cry at the same time, and could so act the lunatic and fool that his best friends could not recognize him. He and some others were selected and they started off. Gilmer called at the house of a tory not far in the advance, and told him he wanted to join Ferguson, but could not find him on the road to Ninety-Six. The unsuspecting tory told all he knew about Ferguson's movements. Gilmer slipped away, his information causing the expedition to move toward Cherokee Ford, where it was halted and Gilmer sent forward to reconnoiter. In a little while the scout was heard singing "Barney Linn," a favorite ballad of the time. Since it was a token that all was clear, the river was crossed and Gilmer again sent forward. Rain was still falling and after proceeding several miles, Gilmer's horse was seen tied to the gate at a tory house. The rider was inside, eating a good meal, prepared by two women for whom they supposed to be one of the king's men. "You damned rascal," exclaimed Colonel Campbell, "we have got you." "A true king's man, by God," replied Gilmer. In order to test the scout, Campbell swore they would hang him at the gate and had a running noose thrown over his neck. Chronicle begged for Gilmer's life, and said if he were hanged here the scout would haunt the two women who were entreating that he be spared. Campbell then said the hanging would be postponed until they found a big tree in the nearest woods. When they were out of sight the rope was taken from Gilmer's neck. He then mounted his horse and rode on to the battle. Thus a grim time was not devoid of humor.

Gist. Benjamin was with Sevier. In 1778 he was a justice of Washington county, North Carolina, and in 1780 was a captain in its militia. His company was also in the fight at Boyd's Bridge, which took place soon after King's Mountain. Captains Russell and Gist were sent ahead by Sevier to head off an Indian uprising, and thus give time for the expedition to get home. Gist was a supporter of the state of Franklin.

Joseph and Joshua were in the border wars and were undoubtedly at King's Mountain.

The record of Mordecai is in Lineage Book 12, D. A. R.

Nathaniel was under Campbell, and was killed at nearly the same moment as Edmondson, his captain. He, also, had been in the border wars, and was a trader with the Indians. In 1761 he bought from the Cherokees Long Island in the Holston, and it was here that a treaty was made with them in 1777.

Richard and Thomas, who seem to have been brothers, were also in Edmondson's company. Thomas was in the battle at Boyd's Bridge.

Given. James was with Colonel Campbell at King's Mountain and also at Green Spring in 1781. He was born in 1764, and was living in 1844.

Godwin. Joseph, Robinson, and Samuel were from Lincoln county, and served under Cleveland. They were pensioned in Lincoln in 1833.

Goforth. Preston was in the Rutherford troops under Colonel Hampton and was killed. Three brothers were on the tory side, and they were likewise killed. One of them, whose name was John, is said to have been slain by Preston, who in turn was killed by John. Mrs. Arthur Patterson, who lived near, went there in the afternoon to assist in caring for the wounded. Bettie Goforth, a neighbor, hauled her dead husband home on a sled.

Goff. Andrew, an ensign, and William were in Campbell's regiment. Andrew was in Shelby's company at Point Pleasant.

Gordon. Charles was a native of Virginia who moved to Wilkes county, North Carolina, where he filled public positions, and became a major of militia. At King's Mountain he was in Cleveland's command. There were many hand to hand combats in the battle. Gordon grabbed a tory officer by the queue and while dragging him down the mountain he was shot in the left arm. The whig then drew his sword and dispatched his captive. His wife was a daughter of General Lenoir. He died in 1790 at the age of thirty-seven. His widow married Colonel William Davenport, founder of the Davenport Female School at Lenoir.

Chapman and George were also in the North Carolina troops. Their record is in Lineage Book 8, D. A. R.

Gourley (also Gorly and Gorely). Thomas was an early settler on the Watauga and served under Sevier. When the state of Franklin fell into trouble, Gourley sided with the Tipton faction, and was one of the guards to take Sevier to Morganton. When French, the other guard, wanted to kill the prisoner, Gourley prevented this and told Sevier about it.

Graham. James was in Campbell's Virginia troops. Colonel William was born in Virginia in 1742, and died in Shelby county, North Carolina, 1835. A short time before the opening of the battle of King's Mountain he was urgently asked to go home because of the serious illness of his wife. Some of the men detailed to accompany him heard the firing and hastily returned to the field, but arrived only in time to guard the prisoners. Graham was in the Provincial Congress of 1775, and was colonel of Tryon county. Among the battles in which he took part were Cedar Spring, Thicketty Fort, and the Snow, so called because of the unusually deep snow at the time. See Hunter's Sketches.

Gray. James was from Rutherford. While looking after the tory wounded the morning after the battle, he came upon a neighbor unable to walk because of a wound in the ankle. Knowing he was a tory by principle and not one of the thieving sort, Graham took out his handkerchief and dressed the wound. The tory was ever after a friend and a useful citizen of Rutherford to the end of his life.

William was a second lieutenant under Cleveland. After the war he moved to Wilson county, Tennessee, and was one of its first magistrates. He was there pensioned in 1833, when seventy-seven years old.

Green. Jesse appears early in the Watauga settlement, and was active in the border wars. Before going to King's Mountain, Jesse Green and John Gibson hanged Dykes and Bradley, two malicious tories. The court of Washington passed an act of oblivion for their relief. Both men went to Morganton to rescue Sevier. Green was pensioned in 1833.

Greer. Alexander was an early settler of Watauga, and signed the petition sent to the Provincial Congress at

Halifax, asking annexation. He was in Sevier's regiment, and in 1792 was a captain in the Territory South of the Ohio.

Andrew* also signed the petition above named, and was one of those affected by the Cherokee land purchase of 1775. He located on the present site of Elizabethton, near where the Naves live. When in a Cherokee town in 1775, he suspected harm, because of the queer conduct of another trader named Walker. He quietly slipped away with his furs, not taking the usual way back. Boyd and Doggett took the other path, were killed by Indians, and their bodies thrown into a creek. The stream, which is in Sevier county, has since been known as Boyd's Creek. When chief Abraham of Chilhowee attacked Watauga fort in 1776, Greer had a hand in his defeat, but the Indian captured Mrs. William Been. This affair was called the siege of Watauga, the Indians blockading the place twenty days. Greer was a magistrate in 1778, and on the formation of Carter county was one of the commissioners to select a site for the courthouse and erect the county buildings. He was one of Sevier's men at King's Mountain.

Andrew Jr., son of the foregoing, was also under Sevier, and he signed the petition to Halifax.

Joseph also signed the Halifax petition, and was one of Sevier's sharpshooters at King's Mountain. When Knoxville was laid out by James White in 1792, Greer was one of the first lot-buyers and descendants are still in Knox.

Gregory. John and William were of Lincoln county, and were there pensioned in 1833.

Grier. John and James were from Washington county, Virginia.

Griffing. Joseph was a South Carolina soldier. See Lineage Book 10, D. A. R.

Grimes. George and James were from Washington county, Virginia.

Gwaltney. Nathan was from Lincoln and was pensioned in 1833.

Hackett. John was one of the two hundred picked up by Colonel Arthur Campbell to go to King's Mountain. He located a land grant near Campbell Station.

Hafner (Hofner). Nicholas was a soldier under Colonel James Johnstone of Lincoln, and was pensioned in Lincoln 1833.

Hager. Simon was also under Johnstone, and was pensioned in Lincoln in 1833. The following letter would seem to indicate that there were two of this name.

Mr. Speaker and Gentlemen: The resolve of your House permitting Joseph Taylor, Esq. to resign his appointment as clerk of the Superior Court for the District of Hillsborough, we return concurred with, whereas it appears to the satisfaction of the General Assembly that William Graham, a colonel of the county Lincoln hath been guilty of receiving a bribe for procuring the discharge of a prisoner named Simon Hager, taken at Kings' Mountain, that the said Graham as an officer has been guilty of a misdemeanor, therefore,

Resolved, that the aforesaid William Graham be discharged from the said office, and that Joseph Dixon be appointed Colonel of the said county of Lincoln.

Haile. John was one of the early settlers at Watauga, a signer of the Halifax petition, and one of the three to represent the district in the Provincial Congress, the others being John Carter and John Sevier. Descendants are in Hawkins county.

Hall. David was under McDowell. He was present in other engagements. See Register of Bonny Kate Chapter, D. A. R., Knoxville, Tennessee.

John was with Colonel Williams, received a pension in South Carolina, moved to Knox county in 1783, and upheld the state of Franklin.

Jesse of the Montgomery militia was one of Arthur Campbell's troop, and was pensioned in Montgomery, 1833.

Hambright. Frederick was born in Germany in 1727, came to Pennsylvania in 1740, and by 1755 was in Virginia, where he married Sarah Hardin. Before the Revolution he moved to Long Creek in Tryon county with his brothers-in-law, John, Joseph, and Benjamin Hardin; also James Kuykendall, Nathaniel Henderson, Robert Leeper, and others. Just before the battle of King's Mountain he built a cabin on a large purchase on King Creek, intending to live there. He entered the Revolution early and became a lieutenant colonel in 1777. He was an active and courageous officer, and a terror to the tories, who well knew the vigor of his determination to rid his county of a malicious and plundering nuisance. By the first wife Hambright had John H., Elizabeth, Frederick, Sarah, Benjamin, James and four others. The first, John Hardin Hambright, was at King's Mountain. By the second wife, Mary Dover, there were ten more children. At King's Mountain Colonel William Graham had charge of the Lincoln county men, but having to go home because of his wife's illness, his place was taken by Hambright. No command suffered more severely. Major Chronicle fell at the first fire. Captain John Mattocks, Lieutenants Robb and Boyd, and several others also lost their lives. Hambright was badly wounded at the beginning, but kept cheering his men to victory. After the battle he refused aid until the most severely wounded were attended to. He was cared for at his King Creek home until he was well. He was a worthy elder of the Shiloh Presbyterian Church. On his tombstone are these words: "In memory of Colonel Hambright, departed this life, March, 1817, in his ninetieth year."

Hamer. James was in Campbell's regiment. See Historical Collections, Joseph Habersham Chapter, D. A. R.

One John* Hamer voted against the state of Franklin.

Hamilton. Alexander* was pensioned in Augusta county, Virginia, 1833.

John was one of the 200 raised by Arthur Campbell. When Summers county was formed in 1787, the first court met in his house. David Shelby was clerk and John Hardin sheriff. He and Alexander were brothers or otherwise near of kin. Both are of the Archibald Hamilton family of Augusta.

Robert was a soldier under William Campbell and received a bounty warrant.

Hammond. Charles was born in Richmond county, Virginia, 1716, and died in Edgeville district, South Carolina, 1794. He was present at King's Mountain under Captain Candler. His wife Elizabeth Steele died in 1798. Descendants are in Georgia. His son Abner (1750-1810) was a lieutenant in South Carolina, and descendants hold that he too was in the battle. Lineage Book 31, D. A. R.

Samuel was born in Richmond county, Virginia 1737

and died in South Carolina in 1842. Colonel Hammond
was in the battles of Point Pleasant, Great Bridge, Cedar
Spring, Musgrove's mill, Stono, King's Mountain, Blackstock, Augusta, Ninety-Six, and Eutaw, being wounded
in the last engagement.

Hampton. Andrew was born in England, but in
1751 was living in Rutherford county, North Carolina.
He was a captain in 1776 and colonel in 1779. He fought
the tories who were overrunning his part of the state and
was present at King's Mountain and Blackstocks. He
died in 1805. There are many descendants.

Edward was a brother and a captain. He also saw
service prior to King's Mountain.

Jonathan was with the Rutherford troops.

Handly. Captain Samuel and his brother Robert
were in the Point Pleasant expedition of 1774. Samuel
was at King's Mountain under Sevier and is mentioned by
Draper. As a captain he was with Sevier at Boyd's Creek
mentioned by Ramsay as the best fought battle in the
Indian wars of Tennessee. It took place in December,
1780. In the state of Franklin he sided with Tipton, but
when Pemberton reenforced Tipton with thirty men from
Sullivan and captured John Cowan, Handly made Tipton
release Cowan. In 1793 his company of 42 men was attacked near Craborchard while defending the stations on
the Cumberland. The Indians, 56 strong, mostly Cherokees, and led by Middle Striker, effected a surprise and
created a panic. A man named Lieper was unhorsed near
the Indian line. Handly at once seized the horse and led
it near him, so that Lieper might mount again, but his
own horse was shot from under him and he took a tree,
where he was met by an Indian with uplifted tomahawk.
He caught the foeman's arm and uttered an Indian word
meaning friendship, which the brave reciprocated and
led him to the chief, where for a time he was free from
danger. While this was being done, every Indian near
enough struck him with the flat side of his tomahawk.
This diversion was in favor of the panic-stricken men,
only Lieper and two others being killed. Captain Mc-
Clelland, then where Kingston now is, set out with a relief party to bury Handly, who was thought to be killed.
He found the tree where the prisoner had been tied and
fragments of the paper containing the roll of the company, this having been torn in pieces by Handly. The
captain was taken to Will Town, where his fate was in

suspense three days. He was made to run the gauntlet. His feet and hands were made fast and the Indians threw him over their heads to see what the effect would be on his nose. But his life was spared and he was adopted into the Wolf clan of the Cherokees. His captors wanted peace and allowed him to write the following letter to his brother-in-law, Colonel James Scott:

Will Town, Dec. 10, 1792.

Dear Sir:—I am a captive in this town in great distress, and the bearer hereof is a runner from the Upper Towns, from the Hanging Maw, and is now going with a talk from Colonel John Watts, with the Governor, on the terms of peace. These people are much for peace. . .

Dear sir, I have been much abused and am in great distress. I beg for you and John Cowen, and every good friend would go to the Governor and try all you can to get him to send a good answer so I may get away, for if an army come before, I am sure to die. Send word to my wife, and send me a horse down by the Hanging Maw's runner, for I am not able to come without. Dear friend, do what you can, for I am in a distressed way. No more but—

Samuel Handly

To James Scott, Nine Mile, Henry's Station.

Governor Blount was more than willing to rescue Handly, so his answer was favorable to peace. Eight of the braves escorted Handly to his home in Blount, the only ransom asked being a keg of whiskey. Handly was about forty at the time and his hair brown, but when he returned his hair was gray and he was much broken. He resided for some time near the Tellico blockhouse, where the Indians came to trade. When a native from Will Town came across the river he would cry, "canawla, canawla (peace, peace)", and then spend days with their white brother of the Wolf clan. Handly finally settled at Winchester, Tennessee, where he located a land grant, and died there in 1840. He married a Miss Cowan of a prominent East Tennessee family. His son Samuel, while living at Pontotoc, Mississippi in 1842, was interviewed by Draper on what he remembered his father having said about the battle of King's Mountain. The inscription on Handly's grave reads as follows:

Samuel Handly born 1748; died Aug. 4 1840
He was a Revolutionary Soldier and a member

Of the first Convention that formed the State of
                                                Tennessee
Born in North Carolina; Died in Winchester,
                                                Tennessee
He was a Captain in the Indian war.

Hanna. Robert (1744-1821) served in many skirmishes and was a private at King's Mountain. His wife
was Mary Parks. The battle of Cowpens was fought on
the plantation of his son Joseph, who married Sarah
Adair.

Hannah. Captain Robbin of South Carolina lived on
Hannah Hill on the road to Musgrove's mill.

Hansley. Robert was in the North Carolina militia.
He was pensioned in Hawkins county, Tennessee, in 1834.
A William in the Albemarle militia was not at King's
Mountain.

Hardeman. Thomas was with Captain William
Been at King's Mountain, and also at the capture of Isam
Yearly and other tories. After the war he moved to
Davidson county, which he represented in the first state
convention.

Hardin. Abraham was at Musgrove's mill, King's
Mountain, Whetzell's mill, and Guilford, according to
Draper.
Colonel Joseph and his sons Joseph, Jr. and John
were at King's Mountain, according to a family tradition
discussed by Dr. George F. Mellen.

Harkleroad. Henry is listed by Summers. He seems
to have been the only Revolutionary soldier of that name.

Harlison. There is a tradition that Herdon was at
King's Mountain. He was living in Brownsville, Tennessee in 1840. See Draper.

Harrell. Reuben was under William Campbell, and
was pensioned in Washington county, 1835.
John*, Joseph*, and Kidder* were pensioned by
North Carolina.

Harris. James was born in North Carolina 1736 and
died in Spartanburg, South Carolina, 1804. He was at
King's Mountain under Sevier. He married Priscilla Gilliam. A son born 1788 married Elizabeth Golightly.

Harrison. Gideon served under Sevier.

Hawthorne. James was born in Ireland in 1750. His parents located on the South Carolina frontier and were much molested by the natives. In 1762 the mother and two daughters were killed and the son carried into captivity. After his release he learned blacksmithing in York county, and there married Mary, daughter of Colonel Thomas Neel. He served under Neel in the Snow campaign of 1775, and was in Williamson's expedition of 1776. In the Florida campaign of 1778 he was made captain, and afterward was in several of Sumter's battles. Colonel Hill, so active in planning the King's Mountain expedition, could not lead his troops on account of a serious wound, and Hawthorne, now a lieutenant colonel, took his place. Afterward, he was again with Sumter at Blackstocks and Fishdam Ford. He was twice wounded. After the war he moved to Kentucky, settling in Livingston county, where he died in 1809. There are many descendants.

Hayes. Joseph of Laurens county, South Carolina, was first a captain, and served under Colonel Williams at Brier Creek, Stono, and other engagements with the British and Cherokees, succeeding Williams after the latter was mortally wounded at King's Mountain. He was also present at Blackstocks, Hammond's store, and Cowpens. November 19, 1781, he was besieged at Hayes Station by the infamous tory, Bloody Bill Cunningham. Among his thirteen comrades were two sons of Colonel Williams, Captain Daniel and Joseph, the former eighteen, the latter fourteen. The buildings were fired, the little garrison surrendering on the assurance of being treated as prisoners of war. But Cunningham was destitute of honor and hanged them all. When he was about to hang Colonel Hayes and Captain Williams on the pole of a fodder stack, Joseph cried out in anguish, "Oh, brother Daniel, what will I tell mother?" "You will tell her nothing, you damned rebel suckling," answered Cunningham as he hewed him down. The pole above the two men breaking, the fiend finished the victims with his sword.

Hayter. Israel was in William Campbell's regiment, and said the following of his commander: "He from the commencement of the battle until near the close, when he was wounded and the enemy had hoisted a white flag, he saw Colonel Campbell constantly the whole time encouraging his men and leading them up the mountain. His regiment twice gave way and retreated some distance, and he rallied them each time in the most gallant manner."

Helm.   John was in the Lincoln militia, was pensioned in Lincoln in 1833, and it is a family tradition that he was in the battle.

Meredith* Helm was one of the justices of Frederick county, Virginia, on its organization in 1743.   See Cartmell for a genealogy.

Helton.   Abraham, of the North Carolina militia, moved to Bedford county, Tennessee, soon after the war, and was pensioned in 1833, when eighty years old.   He was in other fights also.

Hemphill.   Charles was from Washington county. Virginia.

Thomas was a captain in the battle.   Just before the engagement, Colonel McDowell wanted the Hemphills to corral cattle for the whigs, but not liking the method suggested they would not comply.   In the diary of Lieutenant Allaire is this entry: "Got in motion at five o'clock in the morning and marched eleven miles to a rebel Dr. Hemphill's plantation and halted."

Henderson.   John is listed by Summers in the militia of Washington county, Virginia.

In Greene county, Tennessee, in 1783 were also Daniel*, Joseph*, and Robert*, with Virginia bounty warrant and William* located land here.   The Hendersons were prominent in early Tennessee history, there being the brothers, Richard, Nathaniel, and Pleasant, Andrew, a first justice of Jefferson, and Thomas, who represented Spencer in the state of Franklin.

Hendrick.   David was in Shelby's regiment.
Moses was under Campbell, and was pensioned in Logan county, Kentucky, 1833, when seventy years old.

Henniger.   Henry, Jacob, and John were under Campbell.   Jacob was an ensign and Henry was killed. Conrad, perhaps their father, was on the Middle Fork of Holston in Fincastle in 1774.

Henry.   Henry, James, and Moses were brothers living in Gaston county, North Carolina.   James captured a fine horse from a British officer, but his mother would not let him keep it, because it had belonged to a tory.   Moses, ho soon died of his wounds at Charlotte, left descendants, Colonel Moses Henry Hand of Gaston being a grandson.

John, Henry, and Robert were in the Virginia troops. John was pensioned in Jefferson county, Tennessee, in 1833, when seventy years old.

In the Habersham Historical Collections is a letter from Robert C. Gilliam to Dr. J. H. Logan. It was written from Asheville, North Carolina, September 29, 1858, and thus reads: "I have called to see Mr. Robert Henry at your request, and have taken down what he said about the battle of King's Mountain. He says that he was thirteen years of age, and joined in with the over-mountain men under Colonel Chronicle with twenty other recruits at Probert's place on Broad River. He went into action with and was standing very near Colonel Chronicle when he was shot. They surrounded Ferguson and charged up the mountain. Early in the engagement he was run through his hand and hip, by a British bayonet, and he tumbled over a log and lay still, until all was over. They charged over him two or three times in the attacks and retreats of the regulars, but he kept dark until he was relieved by a friend who pulled out the bayonet and let him up. He had shot the British soldier who had transfixed him, but was not able to free himself from the bayonet." Draper says Robert Henry was born in a rail-pen in Roane county, January 10, 1765. In 1795 he helped to run the line between North Carolina and Tennessee. He practiced law many years in Buncombe county, and died in Clay, January 6, 1863, being undoubtedly the last of the heroes of King's Mountain. He was a clear and forcible speaker.

Samuel, of Augusta county, moved to Henry's Station on the French Broad. Here the Dumplin Creek treaty with the Indians took place. Samuel was one of the commissioners to select a county seat for Blount. Many descendants are in and about Maryville.

Hensley. Samuel is listed by Summers.

Hereden. It is a tradition that James and his brother Edward were in Arthur Campbell's troop of 200. James was pensioned in Warren county, Tennessee, 1834, when seventy-four years old.

Hickman. James was a Virginia captain, married Elizabeth Bryan, and died in Kentucky in 1828.

James was a private under Shelby, and was pensioned in Shelby county, 1833, when seventy-two. Lineage Book 9, D. A. R.

Joel, also under Shelby, was pensioned in Clay county, Kentucky, where he died in 1833, aged seventy-two.

Thomas was one of William Campbell's men.

Hider (Hyder).   Michael lived on Powder Branch, and signed the Halifax petition of 1776. He was under Sevier at King's Mountain. A direct descendant is Senator R. E. Patton, of Knox county.

Higgenbottam. Robert is listed by Summers.

Higgens. John was under Shelby. See Draper manuscripts.

Hill. James was from Lincoln and was there pensioned for service under Cleveland.

James of North Carolina died in Blount county, Tennessee where he was pensioned in 1834, when seventy-four years old.

Colonel William was not in the battle because of a wound, but did good service in aiding the expedition. He was again wounded at Blackstock. He moved from South Carolina to Livingston county, Kentucky, where he died 1809, aged fifty-nine. There are many descendants.

Hillian. James is listed by Summers. Eckenrode mentions John, who was pensioned.

Hobbs. Thomas is listed by Summers. He was afterward wounded in service against the Cherokees.

Hollingsworth. Benjamin was a South Carolina man under Williams. Lineage Book 6, D. A. R.

Hollis. Captain John was in Colonel Lacy's South Carolina men. Lineage Book 15, D. A. R.

Holloway. Charles of South Carolina was under Lacy. He was a great friend of Joel Culbertson. Draper mentions his prior service.

Hood. John, a Virginia soldier, died in Roane county, Tennessee, and was buried on Wolf Creek.

Hortenstine. Abraham is listed by Summers. (Editor's note: He was perhaps the same as Abraham Hempenstall or Haptonstall).

Horton. Daniel*, Henry*' and Joshua* were early Watauga settlers. In 1766 Colonel James Smith set out to explore the lands toward the Ohio. From the Holston he traveled with Joshua Horton, Uriah Stone, and William Baker, all from Pennsylvania, and a slave belonging to Horton. At the Cumberland they halted and returned to the Watauga, where Smith, Horton, and the negro again entered the wilderness. The residence of Joshua, near Watauga Springs, was known as Green Hill. His sons Joshua and Richard are supposed to have been with Sevier. I have many letters inquiring for the Revolutionary record of Joshua, Daniel, Henry, and Richard.

Henry was a Watauga sharpshooter. See Lineage Book 6, D. A. R.

John, a North Carolina man, was pensioned in Greene county, Tennessee, in 1833.

Daniel, whose service is mentioned by Carruther had a father and six brothers on the tory side.

Zephaniah* of North Carolina was pensioned, but his application does not say whether he was in the battle.

Houghton. Thomas, an early justice of Washington, was under Sevier.

Houston. James and John, both ensigns, are listed by Summers. James in 1783 was a justice of Green county. William was pensioned in Greene in 1833. In 1784 there was a Houston Station on the Little Tennessee.

Howard. William was under Campbell. He may have been a son of John, a magistrate of Botetourt in 1770.

Hubbard. James was a private under Sevier, but was a captain in the Boyd Creek battle. In 1782 he and Jonathan Tipton were made majors and marched with Sevier against a band of Cherokees and Creeks under Tassels. At Citico John Watts and Hanging Maw held a peace talk, but the truce was disturbed by Hubbard. While he and a companion were shooting at a mark, Hubbard hit an Indian, intentionally, as it was charged, and the companion of the Indian fleeing to his tribe, another uprising was the result. Hubbard was one of the first justices of Jefferson in 1782. All his family except himself having been killed by the Shawnees, he became a sworn enemy of all Indians, and was said to have slain more than any other man of his time. He owned Hubbard Island in French Broad, where many persons went to find pearls.

Hudson. John was under Shelby, and was pensioned in Sullivan county in 1833 when eighty-four years old.

Hufacre. George was with Shelby. He is often mentioned in the Washington county records of 1777-80. When seventy-seven years old, he was pensioned in Knox county, where descendants are still found.

Hughes. Joseph was a lieutenant under Colonel John Brandon, of South Carolina, and fought at Musgrove's mill, King's Mountain, Hammond's store, Cowpens, Hanging Rock, and Rocky Mount. A son said that the father of Joseph was murdered by tories when in search of his hogs, his body being pierced by seven balls. Joseph then swore he would kill every tory he met. He was famous as a rifleman and very quick on the trigger. He was a giant in size, very active and strong, and fearless to the point of recklessness. In Chester county some tories were besieged in a log house in an open field. When the assailants were about to withdraw, Hughes swore he would never leave a tory in the house. He kindled a torch, approached the house under cover so far as possible, then darted the remainder of the distance exposed to the fire of the whole platoon. He stooped, the balls flew over his head, and the next instant he was under the house creating a blaze. The tories then surrendered. Hughes was also famous for his independence and moral courage. In a case before the court of Chester it became necessary to determine whether a notorious tory by the name of M——— was alive or dead, and if dead at what time he died. Hughes fearlessly acknowledged that he had shot the marauder himself. With his family and Jack Mabry, a son-in-law, he at length removed to Alabama. Meanwhile he had become a Presbyterian elder and given up profanity. In passing through the Indian country he came upon a tory refugee by the name of Radcliff. Hughes eyed him closely and then exclaimed: "I know you, sir. You are a scamp of a tory. I ran you from Chester district, and nothing but an accident saved your life. I have a good mind to make away with you now. Hop about now, or I'll do it yet." Mabry was alarmed. Indians and negroes devoted to the refugee were standing about, and Radcliff himself was no mean antagonist. But the ex-tory was thoroughly cowed and was annoyingly obsequious. Mabry could not sleep that night, but the colonel was soon snoring as though nothing had happened. Hughes lived to old age, but to the last was able to bring down a buck in the wilds of his adopted state. The worst thing ever said of him was his firing at a woman. She was a tory and had done much mischief in informing the royalists of the hiding places of the whigs. The ball struck a sapling and thus the woman escaped. At Cowpens he became separated from his troops and was attacked by two dragoons. He ducked to save his head from a sword cut, and with his rifle warded off a stroke by the other Briton. A comrade ran to the assistance of Hughes and shot one of the dragoons. Hughes then clubbed his rifle and dispatched the other.

David, Francis, and Thomas were early Watauga settlers and were with Sevier at King's Mountain. David was pensioned in Sullivan in 1833, when eighty-two years old. Francis was pensioned in Greene the same year at the age of seventy-five.

Hunter. Thomas was in the battle from Gaston county. He migrated to Blount county and built Hunter's Station near where Maryville now stands. He was pensioned in Blount in 1833 when eighty-one years old. It is supposed he was a near relative of the Rev. Humphrey Hunter of Gaston, who was in many a contest with the tories.

Hyce. Leonard of Campbell's regiment was wounded. There was a George on the Middle Fork of Holston in Washington county, Virginia.

Hyden. William was from Washington county, Virginia, and was pensioned in Roane county, Tennessee in 1833 when eighty-four.

Ingle. John and Michael of Washington county, Virginia, settled in Washington county, Tennessee, where they were pensioned in 1833, Michael being seventy-eight and John seventy-six. John died May 13, 1824.

Ingram. Jeremiah of the Virginia militia settled in Adair county, Kentucky, where he was pensioned in 1833 at the age of seventy-six.

Inman. Abednego was under Sevier. He carried scars received at King's Mountain and in skirmishes with the Indians. He settled in Jefferson county, Tennessee, where he located a landgrant and died in 1831 aged seventy-nine. His wife was Mary, daughter of Alexander Ritchie. His son, William Hardin married Eleanor Wilson, and another son, James Wilson, married Annie Lea.

Captain Shadrach Inman is erroniously said to have been at King's Mountain. He was killed at Musgrove's mill, two months earlier.

Ireland. Hans was under Shelby. See Draper manuscripts.

Isaac. Samuel (1759-1845) was born in Frederick county, Virginia and died in Lincoln county, Tennessee. He had service under General Marion. He was pensioned in Lincoln in 1832. His wife was Mary Wallace, and a daughter married Captain Jacob Van Zandt.

Isbell. James, Francis, Livingston, Thomas, and William were brothers, and are said to have been in the same company at King's Mountain.

Zachary, an early Watauga settler, was in the battle. He was one of thirteen commissioners elected by the convention of 1772 to formulate laws. The others were William Been, Jacob Brown, John Carter, John Jones, Robert Lucas, Jacob Nomack, Charles Robertson, James Robertson, George Russell, John Sevier, James Smith and William Tatham. All were present at King's Mountain. Zachary Isbell was a justice of Washington in 1778 and a signer of the Halifax petition.

Godfrey was under Sevier. At a militia meeting of March 19, 1780 there were present Colonel John Sevier, Major Jonathan Tipton, Captains Godfrey Isbell, John McNabb, James Stinson, William Trimble, and Joseph Wilson, and Lieutenant Landon Carter, acting in the absence of Captain Valentine Sevier. It was ordered that 100 men be raised agreeable to the command of General Rutherford, to serve in South Carolina. These men were at Musgrove's mill as well as King's Mountain.

Henry,* pensioned in Kentucky as a Virginia militiaman, went to Kentucky in 1818 when seventy-eight. He is not claimed as a King's Mountain man.

Jack. James was a private under Shelby, and was pensioned in Greene county, Tennessee, in 1833 when seventy-seven.

Jeremiah, a Watauga settler, was under Sevier at King's Mountain and Boyd's Creek. He was present at the siege of Watauga in 1776. In the early settlement of

Nollichucky, corn became very scarce. Jack and William Rankin went in a canoe down the Holston to the present vicinity of Knoxville to see if they might not trade clothes for corn. The Indians at first refused and intended harm, but through the influence of Nancy Ward an exchange was effected. On the return they camped one night a mile above the mouth of French Broad. Jack was so well pleased that he settled here in 1787. He was conspicuous in the history of Franklin and early Tennessee, and was a justice of Knox in 1792.

Captain James Jack, who carried the Mecklenburg Declaration to Salisbury and Philadelphia, is said to have been at King's Mountain under McDowell.

Patrick* was one of the three men who escaped in the Fort Loudoun massacre. In the records of Knox is a grant to him signed by Governor Dobbs of North Carolina. It is dated 1764 and is for fifteen square miles south of the Tennessee River, the consideration being four hundred pounds. Patrick was in the Revolution, but I fail to find his record, and it is not certain whether he was at King's Mountain. His son, John Finly Jack, was a prominent lawyer of East Tennessee, and at Rutledge was a partner of General John, son of General William Cocke. Jacksboro is named for him. He married Elizabeth, daughter of William Cocke. Mrs. Carriger and Mrs. Rhoton of Morristown were two of his eight children. See Hunter's Sketches.

Jackson. William was a captain under Cleveland. A William of the North Carolina line was pensioned in Franklin county, Tennessee, in 1833. A William was pensioned in Blount in 1833 for service in the Virginia militia. He was then eighty-seven.

Jamison. John was a lieutenant from Washington county, Virginia.

Samuel and Thomas were privates under their brother, the above John.

One Robert was pensioned in 1835 and went to Missouri.

Jarnigan (Jernigan). Thomas and William were under Shelby, and were pensioned in Jefferson. The Jarnigans of Tate Springs are descendants. Thomas married Margaret Evans.

George, a lieutenant of North Carolina, is thought to have been present under Johnston. He was pensioned by North Carolina in 1844.

Jefferies. John was under Johnston and was pensioned.

Nathaniel, born in Virginia 1735, died in Kentucky 1812, served with Brandon's South Carolina men at Hanging Rock, Musgrove's mill, and King's Mountain. He married Sarah Brownsteen and their son John Randolph married Sarah Barnett.

Jean, Philip, and Nathan of Cleveland's command were pensioned.

Jenkins. Jacob, living near Dandridge, was badly wounded by Indians in 1793. He had a bounty warrant, and it is a tradition that he was in the battle.

Thomas and William are listed by Summers.

Jennings. David was under Shelby. See Draper manuscripts.

Johnson. Barnett was also in Shelby's Chickamauga campaign of 1779. See Draper manuscripts.

James, a son of Henry of Ireland, was born in Lincoln county in 1742. Besides his service at King's Mountain, he was in the Snow campaign, the siege of Ninety-Six, and various engagements with the Cherokees and tories. In a hand to hand fight with Patrick Moore, he captured this tory officer, although he received a saber cut in the hand. Thus he could not fire his rifle when some British rushed upon him, and Moore got away. At King's Mountain he commanded a troop of ninety reserves, who were called into action. Johnson died in 1805. His great estate on the Catawba was known as Oak Grove. He married before the war Jane, eldest daughter of Robert Ewart. She died in 1795. They had twelve children. Several of their descendants won some distinction.

Johnston (Johnstone). John was born in Scotland in 1740 and died in Maury county, Tennessee, in 1818, his widow being pensioned there in 1841. After five campaigns under Captain Moffett he fought at King's Mountain and Hanging Rock. His wife was Martha Allison. His son Alexander (1791-1822) married Eleanor Craig. Descendants are in Wayne county, Tennessee.

Robert, pensioned by North Carolina 1835, was a private in William Johnston's company.

Captain William was in the battle, and was pensioned in North Carolina.

Jones. Daniel of North Carolina was pensioned in Hawkins county, Tennessee, in 1833 when eighty-seven.

John, a Watauga rifleman, was present under Campbell. He and his brother Lewis had a large grant from the Indians in 1775.

Thomas of Washington county, Tennessee, was pensioned in 1833, when seventy-four.

John and Joseph of the North Carolina militia were pensioned in Giles county, Tennessee, when the former was ninety, the latter eighty-two.

Judd. When Colonel Shelby made his last appeal, immediately before the battle, he said that if anyone wished to stay back he must go at once. One man, John Judd, offered to hold the horses. Rowland was in the thickest of the fight. In 1778 the Judds were at Greasy Cove, where now is the town of Erwin.

A Judd was one of the officers at the surrender of Fort Loudoun to the Cherokees in 1760.

Karr. (Carr). Robert lived in what is now Greene county, North Carolina. The first session of the county court was held in his house. Under the state of Franklin, he was county register. He fought at Point Pleasant under Evan Shelby and at King's Mountain under Isaac Shelby.

Matthew, probably brother to Robert, was also at King's Mountain. In 1792 he was living in Knox, and as a sergeant commanded eight men at Ish Station.

Keeps. James was a sergeant under Campbell.

Kendrick. Benjamin and Samuel were in Aaron Lewis's company of Campbell's regiment. Benjamin was pensioned in Kentucky, 1830.

John was another of the family. He and John Maxwell were wounded by Indians in Davidson county.

Solomon was with the Washington troops, and was also at Point Pleasant.

The Kendricks lived on the Holston near Abingdon.

Kennedy. Daniel settled in Greene county, Tennessee, and was its first clerk. He was conspicuous in forming the state of Franklin, and was one of its two brigadier generals. A certified copy of his services in the expedition to King's Mountain is in the minutes of the Masonic lodge at Greenville. He was steadily loyal to Sevier.

Thomas (1756-1836) was a captain under Mc-

Dowell. He was wounded at Ramseur's mill, present at Earle's Ford, Cane Creek, and King's Mountain, serving under General Rutherford in 1781. He moved from Burke county, North Carolina to Garrard county, Kentucky. He served in the legislatures of Virginia and Kentucky, and was in the Kentucky convention of 1791.

The record of Moses is given by Summers and Eckenrode.

William served under Brandon, near whom he lived. He was considered the best shot of his section, was always active against the tories, and performed many heroic deeds in the Revolution. He refused all opportunities for office, although he had great executive ability, was quick in any emergency, tall athletic, and very handsome in face. He was pensioned in Wayne county, Tennessee, in 1833, when seventy-four.

Robert* was a cavalry officer in Washington county, Virginia.

Robert is mentioned by Heitman as a captain in the North Carolina service.

Kerby. Henry was in the North Carolina militia, moved to Jackson, Tennessee, about 1783, and was there pensioned in 1833.

Kerr. Adam was under Campbell. In 1777 he was a commissioner to view a road from Washington courthouse to Phillips' mill on the Watauga. James settled very early on the upper Holston.

Joseph, known as the "crippled spy," was born in Chester county, Pennsylvania, in 1750, the family moving to North Carolina when he was very young. Though lame from infancy, he offered his services as a spy to Colonel McDowell. His first work as such was at Blackstock ford on Tiger River, where the enemy were 1500 (150?) strong. Hiding his horse he entered the British lines as a beggar, and after learning all he could, reported to McDowell. On his information the Americans attacked and won a victory. At King's Mountain he reported to the whig leaders where Ferguson was located and what his strength was. Upon this information they made a forced march in thirty-six hours, with only one hour for rest, reaching the mountain at three in the afternoon. In South Carolina he was recognized and barely got away in time. After the war he settled in White county, Tennessee, where he was pensioned in 1833.

Keys. James, a lieutenant in Washington county, Virginia, served under Shelby, and was pensioned in 1835.

Kidd. John was with the Lincoln men and was pensioned.

Kincannon. Andrew, James, and Matthew of Washington county, Virginia served with William Campbell. Andrew was one of the sureties of Arthur Campbell, when the latter was appointed sheriff in 1779. James was a road overseer in 1774 and 1777. Matthew was an ensign at King's Mountain, and after Captain Dysart was wounded, Andrew took command becoming a full captain in 1782. He was born on the Holston in 1774 (?) was a blacksmith and gunsmith, and is said to have made the first horseshoe in Kentucky. He was tall and large, and of fine character and intelligence. After the war he settled on Tom's Creek in Surry county, North Carolina, where he had ironworks and a large plantation. His wife was Catharine McDonald, and he had nine children. He died in 1829.

Kinkead. John was a captain under Campbell. In 1774 he was a sergeant in command of fifteen men at Elk Garden. The same year he fought at Point Pleasant. He was one the first justices of Washington, the court sitting near his home at Black's Fort, now Abingdon. In 1777 he was one of a committee to locate a road over Clinch Mountain to Halbert McClure's and Robert and James Logan's. With Captain Callaway he located the Wilderness Road to Kentucky, this road passing through Abingdon.

Kilgore. Charles was a private under Campbell, and was wounded. In the pension list of Greene county, Tennessee, in 1820, he is named as an invalid with an allowance of $48 a year.

There was a Kilgore Station in the basin of the Cumberland.

King. Robert was under Campbell. He was conspicuous in the early history of Tennessee. As a major he was sent by Governor Blount to invite the Cherokees to White's Station for a treaty. He found the tribe divided into two parties, Hanging Maw leading the northern wing and Little Turkey the southern. The town of Kingston in Roane was laid out on his land in 1799. He lived on a small cabin on the site of the Exchange Hotel, and opened a store as soon as the town was established. Kingston was the state capital two days in 1805, but though on a line of much travel, the accommodations were so poor that the legislature returned to Knoxville. A mile distant in 1792 was a fort called Southwest Point.

William served under Shelby, and was pensioned in Sullivan in 1833, when eighty-eight years old. When Hawkins county was established in 1786, he was on the committee to choose a site for the courthouse, which was built of logs. The town of Kingsport was in part named in his honor.

Knox. Robert was in the militia of Lincoln county, North Carolina, where he was pensioned in 1833.

Benjamin*, James*, and Samuel* are on the pension list of North Carolina, and a Colonel John Knox is mentioned in Hunter's Sketches.

Kusick (Cusick). —————, serving under Sevier, is said to have been the man who shot Ferguson.

There was a John* Cusick in the militia of Washington county, Virginia.

Kuykendall. Matthew was in Campbell's regiment.

Benjamin* and Joseph* located grants in Summers county, Tennessee, and both were killed by Indians in 1792.

Lacy. Edward was born in Pennsylvania in 1742, is said to have been present at the Braddock defeat, went to Chester district, South Carolina when still quite young, and bound himself out to William Adair to learn bricklaying. He was a captain at the beginning of the Revolution, was in the Cherokee wars and at the battles of Hanging Rock, Rocky Mount, Carey's Fort, and Fishing Creek. At King's Mountain he led the Chester troops and was wounded. He had a large landgrant in Tennessee. Colonel Lacy was drowned in Kentucky in 1833, while attempting to go through the swollen waters of Dove Creek in Livingston county.

Laird. David, James and John were in Campbell's regiment. James and John were killed. They are mentioned by Summers, Draper, and others.

Lane. Isaac was in Russell's company of Sevier's regiment.

Tidence, born 1764, was in the North Carolina line, and was pensioned in Jefferson county, Tennessee, in

1833. He seems to have been one of the eight sons of Tidence Lane, a Baptist preacher, all of whom were in the Revolution. The will of Tidence Sr., is on record at Dandridge, Tennessee.

Aquilla was in the battle and was pensioned.

John was under Shelby.

Lang. John was in Shelby's troop.

Langston. John and Robert were South Carolina men under Lacy.

Lankford. Thomas was in Cloud's company of Cleveland's regiment. He was one of the scouts in the advance of the expedition, and the tories came near capturing him when they wounded John Martin.

Benjamin was a Virginia soldier and pensioner.

Large. Joseph, one of Cleveland's men, was pensioned in Jefferson county, Tennessee, 1833, when seventy-four.

Latham. John was in Russell's company. He was living on Long Island in 1776, and in 1779 was a justice in Washington county, Virginia.

Latman. Joseph was under Shelby. See **Draper** manuscripts.

Lawson. William is listed by Summers.

Ledbetter. George was a captain of Rutherford troops. He was also at Blackstock and was a member of the North Carolina convention of 1778. His son William married Elizabeth Welborn of North Carolina.

Lee. James (1748-1810) was born in Virginia, and settled at High Shoals, North Carolina, where he married Mary Lewis. He was at King's Mountain and Cowpens. Lineage Books 17 and 27, D. A. R.

Leeper. James was a second lieutenant under Campbell. He moved to Davidson county in the winter of 1780-81, and was a captain on the border. In April, 1781, he was killed from ambush. The first marriage solemnized by James Robertson in the Cumberland settlement was that of James Leeper.

A Samuel* was killed by Indians on Cumberland Mountain when Captain Handly was captured.

Lefy. Shadrach was a Lincoln county man and pensioner. Lineage Book 9, D. A. R.

Lenoir. See Chapter XI.

Leonard. George and Frederick are listed by Summers.

Henry, living on New River in 1756, was captured at the same time with Mrs. Draper. The same or another Henry, and Robert* were pensioners in Washington county, Virginia.

Lewis. The following Lewises were at King's Mountain: Charles, James, Joel, John Martin, Micajah, and William Terrell, Jr.

Major Micajah was born in Virginia in 1755, moved to Surry county, North Carolina, was in the battle of Stono, and as one of Cleveland's men was wounded at King's Mountain. At Pyle's defeat in 1781 he was so badly wounded that he died the next day.

Captain Joel was born in Virginia 1760, also moved to Surry, and led a company at King's Mountain. In this troop were twenty-two of his family connection. He married Miriam Eastham and had eighteen children. In 1789 he was a tavern-keeper in Nashville, where he died in 1816. He held several offices.

James M., a third brother, was born 1762 and died in Columbia, Tennessee in 1830. He was a lieutenant under Micajah. His wife was a daughter to Colonel Benjamin Hardin.

All three brothers were wounded at King's Mountain.

For record of Charles see Lineage Book 9, D. A. R.

Lindsay. James was captured by Ferguson's foragers the day before the battle, but after the fight began he and the Pattersons escaped and joined the patriots.

John is listed by Summers.

Linn. Andrew, Daniel, and William were under Shelby. See Draper manuscripts.

William was pensioned in Maury county, Tennessee in 1830, when seventy-eight.

Litton. Catel was under Shelby. See Draper manuscripts.

John is listed by Summers.

Livingston. David is listed by Summers.

Logan. Joseph and William were Lincoln men in the company of Mattocks, and were close to their captain when he fell early in the engagement. The Logans were from Virginia. William married Jane Black, was pensioned, and after the war removed to York district, South Carolina, where he died in 1832, aged eighty-three. There are many descendants. His brother Joseph became a Baptist minister.

James is listed by Summers.

Long. John, Richard, and William were in the battle. John and William were under Shelby. John settled in Sullivan county, Tennessee. For record of Richard, see Draper manuscripts.

Looney. For record of John, Robert, and Major David (1738-1800) see Lineage Book 4, D. A. R. David was wounded in the battle.

Moses, a lieutenant, is listed by Summers.

Absalom*, son of Major David, married Nancy Long and settled in Knox county, Tennessee.

Love. Robert is mentioned by Hunter. See also Lineage Book 12, D. A. R.

For Hezekiah see Chapter XI.

Lowery. John, a second lieutenant, and William are listed by Summers, were pensioned, and in 1792 were living in Knox and Sevier counties, Tennessee.

Loyd. John is listed by Summers, and was pensioned in Washington county, Virginia.

Lucas. Robert was on the Watauga in 1772, and in 1778 was a justice of Washington. At King's Mountain he was a captain under Sevier.

Major Isaac was a brother to Robert, and in 1781 moved to Davidson county, where he had fighting against the Indians.

Captain Joseph, an early Watauga settler, was probably in the battle. In 1791 he was in the Miro district defending the frontier.

Lusk. Captain Joseph* was on the Watauga in 1776, and in 1792 was in Summers county.

In 1793 Samuel*, a scout in Robert Crockett's company, was captured by Indians.

Lyle. Henry was an early settler on the Nollichucky, was with Sevier in his border campaigns, and was probably at King's Mountain.

Samuel* was in Jefferson county, Tennessee in 1792.

Lynn. David is listed by Summers.

Lyon. Humberson and William were under Campbell. Humberson, an ensign, was killed. William was pensioned in 1833.

Lytle. Captain Thomas was in McDowell's regiment, and is mentioned by Draper.

Archibald, Micajah, and William are mentioned by Heitman.

McAden. William was in Shelby's command. See Draper, including Draper manuscripts.

McAdoo. John was an early settler on Watauga, and in the Washington records of 1778-80 appears as an exemplary man for the strenuous times. He was at King's Mountain under Sevier. His son, William C. married in 1848 for his first wife Annie Hornley of Columbus, Georgia, and for his second, Mary Faith Floyd.

John settled in Jefferson county after the war and married Mary Gibbs, daughter of a soldier in the French and Indian war. A grandson is William Gibbs McAdoo of the Wilson cabinet.

McBee. Silas was born November 24, 1765, and therefore was not quite fifteen when fighting at King's Mountain under Colonel Williams. He lived at Thicketty Ford, South Carolina, and was there at the time of the capture of Captain Moore and his men. He was a member of the first legislature of Alabama, but in 1842 was living in Pontotoc county, Mississippi, where he died three years later. Draper had several interviews with him.

McCafferty. William was an Irish merchant near Charlotte who turned the British army into a wrong road in order to protect the whigs on their way to King's Mountain.

McCampbell. John was born in Augusta county, Virginia, 1742, and died at Abingdon in 1808. He commanded a company of Washington county men, and was also at Musgrove's mill, Cowpens, and Guilford. His wife was Ruth Edwards. His sons Archibald and Walter married, respectively, Catharine Lewis and Sarah Moore.

McCarthy. William was under Cleveland and was pensioned in Lincoln in 1833.

McCulloch. Thomas was a lieutenant in the Washington county line and was killed.

McClelland. Abraham was in the Virginia troops under Campbell. John was under Shelby. In 1790 he was sent to Westpoint Station to keep the Indians from molesting the Cumberland settlement.

McClough. James was with the Virginia troops.

McClure. John was with the Botetourt militia. See Lineage Book 2, D. A. R.

McConnell. Abram was with the Virginia men under Campbell. After the war he received a landgrant and settled in Blount county, where he founded McConnell Station very near the Houston settlement.

McCorkle. Francis entered the army at the beginning of the Revolution, and was also at Ramseur's mill and Cowpens. In 1774 he was on the committee of safety for Rowan county, North Carolina. His second wife was Eliza, daughter of Richard Brandon. He left a large family.

McCrory. Matthew was under Colonel Williams.

McCroskey. John was a private in Captain William Beattie's company. After the surrender he went in search of Captain Robert Edmondson, told him of the victory, to which the prostrate officer nodded his satisfaction and then died. McCroskey was pensioned in Sevier county, Tennessee, in 1833, when seventy-six years old.

McCulloch. John, a soldier under Campbell, was pensioned in 1833.

Robert, a lieutenant of the Washington county men, was wounded.

McCutchan (McCutcheon). John was an Augusta man under Campbell. In 1778 he served a three months tour against the Indians, and in 1779 was one of Captain John Walkup's men, stationed at Warm Springs to protect that point. He was pensioned in Augusta county in 1835.

Samuel was a captain of Augusta militia.

William was also in the Augusta militia, but his first service was in the New Jersey line. He was at the surrender at Yorktown. He was pensioned in Augusta in 1835 and lived to be very old.

McDonald. Magnus was in the North Carolina militia.

McDowell. Charles was born at Winchester (?), Virginia, in 1743, and died at Morganton, North Carolina in 1811. He was in Rutherford's campaign against the Cherokees. He and his younger brother Joseph were at Musgrove's mill and King's Mountain. He married Grace Greenlee Brown. His sons Ethan Allen and Charles Gordon married, respectively, Ann Gordon and Lucinda Jones.

Colonel Charles was conspicuous in organizing the expedition to King's Mountain, but gave the actual lead to younger men. Through him many have joined the Daughters of the American Revolution.

Major Joseph, brother to the colonel, commanded a regiment at King's Mountain. In 1776, when hardly grown, he fought under Charles against the tories. He served under Rutherford, and was at Stono, Ramseur's mill, Earle's ford, Musgrove's mill, and Cowpens. He died in 1801, aged forty-four. His wife was Margaret, daughter of Colonel George Moffett. He left two sons and six daughters.

Mrs. Ellen McDowell and her daughter Jane heard the firing from their home near King's Mountain, and spent several days on the battlefield nursing the wounded.

McElwee. James (1752-1820) was under Colonel Campbell. John and William were in the same regiment. See Lineage Book 16, D. A. R.; also Habersham Collections, Volume 3.

James, a native of North Carolina, came to Tennessee about the time Daniel Boone visited the Watauga. He is thought first to have settled on the Nollichucky, but his military landgrant was four miles below Knoxville. He was with Sevier at King's Mountain, and was the first to reach Cavett Station after the massacre there of thirteen people. His son William married Lucinda Eblin, and descendants are in Knox and Roane.

McFarland. Robert was a lieutenant in the battle. He moved from North Carolina to Wythe county, and later to Hamblin, living until 1837. He was the first sheriff of Jefferson, and a colonel of militia. His first wife was a Barton, the second was Mary Ann Scott. His son William was in the war of 1812. Many of his descendants are in Jefferson and Hamblin.

McFerren. John, an ensign, came from Botetourt, and was with the Washington county men. It is claimed that his brother Martin was also in the battle.

McHenry. John is listed by Summers.

McJucken. Joseph was born in Carlisle, Pennsylvania, 1755, and died in Union district, South Carolina, 1841. He was also at Musgrove's mill. His son Samuel married Ann Bogan, and their own son Joseph married Annie Thomas.

McKee. The mother of Major William Chronicle first married a McKee in Pennsylvania. He died in Lincoln county, North Carolina. The major was the only son by her second marriage; James McKee was given the sword and spurs worn by the major at King's Mountain, and they are still in the possession of descendants.

McKissick. Captain David was wounded at Ramseur's mill, but it is claimed that he was present at King's Mountain. He represented Lincoln in the legislature, 1783-87.

Thomas was in the battle and was pensioned in Blount county, Tennessee in 1823.

McLain. Alexander came from Ireland to North Carolina, where his son William became a physician, and attended the wounded after the battle. He was afterward with the army of General Greene, and served till the end of the war. In 1815 he erected a monument on the battlefield at his own expense. He was pensioned in Lincoln in 1833, and attained the age of ninety-six. Dr. McLain was buried in Bethel Cemetery, York county, South Carolina. His brother John, born in Rowan, was killed at Buford's bridge.

McMillian. Alexander was born in County Derry, Ireland, came to America in 1775, and at once entered the American army. He was at Quebec, where a finger was frozen while on picket duty. In 1778 he married Margaret McMillian, his first cousin, and shortly after the battle of King's Mountain they settled in Washington county, but moved to Knox. Though sixty-three years old, he was present at the battle of New Orleans, serving as a volunteer. He died at McMillen Station in 1837 and was buried near Calidonia church on the Philip Sherrod farm.

McMillen. William was with the Washington county men, and is listed by Summers. He married Mary Leeper 1759, and died 1810. His eldest son, William, graduated from William and Mary College, becoming first a Presbyterian minister and afterward a lawyer. McMillen Street in Cincinnati is named for him.

McNabb. John was an early settler in Washington county, Tennessee, and a justice in 1777-80. He was active in the border fighting, was a captain in the Boyd Creek affair, and was with Sevier at King's Mountain. The first mill in his neighborhood was on Buffalo Creek on land patented by himself and his brother Baptist.

David was also at King's Mountain, and was a captain in the fight shortly afterward at Greasy Cove. In 1793 he was a lieutenant colonel under Sevier in his Cherokee campaign.

McNutt. George was the first settler in Jefferson, but with Moses Brooke he relocated a few miles above Knoxville. He was an elder of Lebanon church at the mouth of the French Broad, and a trustee of Washington College. For a man of his time he was the owner of many books, chiefly theological. He came from Rockbridge, and was an uncle to Governor McNutt of Mississippi. His daughter, the first white child born below the French Broad, married Colonel Robert McFarland. George McNutt died 1857 (?), and was buried in the family cemetery.

McQueen. James was under Cleveland.

McShaney. For the record of William see Draper manuscripts.

McSpedden. It is claimed that William was one of Shelby's men. He was with Evan Shelby in his Chickamauga expedition.

Magill. James and John were with the Virginia troops. James was pensioned in Monroe county, Tennessee, in 1833, and John in the same year when seventynine years old. The latter moved to Franklin county with Samuel Handly.

Mahannas. Tapley was from Lincoln county, North

Carolina, and pensioned there.   See Lineage Book 9, D.
A. R.

Mahoney.   Michael was born in the south of Ireland
and came to America when young, settling on the Nollichucky.   He was in the battle under Sevier, and appears
to have been one of the killed, since John Black was made
his administrator, November 17 following, the bond being 10,000 pounds in depreciated currency.

Main.   Tobias, an ensign in 1777-78, was at King's
Mountain under Campbell.

Henry was one of the foot soldiers left behind, and
unable to be present in time.

Manor.   Josiah was in the North Carolina troops,
and is said to have been in the battle, although his pension application is silent on the matter.

Thomas was one of Shelby's men.   See Draper manuscripts.

Maples.   Marmaduke was a private under Chronicle,
and was pensioned 1833.

Martin.   Salathiel was in the North Carolina troops
and died May 6, 1827.   His widow applied for pension
in Claiborne county Tennessee, in 1845, when eighty-one
years old.   She stated that Salathiel was a captain in
Armstrong's regiment, and was present also at Guilford,
serving eighteen months in all.   His wife Mary married him in Surry county, North Carolina, April 23, 1782.
Martin was very tall, of great physical strength, and was
reputed to be an excellent officer.   His service was with
the dragoons.

John was in Cloud's company of Cleveland's command.   While on a scout with Thomas Lankford, both
men were wounded, and Martin was left for dead, but
recovered and rejoined his company.

Robert was also under Cloud.

William was pensioned in Woodford county, Kentucky, when seventy-two.

Samuel was a captain of twenty of Chronicle's men.
Four were killed and two wounded.

Joseph was a captain in Washington county, Virginia, but moved to Sullivan in 1782.   He was also in the

Boyd Creek battle and became a major. Ramsay says much of him.

Matthew, born in Charlotte county, Virginia, 1763, died in Bedford county, Tennessee, in 1846. He was a private under his brother, Lieutenant George, and was pensioned in 1831. He was the youngest of eight brothers, all of whom were in the army.

Mason. Thomas and Patrick of Lincoln county were pensioned 1833.

Massingale. Michael of Grainger county was under Captain Been. Many descendants are in Grainger and adjoining counties.

James* is mentioned in the Washington records of 1778-82.

Mattocks. Captain John of the Lincoln county men was killed. His brother Charles was also in the battle, but the life of their brother Edward, a tory, was spared at his intercession, and he also became a whig. They moved to Georgia.

Maxwell. George was born in Virginia in 1751, went early to the Holston, and became a lieutenant in 1777. When the Ingles were captured by Indians he went to the rescue. He commanded a company under Shelby at King's Mountain. He was one of the first justices of Sullivan and held other important offices.

John was under Campbell. In 1781 two of his daughters were scalped by Northern Indians. Maxwell's Gap in Washington county, Virginia, is where the capture and murder of the Ingle family took place.

James was also at King's Mountain. He was killed while pursuing the Indians who had murdered the daughters of John. His white hunting shirt made a conspicuous target.

Thomas of the same county was under Shelby. He said the action began at the east end of the mountain, Campbell and Shelby there being opposed by the British regulars led by Ferguson in person.

All these Maxwells seem to have been brothers, or otherwise near of kin.

May. Humphrey and John were Virginians, and it is claimed they were in the battle. Humphrey, a sergeant, was pensioned 1833, when seventy-six. John was clerk of Botetourt in 1773, a lawyer in Fincastle county in 1774-75, and received a bounty warrant.

Mayes. William was a North Carolina soldier, and was pensioned in Lincoln as a private, 1833.

Meaden. Andrew and John were at Ramseur's mill and Cowpens, and descendants claim they were also at King's Mountain. They were pensioned 1833 in Jefferson county, Tennessee.

Meek. Adam came from Ireland while young, settled in Mecklenburg county, North Carolina, and was a signer of the celebrated Mecklenburg petition. He was a lieutenant at King's Mountain. His was the first cabin in Jefferson county, Tennessee. No neighbor was west of him, and the nearest mill was at Greenville. He was a surveyor, and was buried at Strawberry Plains. He married a Miss Childers of Mecklenburg. His son, Adam K., was in the Seminole war. The Habersham Collections say this of the Meeks: "On Bullock Creek (South Carolina) were the Meeks, three of whom, Moses, James, and Adam were in the war. The place is still owned by grandsons."

John, a son of James and Annie, was in the battle. He married Jane McCutcheon, June 15, 1770. Her father was also in the battle. Joseph, son of John, married Rebecca Meek.

Mendenhall. Nathan is said to have been with the Lincoln men. He was pensioned in Lincoln, 1833.

Meredith. William was born in Louisa county, Virginia, his parents coming from Wales. On the Yadkin he was a neighbor to Colonel Cleveland, and commanded a company under him at King's Mountain. He went into the war at the beginning. Afterward he taught school. He died on the Tugalo River.

Miller. James (1740-1812) was born in Pennsylvania, saw much military service, commanded a company under Hampton at King's Mountain, and in 1781 was made a colonel. Next year he led the Rutherford troops against the Cherokees. He was state senator four terms. In 1767 he married Agnes Miller, his cousin.

John, an ensign, was with the men from Orange, and was pensioned 1833. His wife was a sister to William Twitty, also a King's Mountain soldier. On one occasion she made a successful dash for guns and ammunition, although under the fire of tories.

Robert of Chester district was under Lacy, and was wounded.

Millon. ———— was in Evan Shelby's troop, and was also in the Chickamauga campaign.

Mitchell. Elijah was born in Mecklenburg county, North Carolina, April 8, 1761, was in the battle under McDowell, and was pensioned 1832. He died in Warren county, Indiana.

James was also under McDowell and pensioned 1832. He married Mary Craig, and died in Maury county, Tennessee. His son Andrew married Mary McGovern.

Edward (1760-1837) was a private in the Virginia militia, was pensioned 1835, and died in Illinois. His first wife was Mary Halse, his second was Eleanor Essex.

Moffett. John was born in Virginia and settled in Chester district, South Carolina. He was at King's Mountain under Lacy. He also served under Sumter, in the Snow campaign, and in 1776 against the Cherokees. Before the close of the war he was made a colonel. He died in DeKalb county, Georgia, 1829, aged eighty-six.

Monroe. William, as is claimed by descendants, was with Campbell at King's Mountain, having already served under him. He was born in Frederick county, Virginia (?), and was pensioned 1835.

Montgomery. Alexander lost a saddle in the fight. The same year he was a coroner of Washington.

James married Mary Robinson and a daughter married Walter Preston.

Richard was with the Washington men.

Robert was under Campbell.

It is claimed that John of Botetourt, who led a company in the Big Sandy expedition of 1757, was at King's Mountain, but it may have been a younger John.

Thomas was a brother to Alexander.

Mooney. Martin was in Fontaine's company of the 14th Virginia, and was with Cleveland at Long Bridge, King's Mountain, and Ninety-Six. See Wood's History of Albemarle.

Richard* was in Greene's battles in the Carolinas and was pensioned in Albemarle in 1835, but there is no mention of King's Mountain.

Moore. Alexander was in the Lincoln militia, was pensioned in Lincoln in 1833, and there is a tradition that he was at King's Mountain.

John was born in Lincoln in 1759. His father was William Moore, one of the first settlers. John and his brothers, Alexander, James, and William were in the Revolution, were pensioned, and all are claimed as King's Mountain men.

Samuel of York county, South Carolina, was under Hambright. He was also at Ramseur's mill and Musgrove's mill. In the latter skirmish Moore led a party of twelve up the river, crossed, and attacked with such vigor as to decide the action. When Colonel Hambright was wounded at King's Mountain, he declined an offer by Moore to assist him from his horse.

William lost a leg by amputation, and was left at the house of a friend. Hearing of his plight, his wife rode a horse all the way from Washington county, and nursed him until he could go home. He was pensioned in Washington and lived until 1826. His son William married Elizabeth Steele.

Morehead. John was born in Richmond county, Virginia, 1766 and died in Rockingham county, North Carolina, 1832. He was also at Guilford. His wife was Obedience Morehead.

Morgan. Isaac was one of Shelby's men.

Thomas was also under Shelby. Warm Springs on the French were discovered by him and Henry Reynolds, while on a scout in 1778.

Morrison. By tradition, Peter and William of Burke county, North Carolina, were under Cleveland. William, a private was pensioned in Dickson county, Tennessee, in 1833, when seventy-five.

Munday. Jeremiah was a Lincoln soldier and was there pensioned in 1833. He served under Chronicle.

Murphy. Patrick was born in county Kerry, Ireland, and was in Sevier's regiment. In the battle his windpipe was badly cut by a ball. When his comrades washed the wound with some captured rum, Murphy drank a portion of the liquor, saying "it was as good in as it was out." His home was in Washington county, Tennessee.

William was born in Virginia in 1759, and died in

Missouri in 1799.   He served under Sevier in 1776-78, and was with him at King's Mountain.

Joseph was a brother to William and also died in Missouri near the present town of Farmington.   He was also at Guilford.

Murfree.   Henry is claimed as a North Carolina participant.

John was also in the battle.   He was pensioned in Jefferson county, Tennessee, at the age of seventy-four.

Musick.   Lewis Musick and William Twitty, after the defense of Graham's fort, followed Ferguson as spies. They captured his cook at King's Mountain.   Draper mentions them.

Murdoch.   John was born in Ireland, was with the Washington troops, and in 1782 entered a landgrant at Abingdon.   His son Joseph married Martha, daughter of Arthur Lee.

Nave.   It is a tradition that Abraham, Conrad, and Henry, sons of Teeler Nave, were under Shelby.   Teeler* was one of the first settlers on the Watauga.   Abraham married Mary Williams and settled in Carter county. Conrad was at Point Pleasant.

Neal.   John, of the North Carolina militia, was pensioned in Hawkins county, Tennessee, when eighty years old.

Captain William was under Campbell, who considered him an officer of character and energy, and left him in charge of the men following on foot to urge them forward.   He received a bounty warrant.

Neally.   B———— was at Point Pleasant and King's Mountain.

Nelson.   John was a North Carolina private, and was pensioned in Warren county, Tennessee, when eighty years old.

Sutney is said to have reached the age of one hundred and fifteen.   His son David married Charlotte Lane.

William was in Tipton's company of Shelby's regiment.   He was pensioned in Hawkins county, Tennessee in 1833 when eighty-seven.

Newall.   Samuel Sr., is listed by Summers.

Samuel, Jr., was sent in 1776 by the commandant at Fort Patrick Henry to bring in Raven, the Indian chief at Choto. In 1778 he was on scout duty with Captain Dysart in the Powell and Clinch valleys. At King's Mountain he was a lieutenant under Campbell. In 1781 he was on an expedition against the Cherokees. He settled in Sevier county. The following letter was written to General John Campbell, when the latter was a member of the Executive Council at Richmond.

Abingdon, Va., June 5, 1825.

Dear Sir:

I have read with great delight the narrative of Colonel Samuel Newell, of Kentucky, and the part Colonel Campbell acted in the King Mountain engagement. Colonel Newell's general character, from the period of manhood to the present time, I have understood has been uniformly good, although I had not the pleasure of an intimate acquaintance with him, yet I have occasionally seen him from upwards of the last thirty years; and heard his character several years before and frequently since my acquaintance with him. He moved from Virginia many years ago, but has left behind him a favorable impression in this country of general good character for intelligence, veracity and respectability, and from all I can learn from others he has sustained the same reputation in the States of Tennessee and Kentucky, where he has resided since. I can with confidence assert that I have never heard him spoken of in any other manner than terms of respect.

I am, dear sir, your sincere friend

Andrew Russell

Newman. Isaac was in the militia from Guilford, and located a landgrant in Jefferson county, Tennessee, accompanied by his son Joseph, who married Catharine Cate. Descendants are in Jefferson.

John, an early immigrant to the Watauga, was one of Sevier's riflemen. In 1782 he was a justice of Greene, and afterward was colonel of its militia. He voted against the state of Franklin.

Newland. Lewis was an ensign at King's Mountain, and by tradition Abram and Isac were also present. Isaac was living near Abingdon in 1790.

Nicholas. Flayl was born on the Sweetwater in Virginia, and was present with Campbell. He married Nancy Hatcher, a cousin to Henry Clay, and spent his last years in Tennessee.

James, a brother to Flayl, was also in the battle.

Nixon. John (1758-1781) raised a company, and in 1780 became a lieutenant colonel. He was in command at Hanging Rock, after Colonel McClure was wounded. Soon after King's Mountain he was killed by marauding tories. He married Mary Adair in 1774. His daughter, Mary married John Hemphill. Descendants are in Chester county, South Carolina.

O'Brien. William was under Sevier and was pensioned in North Carolina.

Oglesby. Elisha of the Virginia militia was pensioned in 1833 in Summers county, Tennessee.

It is claimed that Richard, a captain of Amelia county, in 1780, was also present.

O'Gullion. Barney and Hugh were in Shelby's Chickamauga campaign as well as at King's Mountain.

Outlaw. Alexander was one of the first officers of the state of Franklin and a staunch friend to Sevier. In 1783 he was living in Jefferson. See Lineage Book 9, D. A. R.

Overton. Eli of the North Carolina militia was pensioned in Hawkins county, Tennessee in 1833, when seventy-four. His descendants think he was in the battle.

Owen. John was pensioned in Smith county, Tennessee, in 1833 when seventy-three years old. See Lineage Book 6, D. A. R.

Robert is listed by Summers.

Palmer. John, Peter, and Thomas were in Marion's brigade, and according to tradition were at King's Mountain under Lacy. Thomas (1763-1811) married Elizabeth Richburg. Their daughter Narian wedded a son of Peter Gaillard, one of Moultrie's soldiers.

Thomas was a private from Botetourt, and was pensioned in Cocke county, Tennessee when seventy-three.

Parke. Ezekiel Evans Parke was present. See Lineage Book 2, D. A. R.

Parke. George (1759-1837) was born in Amherst county, Virginia, and when a boy went with his father to the Yadkin. At King's Mountain he was in Captain Lenoir's mounted riflemen. He was pensioned 1832 for one year's service and died in Monroe county, Indiana. His wife was Milly Davidson.

Another George was present under Shelby, and was also in the Chickamauga campaign of 1779.

Parker. Humphrey was from Lincoln county, where he was pensioned. He was also in the border wars.

Patterson. Arthur and his three sons, Arthur Jr., Thomas, and William, were in the battle. The father was killed. He was a native of Ireland and settled near King's Mountain. The day before the battle the boys were captured by Ferguson's foragers and placed under guard. The father came to secure their release, but just before he could reach Ferguson's camp the action had begun. The sons escaped and joined the whigs. Arthur Jr., located a landgrant in Tennessee.

William of Patterson's mill on the Watauga was in the battle.

Patton. Captain Matthew is mentioned by Draper as in the King's Mountain campaign.

Robert was also in the battle according to the same author, as a soldier under McDowell.

Mrs. Mary Patton is said to have made powder used in the battle. Her maiden name was Mary McKeehen, and she was born in England. She married John Patton at Carlisle, Pennsylvania, and they settled on Powder Creek in Carter county. She had learned how to make powder and when Nathaniel Taylor, who had married her cousin, settled also in Carter, he built a powder mill. Here Mary Patton made powder for years before and after the battle of King's Mountain. It is said she furnished five hundred pounds of powder for the expedition, asked no pay for it, and received nothing. Her price, when she sold powder, was one dollar a pound, and a portion of her product was marketed east of the Blue Ridge, being carried by a footpath. Her life was very active, for in addition to the mill, she managed the farm at the head of Powder Branch which is now owned by James Moffett. She died in 1836 at the age of eighty-five. This story of her life was told me by T. V. Patton, a great grandson. On the monument on the public square in Elizabethton, dedicated to the soldiers of all the American wars, appears the name of Mary Patton.

Pearce. Joshua moved from Baltimore, Maryland, to Sullivan county, and is thought to have been in the battle.

Pearson. Abel was at Boyd Creek as well as King's Mountain.

Peebar. Elias, one of the early Watauga settlers, signed the Halifax petition.

Peery. John and Thomas were of the company that joined Campbell on Wolf Creek. The Peerys were early settlers on the Clinch, and took part in the warfare with the Indians. In 1773, three brothers, Thomas, William, and George, and a cousin, John Peery, were living in Tazewell, where the name is still prominent. At Guilford, John was badly sabered by Tarleton's men and his son Thomas was killed. Pendleton, in his History of Tazewell, says, "No roll of the company has been preserved, and therefore it is impossible to give all the names from Tazewell that were in the King's Mountain battle. Traditions and imperfect records show that David Ward, Thomas Maxwell, James Laird, Thomas Witten, Jr., John Skaggs, and John and Thomas Peery, father and son, were members of the company that went from Tazewell and joined Campbell at Wolf Creek."

Peck. Adam came from Botetourt and was one of the first pioneers on Mossy Creek. He served under Campbell and was pensioned in Jefferson. Of his twelve children, Jacob, the eldest, became a lawyer and settled in Missouri. M. L., who remained on the homestead, was a pensioner of the war of 1812. He married Susan, daughter of a man prominent in the early history of East Tennessee. The homestead is yet in the family.

Pemberton. Captain John was in Shelby's regiment. He was in the feud between Sevier and Tipton. At the request of Tipton, Pemberton came with thirty men, stationing them unperceived in front of Sevier's camp, and ordered a volley fired, but with care not to hit anyone on the other side. After the fusillade John Cowan went out from Sevier's camp with a white flag for the purpose of a parley, but was arrested and taken away. Since the men of both factions had been comrades at King's Mountain, their hostilities were limited to angry words. Perhaps the many Pembertons in Anderson county, Tennessee, are of this family.

Pendergast. Garrett was under Shelby. See Draper manuscripts.

Pepper. Elisha, a Virginia soldier, was killed in the

battle. He seems to have been of the family of Samuel, who lived near Fort Chiswell, county seat of Fincastle county.

Perkins. Elisha was in Shelby's command. See Draper manuscripts.

Perry. Solomon is listed by Summers.

There is a tradition that Jesse, pensioned in Knox in 1833 for service in the North Carolina militia, was in the battle.

Pertle. George, an ensign, is listed by Summers.

Peters. John served under Captain Pemberton.

Pettiford. Edward was under Campbell and located a landgrant in Tennessee. See Lineage Book 4, D. A. R.

Phillips. James, an ensign, was killed.

Samuel was related to Colonel Shelby, and conveyed from and to him a verbal message from Ferguson. It said that if Shelby and the other officers of the over-mountain men did not desist from their opposition to the British arms, he would march his army over the mountains, hang their leaders, and lay their country waste with fire and sword. King's Mountain was the answer to this threat.

Joseph served under Cleveland. He moved from Surry county, North Carolina, to Claiborne county, Tennessee, where he was pensioned 1833, at the age of eighty-one.

Pierce. James was one of Sevier's riflemen. He is mentioned by Draper.

Joseph was one of Shelby's men and was in the Chickamauga campaign of 1779.

Piper. James was with Campbell. His son Joseph moved to Tennessee, where descendants still live.

Pippin. Robert was of the Virginia militia, and was pensioned in Washington county, 1833.

Pitman. William was in the Virginia militia and received a landgrant for service.

Pitts. Lewis was from Washington county, Virginia.

Plonk. Jacob was under Cleveland and was pensioned in Lincoln.

Polk. Ezekiel signed the Mecklenburg declaration.

See Hunter's Sketches, Wheeler's Reminiscences, and Lineage Book 10, D. A. R.

Polson. Andrew was with Captain Shelby at King's Mountain and in the Chickamauga campaign.

Porter. Major James was born in Pennsylvania in 1754 (?), and died childless in Greenville district, South Carolina. He was with the Rutherford men under Hampton, and was wounded.

William was a brother to James and was in the same troop. He served nineteen years in the legislature and was killed by lightning in 1817, at the age of seventy-one.

Robert was a cousin to the above and was an officer in the battle.

Potter. William of the Lincoln militia was pensioned in North Carolina, and it is claimed he was in the battle.

Poston. Richard was in Virginia on the North Fork of Holston. He was in the battle under Campbell.

Prather. Charles was with Shelby at King's Mountain and Chickamauga. See Draper manuscripts.

Preston. Robert was a Virginia soldier under Edmondson. In 1781 he was a deputy surveyor of Washington.

Walter was a brother to Robert and was also under Edmondson. He was born in Ireland in 1765, and died at Abingdon in 1834. He was a graduate of William and Mary, and after the war held many important positions in Washington. He married Annie, daughter of James Montgomery. See Lineage Book 56, D. A. R.

Thomas commanded a company, serving under Sevier. In the Watauga purchase of 1775 his name appears with that of Sevier. In his dealings with the Indians in 1777 he is called Captain Thomas.

Price. James came early to the Holston, was in many skirmishes before King's Mountain, where he served under Campbell.

Samuel was with Shelby at King's Mountain and Chickamauga.

The Thomas Preston named above may have been a Price.

Jonathan served under Colonel James Johnson. He

married Betsy, daughter of Robert Ewart, whose father was also in the battle.

Purviance. William is listed by Summers.

Rabb. William was killed in the battle soon after Chronicle. His name is on the McLean monument. See Lineage Book 9, D. A. R.

Rankin. William was with the North Carolina troops, and was pensioned in Greene county, Tennessee in 1833. It was he and Jeremiah Jack who went down the Holston to barter for corn, and would not have secured any but for Nancy Ward. He represented Greene in the first convention called by Governor Blount.

David and William were prominent in Franklin.

Reanney. Daniel is listed by Summers.

Reazer. Peter is also listed by Summers.

Reed. James had seven sons at King's Mountain, namely: Benjamin, James, John, Joseph, Samuel, Thomas, William. See Lineage Book 9, D. A. R. John, Joseph, and Samuel were pensioned.

Reep. Adam lived on the west bank of the Catawba and served under Graham against the tories; at King's Mountain under Dickson.

Michael* was pensioned in Lincoln county, North Carolina, although his name does not appear as a King's Mountain man.

Regan. Charles was likewise pensioned in Lincoln, and it is the tradition that he was in the battle.

Remfeldt. Henry* was pensioned in Lincoln in 1833, but I am not sure he was at King's Mountain.

Reese. James was with Shelby. He lived in Greene county and voted for the state of Franklin, the others from that county in the same convention being Daniel Kennedy, Joseph Hardin, John Newman, and James Roddy. All were King's Mountain soldiers.

David was a signer of the Mecklenburg Resolutions.

Reeves. William was on Watauga in 1775, and signed the Halifax petition of 1776. He was under Sevier in the border wars, and was almost certainly at King's Mountain. His son, William P., born 1773, died 1835, married Mary, one of the eight children of William Devalt. Descendants are numerous in Washington county, Tennessee.

Reynolds. Elisha was born in Wilkes 1755, was in skirmishes under Rutherford in 1776, fought the tories on New River, and served with Cleveland at King's Mountain. After his colonel was captured by Riddle, he went to his relief under Captain Johnson, and the tory gang was broken up. He became a lieutenant, and died in 1836 aged eighty-one.

Henry was a scout in the summer of 1778, when he was one of the discoverers of Warm Springs. While looking for some stolen horses, they tied their horses on the north bank and waded the French Broad, when a current of warm water attracted their attention. Next year the springs became a health resort. Reynolds moved to Illinois.

Nathaniel was in Gaffney's company, and located his landgrant near Concord, Tennessee. See Lineage Book 4, D. A. R.

Rhea. Until 1779 Sullivan was thought to be in Virginia, and the first grants of land were by that state, Pendleton in 1756 acquiring 3000 acres. Joseph* Rhea, a Presbyterian minister, of Maryland, came to remain in 1776, and was with an expedition against the Cherokees. John came also in 1776, and bought land on Beaver. Mrs. Rhea came as a widow in 1778, with the others of her family, John, Matthew, James, Samuel, Joseph, Robert, and William. John was at King's Mountain, was the first clerk in his county, was also a lawyer, and was in Congress from 1803 till 1823. He never married and died 1837.

Ritchie. Alexander is listed by Summers.

Samuel is also listed by Summers. He was in the fort at Hamblin mills when it was attacked by Indians.

William was from Botetourt county. He was summoned by the court of Washington in 1780 to say why he did not serve on the grand jury.

Roberson. William is listed by Summers.

Roberts. David and James are listed by Summers.

Robertson. Charles was a major under Shelby. He was an early settler, his name often appearing in the court records of 1777-80. He was at Point Pleasant and

Musgrove's mill, and was wounded at Cedar Spring. See Ramsay, Draper, and Allison's Dropped Stitches.

William, of the Rutherford men under Hampton, was wounded.

Robinson. William was from Rutherford and was under McDowell and Hampton. He was shot through the body. He asked the man lying next to him if he were wounded, and the man said his gun was choked and would not go off. Robinson handed him his rifle and shot-pouch, and lay back to die. He was attended to by Mrs. McDowell and her daughter, and lived to rear a family in Rutherford county.

Thomas, a brother to William, was in the same regiment. A tory neighbor named Lafferty saw he was behind a tree and called him by name. When Robinson peered around to ascertain who spoke, a bullet cut the bark near his head. Robinson then fired and hit the tory.

Willaim was a lieutenant under Sevier, and a signer to the Halifax petition.

Roddy. James, an early settler on the Watauga, was under Captain Been when the tories under Grimes were driven out in 1778. They had killed one Millican and tried to kill Roddy, who served under Sevier in Boyd's Creek, King's Mountain, and skirmishes with the tories. He supported the state of Franklin, and represented Greene county several terms. He was one of the first justices of Jefferson after that county was formed.

Roebuck. Benjamin was born in Orange county, Virginia, 1755, moved to Spartanburg district, South Carolina in 1777, and was a lieutenant at Stono and Savannah. He fought under Sumter at Hanging Rock and Musgrove's mill, and commanded a company at King's Mountain. At Cowpens, where a horse was shot under him, he was made a lieutenant colonel. In 1781 he was wounded at Mud Lick, the ball lodging under the shoulder-blade and remaining there. He was likewise captured, being confined at Ninety-Six during the seige, and afterward in a prison ship. He was exchanged in August, but died in 1788 from the effects of his wound. He never was married.

Roler. Martin was at King's Mountain. See De-Peyter.

Roper. Roger was in the battle and was pensioned in Jefferson county, Tennessee, 1833.

Rosebrough. William was a captain and is listed by Summers.

Ross. John was born 1764, served in the North Carolina militia under his brother-in-law, and is said to have been at King's Mountain. He married Edna Walker and was pensioned in Tennessee.

Russell. For record of Andrew see Lineage Book 8, D. A. R.

George was a captain under Sevier. He was then a justice of Washington county, Tennessee, and was one of the thirteen commissioners of the Watauga convention of 1772.

William, Jr., was born in Culpeper in 1758, was a lieutenant under Neel at King's Mountain, and subsequently an adjutant to Colonel Campbell. In 1774 he accompanied Daniel Boone to Powell's Valley. Between 1791 and 1794 he was with Wayne and others in their Indian campaigns. In 1808 he was in the regular army, and he commanded a company in the war of 1812. He died 1825, aged sixty-six.

Rutledge. George was born in Ireland 1755, and died at Blountsville, Tennessee, 1813. He settled in Sullivan 1777, and was with Shelby's men at King's Mountain. He represented Sullivan in the first Tennessee legislature, and in the third was a senator, still being such when he died. In 1796 he was brigadier in place of Sevier. He married Annie Armstrong in 1802. His son married a daughter of one Netherland, a soldier and pioneer settler in Sullivan. A county in Tennessee was named in honor of General Rutledge.

Sample. Captain Samuel was at Point Pleasant and King's Mountain. In 1792 he was with fourteen men at Menifee Station, a frontier post in Knox county, situated where now is Bell's campground on the Clinton pike. He was a neighbor to Colonel Sevier.

Sawyers. John was born in Augusta county, Virginia, 1745, and died in Knox county, Tennessee, 1831. He was in Byrd's expedition and other border campaigns, and moved to the Holston about 1768. Sawyers fought in the Point Pleasant, Chickamauga, and King's Mountain campaigns, and was prominent in his adopted state. He was buried at the Washington Pike church. A history of the family has been published by Dr. M. M. Harris.

Scott. Summers lists Alexander, Archibald, Joseph Sr., Joseph Jr., Robert, Thomas, Walter, and William. Joseph was a lieutenant under Campbell.

Samuel Sr., (1762-1820) was a minute man under Campbell. He was born in North Carolina and died in Kentucky. His brothers Thomas and William were in the militia. See Lineage Book 9, D. A. R.

Self. Thomas is listed by Summers.

Sevier. A sketch of General John Sevier is in Chapter III.

Valentine, a brother, was a captain.

Robert, another brother, was also a captain. He died of wounds on the way home.

Abraham, a brother, was a private.

Joseph and James were sons of General Sevier, the latter being only sixteen at the time of the battle.

Shannon. Robert was a captain of Lincoln county, and when he heard the firing, he hastened with his men to the battle.

Sharp. Benjamin, Edward, James, Richard, Thomas, and William were in the battle. Thomas was an ensign.

Shaver. Michael and his brother Paul were in the battle, and were pensioned in 1833.

Shelby. The Shelbys came from Wales in 1835, and settled in 1771 near North Mountain in Washington county.

Evan Sr.* was active in the border fighting and was early made a captain. He fought at Point Pleasant, finally became a general, and died 1794 at the age of seventy-four.

Isaac, a son of the above, was born 1750, was a lieutenant at Point Pleasant, and as a captain was with his father in the Chickamauga campaign of 1779. The same year he became a colonel and magistrate of Sullivan, and was sent to the Virginia legislature. In 1780 he was in Kentucky, attending to some land he had entered, but hearing of the surrender of Charleston, he returned home and reentered the service, remaining in service till the close of the war. He was at King's Mountain, Thicketty Fort, Cedar Springs, Musgrove's mill, and many other engagements.

Evan, Jr., a brother to Isaac, was in the Chickamauga campaign, and was a major at King's Mountain.
After the war he settled near Clarksville, Tennessee, and
was killed by Indians while returning from the Ohio with
supplies. He married Catharine Shelby, a cousin, and
had two children.

Moses, another brother, was wounded in the battle,
and died at New Madrid, Missouri. His first wife was a
Miss Rentfro, the second, Elizabeth Deal.

John was in the battle under Colonel Shelby. His
wife was Louisa Looney.

David and Thomas were sons of John, and it is
claimed that both were at King's Mountain. David was
seventeen, Thomas about fifteen. David married Sarah
Bledsoe of Summers county, Tennessee, where he died in
1822. But the Thomas in the battle was probably the
Thomas who was a brother to the colonel, as the latter
was with the Mecklenburg troops.

Colonel Shelby's home in Kentucky was called "Tra-
veler's Rest." It was one of the first stone houses in
that state and is still used by descendants.

Sherrill. Adam was born on the Yadkin 1758, and
died in Russellville, Alabama, whither he had gone with
his sister, "Bonny Kate," the widow of Colonel Sevier.
His wife was Mary, a daughter of Cornelius Cormack,
and his son Enos married Mary Abernathy.

Samuel Sr. was in the King's Mountain and other engagements, as were also his sons, Adam, George, and
Samuel Jr. The Indians, two hundred strong, made an
attack on the Sherrill Station on the Nollichucky, in 1788,
and were in the act of firing the buildings when put to
flight by Colonel Sevier with forty men. Adam was in
the battle at Boyd's Creek. The men who returned with
him from King's Mountain and were at Boyd's Creek were
these: Col. Sevier, Majors Sharp, Walton, and Tipton,
Captains Guess, Russell, Pruett, Stinson, Roddy, Carter,
Handley, and Brown, Lieut. Lane, and John Ward, James
and Abraham Sevier, Thomas Gist, Abel Pearson, James
Hubbard, Jeremiah Jack, Isaac Taylor, George Doherty,
and Nathan G———. Tipton was severely wounded at
Boyd's Creek and Adam Sherrill had several ribs broken
by a fall from his horse. In March, 1780, Washington
county raised 100 men to go with General Rutherford to
the aid of South Carolina, and everyone was a King's
Mountain man. Tipton and Joseph Wilson were majors,
John McNabb, Godfrey Isbell, William Trimble, James

Stinson, and Robert Sevier were captains, and **Landon** Carter, Samuel Williams, Josiah Hoskins, William **Been,** **Jacob** Brown, Zachary Isbell, and Robert Davis were **lieu-** tenants.

George Sherrill and John Sevier, Jr., were but **boys** when they went to King's Mountain. A **grandson of** George was Colonel A. S. Colyar, a distinguished **citizen** of Nashville, Tennessee.

Shipp. Thomas was in Cloud's company of Cleve- land's regiment. He was pensioned.

Shirley. John was under Cleveland. See Arthur's History of Watauga County, North Carolina.

Shote. Thomas, an ensign, is listed by Summers. Emanuel* was with Shelby at Point Pleasant.

Sigman. John, of Burke county, was a captain un- der McDowell.

Singleton. Richard was born in 1759 in Brunswick county, Virginia, and died in Lincoln county, Kentucky. He was in several other engagements and was a major in 1780. Later, he served in the legislature, and was **a** sheriff of Rutherford.

Siske. Daniel, of Wilkes county, was killed.

Skeggs (Skaggs). John, a private under Edmond- son, was wounded.
Henry, one of the Long Hunters, was pensioned in Virginia.

Smart. John, a Rutherford soldier under Hampton, **was** killed by a tory named Hughes. In after years, **his** son John heard that Hughes was in west Tennessee, **and** went to take revenge on him, but never returned.

Smith. David was born in Anson county, North **Car-** olina, 1753, and died in Jackson, Mississippi, 1834. **He** was also at Cowpens and Eutaw. His first wife was **Obed-** ience Fort, whom he married in 1771. He **married** again in 1791. Piety Lucretia, a daughter, married **F.** B. Hadley.
Daniel was a major in the Washington county **mili-** tia, and was pensioned 1833. See Lineage Book 10, **D. A. R.**
Edward, a justice in 1779, was in the Washington militia under Campbell, and was pensioned 1835.

John is listed by Summers and was pensioned in Orange county, Virginia, 1835.

Henry, a captain of Washington troops, is listed by Summers.

William was under Campbell and is also listed by Summers.

William was a captain in the South Carolina line, and was also at Wofford's Ironworks.

Minor was a captain under Cleveland and was wounded. In 1781 he was with Rutherford on the Raft Swamp expedition. He moved to the Tugalo in South Carolina.

James was under Campbell.

Snodgrass. James, a major was either with Shelby or Campbell.

William was one of Campbell's soldiers. In the morning he and Edward Smith were sent to turn the foot soldiers up Broad River. He remarked that the enemy were only a few yards away in the battle. He was also in the Chickamauga campaign of 1779, and was pensioned in Tennessee 1833.

Snoddy. John was a justice in Washington county, Virginia, 1777, and at King's Mountain was under Campbell. According to Eckenrode, he was a captain.

Somers. For record of John see Lineage Book 9, D. A. R.

Spelts. John, called "Continental Jack" fought under McDowell. Draper had conversations with him in 1844.

Stamey. John is said to have been in the battle. He was pensioned in Lincoln county, North Carolina, 1833.

Steele. William was killed. John Brown and Michael Mahoney were the only others of Sevier's regiment who are known to have been killed at King's Mountain. He married Elizabeth Maxwell, and his son, General John Steel, born 1764, was in Congress in 1789.

Colonel James was born in Pennsylvania and removed to Union district, South Carolina. He was also at Rocky Mount, Hanging Rock, Musgrove's mill, Cowpens, and the Snow campaign against the Cherokees. While arresting a tory in 1781, he was stabbed by a companion of the latter, and died from the wound a week later.

John was an ensign under Campbell.

Stevenson.   John was under Campbell and had a bounty warrant.

Stewart.   James was a justice of Washington in 1778.   Next year he was one of the commissioners to lay off the town of Jonesboro.   At King's Mountain he was one of Sevier's men.

John was wounded at Point Pleasant, and it is claimed he was at King's Mountain.

William is listed by Summers.

Stinson (Stevenson.)   James was a captain under Sevier and saw much service in the border wars.

Stockton.   John, of the Maryland Battalion, was taken prisoner at Long Island in 1776, but made his escape, and it is claimed he was one of Campbell's men at King's Mountain; also that a brother George was with him.

William was living in Greene County, Tennessee, in 1779, and it is more than probable that he was in the battle, serving with Sevier.

Stone.   William was in Been's company.   He helped to drive the tories under Grimes out of Watauga.

Stovall.   Bartholemew is listed by Summers. He was one of the first settlers of McNairy county, Tennessee.

Sword.   Michael is listed by Summers.

Syles.   James was a captain under Williams and Lacy, a brave soldier and excellent officer, much esteemed by all who knew him.   He was born in Virginia, but finally settled in Fairfield district, South Carolina.

Talbert.   Charles is listed by Summers.

Talbot.   Matthew Sr.* (1729-1812) was an early Watauga settler coming from Bedford county, Virginia, and the Watauga fort was built on his land.   He had a share in the border wars.   By his first wife, Annie Willston of Maryland, he had Matthew, James, and John.   By a second marriage he had Isham and Martha.   Ramsay says he settled in 1775 on the farm owned in his time by Mrs. Eva Gillespie, and that the fort was built on a high knoll a half-mile from Gap Creek, a few graves and a large locust identifying the spot.   It would be a sacrilege to cut down this tree, standing where the soldiery of Watauga assembled, where courts were held, and where justice was administered under a self-constituted legislature, executive, and judiciary. When the King's Mountain men left Sycamore Shoals, the troops passed along Gap Creek and encamped the first night at the mill of Matthew Talbot.

Matthew Jr., born 1769, was with Colonel Sevier. His wife was Mrs. Mary Day, her maiden name being Hale, and she had one son by her first marriage. Her children were Mary, Matthew, Thomas, William, Edmund, and Clayton. William married Mary Bailey, and their daughter, Mary Hale, married William B. Nunnally of Georgia.

James* another son of Matthew Sr., married Elizabeth Smith.

Thomas* was clerk to the first senate of Franklin.

In 1787 William* commanded a company sent by the state of Franklin to aid Davidson county against the Chickamaugas.

Tate. John, a Virginia soldier was pensioned in Botetourt, 1833.

Robert and Samuel were in Been's company in 1778, and were then justices of Washington. At King's Mountain they were in Sevier's command.

Samuel, called George by Draper, was born near Vance's Ferry on the Santee, and died there 1798. He was in many engagements, and had service under Sumter. He was a brigade major.

Tatum. James was in the battle and was pensioned in Watauga county, North Carolina.

Taylor. Andrew, Jr., was in the North Carolina troops. A grandson is Walter Pickens Taylor of Knoxville.

Christopher (1746-1833) was born in Bedford county, Virginia, and moved to Washington county, Tennessee. He was at Point Pleasant, and in 1778 was a captain of rangers. He supported the state of Franklin, and represented his county in the convention at Jonesboro. At King's Mountain he was a captain under Sevier.

Isaac was also at Boyd's Creek. On the return from King's Mountain, two traders brought word to Sevier that the Cherokees were about to descend on the Watauga. As soon as the Catawba had been crossed with the prisoners, Captain Russell was sent ahead and found the information correct.

Leroy was also at Boyd's Creek.

Teeter. George is listed by Summers.

Temple. Major ——— was born in Chester county, Pennsylvania, in 1756, and moved to Mecklenburg, North Carolina, in 1766. He married Mary, a daughter of Daniel Kennedy of Washington, another King's Mountain soldier, and in 1786 moved to Greene county, Tennessee, where he was a large landholder. He was an ancestor of Miss Mary B. Temple, founder of the Bonny Kate Chapter, D. A. R., Knoxville, Tennessee.

Terrell. Richmond, born at Charlottesville, Virginia, 1760, died in Newton county, Georgia, 1856. He married Cecilia Darracott, and his son Thomas D. married Sarah Livingston.

Micajah and William were in the battle. See Lineage Book 2, D. A. R.

Thompson. Alexander (1739-1815) was a refugee to Georgia who served at King's Mountain. He married Elizabeth Hodges, 1760 and his son Alexander married Emma Strickland 1796. See Lineage Book 45, D. A. R.

James, a captain, was under McDowell.

John, of York distrct, South Carolina, was a captain under Williams. He was also at Rocky Mount, Hanging Rock, Fishing Creek, and Cowpens.

Tillman. Philip, a Lincoln man, was pensioned in Lincoln County, North Carolina, 1833.

Tinsley. Golding was born in Culpeper about 1756 and died in Spartanburg district, South Carolina, in 1851. He moved to South Carolina in 1771, served against the tories, and fought at Stono, Savannah, Musgrove's mill, and Blackstock. At King's Mountain he was a sharpshooter under Brandon. He was pensioned.

Tipton. Jonathan was born in Frederick county, 1750, and died in Overton county, Tenessee, in 1833. In 1777 he was a major in Washington, and in constant warfare against tories and Indians. He directed the battle of Flat Rock on the Nollichucky, and was second in command under Sevier at King's Mountain. He was with Colonel Arthur in the Chilhowee campaign, and in 1781 went with Sevier and Shelby to help General Greene in South Carolina.

William was a captain at King's Mountain. See Lineage Book 9, D. A. R.

Todd. For record of James see Arthur's History of Watauga County, North Carolina.

Topp. Roger was under Campbell. He was killed on the Cumberland in 1783. He was one of the guards sent to a bluff with the North Carolina commissioners, and was shot on the Dedrick place.

Tramwell. For record of William see Lineage Book 10, D. A. R.

Trimble. Captain Robert is listed by Summers.

William was an officer in 1780 in the militia of Washington county, Tennessee, and all his company went to King's Mountain. He upheld the state of Franklin.

Turnley. George was in Doherty's company of Sevier's regiment.

Twitty. William was born in South Carolina 1761, lived at Twitty's Ford on Broad River, and died in 1816.

Anthony, an older brother to William, was under Williams. Draper tells how he and Lewis Musick captured Ferguson's cook on their way to King's Mountain.

Vance. David was born in Frederick county, Virginia, 1748, early removed to North Carolina, where he taught school and did land surveying. In the war he fought at Ramseur's mill and Musgrove's mill, as well as King's Mountain. He served in the state legislature. In 1797 he was living in Buncombe, was a colonel of militia, and was one of the commissioners to run the boundary between North Carolina and Tennessee. He died in 1820. He married a Miss Brank. Among his children were Dr. Robert Brank Vance and David Vance. The latter, who married Margaret Myra Baird, was the mother of Zebulon B. Vance, born 1830. He was an officer in the Confederate army and governor of North Carolina.

James, an ensign, was an officer of the Washington militia, and is thought to have been a son of William K., whose wife was a daughter of Charles Robertson.

John was wounded toward the close of the battle. He was a lieutenant under Campbell.

Samuel (1754-1830) enlisted from Washington county, Virginia, for Point Pleasant and King's Mountain, and was pensioned in Greene county, Tennessee, as a sergeant. His wife was Margaret Laughlin. Their daughter Margaret married Abram Fulkerson, and descendants are in Alabama.

Waddell. John was a settler on Watauga in 1775, and his son John continued to live on his landgrant.

Martin*, also an early settler, was pensioned in Greene county, Tennessee, 1833, at the age of seventy-one.

Walker. William of Rutherford county was pensioned in North Carolina.

Wallace. Captain Andrew of the 8th Virginia was killed at Guilford, 1781. According to Waddell's Annals of Augusta, he and Thomas Bowyer were present at King's Mountain and reported killed.

Walton. William (1736-1806) was one of John Brown's mounted riflemen. He was drafted in 1780 into Captain John Loving's company of Virginia men. He married Elizabeth Tolman. His son John was also at King's Mountain. He was born 1767 and died 1844. He married Justina Ginnerick. See Lineage Book 37, D. A. R.

Ward. David, one of the first settlers in Tazewell and one of the best fighters in the border warfare, was at Point Pleasant and at King's Mountain was under Captain Reese Bowen.

William, a brother, was also at King's Mountain and received a landgrant.

Watson. David was a coroner of Washington county, Virginia.

John was pensioned in Rockbridge in 1833.

Samuel (1740-1781) was born in Virginia, moved to South Carolina 1776, fought at Blackstock, Musgrove's mill, and King's Mountain, and was killed at Cowpens. His wife was Frances Lewis. His son Hezekiah married Mary Holmes, and his grandson Arthur Holmes Watson married Frances O'Hara.

William, a soldier under Brandon and Steen, was badly wounded but lived till 1854, when he was ninety-five.

Wear. Samuel, an early settler on the Nollichucky, was a captain under Sevier and a major in the war of 1812. He was also in Arthur Campbell's Cherokee expedition. He was large in body and mind, of strong character, a good neighbor, and a kind, loving father and husband. He lived to be old, and was buried near Henderson Springs in Sevier county. By his first wife, Mary Thompson, he had six children. His second was Mary, daughter of John Gilliland, also a King's Mountain man.

John, a brother, served under him. He was pensioned as a private in 1833, when seventy-nine.

Weaver. John was under Sevier. He was an early settler on the Nollichucky, and his name occurs in the early records as juryman and assessor. He was pensioned as a private in White county, Tennessee, in 1833 when seventy-five.

Webb. George was a man of affairs on Watauga. In 1778 he sold 540 acres and then bought 640, proving each transaction by the oath of David Webb. He was on the grand jury in the examination of the Tory Dykes. Webb was the first settler in Greasy Cove, a company of Indians following him to his cabin and threatening to kill him if he remained there. He gathered up some more settlers and was not molested. George or David, probably the former, was the Captain Webb of Shelby's regiment.

Weir. John was born in Ireland in 1743, where he married a Miss McKelvey. After the birth of their oldest son they settled at Wier's Bridge in Gaston county, North Carolina. In the Revolution he was a scout and then a captain. When he heard the firing at King's Mountain he hurried there with his men, but the engagement closed a few minutes before his arrival. Just before Cowpens he was severely beaten by tories. His wife was also beaten because she would not tell where he was. He died in 1819 aged seventy-six.

Wells. Joseph was under Shelby at Chickamauga and King's Mountain.

Welchiel. Dr. John served under Colonel Williams of South Carolina. In his pension declaration he states that Williams was killed after the enemy had raised the white flag.

Whit. Charles of Lincoln county, North Carolina, was pensioned there.

White. Benjamin was under Campbell and was pensioned 1832.

Isaac, James, and Thomas were born in Pennsylvania moved to Lincoln county, North Carolina in 1779, and were pensioned in Illinois. James was a captain, and the others were lieutenants.

Joseph, a captain under McDowell, was wounded. He was pensioned in Lincoln county, Kentucky.

Richard was a justice of Washington county, 1778-82, and it is probable that he was one of Sevier's officers at King's Mountain. He passed sentence on some tories in 1778.

William was under Lacy. His pension declaration states that Colonel Williams was shot after the white flag was raised. He was pensioned 1833.

Whitesides. John died in St. Clair county, Illinois, 1793, where his brother William, also at King's Mountain, built Whitesides Station in Monroe county, on the road from Cahokia to Kaskaskia. William, their father, married a Miss Stockton in Ireland and settled in Tryon county, North Carolina.

Whitten. Solomon was under Campbell.

John was also in the battle and was pensioned in 1833.

Wiley. Alexander lived near the head of the Clinch, and was a lieutenant under Campbell. In 1789 his home was raided by Indians, who captured Mrs. Wiley and the youngest child and scalped four others. Mrs. Wiley escaped.

Wilfong. John was born April 8, 1762, and died 1838. He enlisted in McDowell's regiment under Captain Sigman and Lieutenant Van Horn. He was wounded in the left arm at King's Mountain, and went home the day after the battle, but was at Eutaw. He married Hannah Sigmore, and his son John married Lavina Sumay.

Williams. Daniel (1747-1827) was a captain under Marion, and was present at King's Mountain. He was born in Wilmington county, North Carolina, and died in Dickson county, Tennessee, where descendants live. He married Sarah Nixon. His daughter Janette married Henry C. Napier.

Colonel James was a son of Daniel and Ursula, and was born in Hanover county, Virginia, moving to Greenville district, South Carolina in 1772, where he was a farmer and merchant. He fought against the Cherokees, and at Brier Creek, Stono, Savannah, Rocky Mount,

Hanging Rock, and Musgrove's mill. He was mortally wounded at King's Mountain after the enemy had raised the white flag. Colonel Williams married a Miss Clark in 1762 and left five sons and three daughters. He was a jurist as were also his cousins, Colonel Joseph Williams and Colonel Richard Henderson.

Samuel was born in North Carolina 1733 and died in Tennessee in 1788. He was a captain under Sevier. His wife was Mary Magdalene —————. His son Samuel married Margaret Crogan.

Wilson. Robert and Joseph were in the North Carolina line. Robert married Jane, daughter of William and Ellen McDowell. Jane and her mother went to the battlefield to care for the sick and dying. It is said that the father gave Jane to Robert Wilson on account of the bravery of the latter.

Mrs. Eleanor, wife of Robert Wilson, Sr., was a courageous hero of the Revolution, and the mother of eleven sons, several of whom were at Musgrove's mill and King's Mountain. About 1792 all the sons moved to Tennessee. It is said that Robert was the first man to cross the Cumberland Mountains with a wagon.

Captain Joseph was a justice of Washington in 1778, and pronounced judgment against the tory Moses Crawford, who was to undergo imprisonment during the rest of the war. Joseph was at King's Mountain under Sevier.

Zaccheus was a signer of the Mecklenburg Declaration of Independence, a member of the provincial congress of 1776, and at the convention of 1788 he refused to give his approval to the Federal Constitution on the ground that it did not afford proper protection to the rights of the people. He led his company to King's Mountain. In 1792 he was surveyor of Cabarrus county. He was born near Newville, Pennsylvania, but finally settled in Sumner county, Tennessee. He married Mrs. Elizabeth Conger Ross, and had two sons, Stephen and Jonathan. A marker was placed on his grave at the request of the Eleanor Wilson Chapter, D. A. R., of Washington, D. C.

Willoughby. Matthew was in Beatty's company of Campbell's regiment. He moved to Lincoln county, Kentucky.

William was a lieutenant under the same Beattie, and also located land in Lincoln in 1831 by bounty warrant.

Winston. Major Joseph was born in Louisa county, Virginia, in 1746. In 1763 he joined a company of rangers under Phillips, who with Captain George Moffett were drawn into an ambuscade at Mann's fort on Jackson's River and severely defeated. Winston's horse was shot under him, and he was badly wounded, concealing himself under bushes. Here he was found by a friend and taken to a cabin. The ball was not extracted and caused him to suffer for some time afterward. In 1769 he moved to what is now Stokes county, North Carolina, and was a member of the Hillsboro convention. In 1780 he served under Davidson against Bryan's tories and under Cleveland on New River. At King's Mountain he commanded a portion of the right wing and was voted a handsome sword by the legislature of North Carolina, receiving also other honors. He was present at Guilford. He died 1815, and there are many descendants. The family was related to Patrick Henry.

Wither. Elisha of the Lincoln men was pensioned in North Carolina.

Witherspoon. David was born in New Jersey, 1758, and died while on a visit to South Carolina in 1828. He was a lieutenant under Cleveland at King's Mountain and in the border fighting.

John, a brother, was born 1760, and was a private in the same command. After the war he represented Stokes two years in the legislature. He died in Wayne county, Tennessee, in 1839.

These brothers were related to John Witherspoon, president of Princeton College.

Withrow. James was born in Virginia, 1746, and died in 1836. He moved to Rutherford county and served under Hampton, being present also at Stono and Blackstock, and against the tories and Indians. He served eight years in the North Carolina legislature.

Wood. Jonathan was born in Loudon county, Virginia, 1744, and died in Russell county, 1804. He was with Campbell's men. He married Mary Osborn, and his son Jonathan married Patsy Saylor.

Samuel, a captain under McDowell, was born in Albemarle, Virginia, 1735, and died in Lincoln county, Kentucky, 1825.

Woolsey. Thomas was under Campbell. He was

perhaps the same as Thomas, a Baptist preacher of Washington county, Virginia, in 1780-81.

Womack. Jacob was on the Watauga in 1772 and he signed the Halifax petition. He served under Sevier. He became a major, and was a justice of Washington, 1778-80. Womack's Station was about three miles from the Virginia line.

Word. Charles served under Washington in the early wars, and was killed at King's Mountain at the age of forty. Four brothers, Thomas, John, Peter, and Cuthbert, were in the war, and some if not all of them were at King's Mountain.

Wynn. William was born in Virginia in 1753, and was in the battle under Campbell. He married Elizabeth Dabney Anderson, and a daughter married Samuel Tucker Woodson. The Wynns were very early settlers in Hanover county, Virginia.

Yeary. Henry is listed by Summers.

Yontz. George is also listed by Summers.

Young. Robert was one of Sevier's riflemen. According to James and George Sevier, George Wilson, and Thomas Shelby, Young was the slayer of Ferguson. John Gilleland, who was wounded and nearly giving out, drew Young's attention to Ferguson and asked him to shoot the British commander. "I'll try and see what Sweet-lips can do," replied Young as he fired, Ferguson falling from his horse. But Ferguson had six or eight wounds, one of them in the head.

Thomas was under Williams and Brandon. His uncle McCreary was a prisoner of the British on Edisto Island. The wife, for fear her husband would be hanged, made her young son Matthew join Ferguson. "Just after we reached the hill," said Thomas Young, "Matthew discovered me, and ran from the British line, and threw his arms around me for joy. I told him to get a gun and fight." Whether he did or not is an unsolved question.

James and William were under Campbell. In 1773 James was at the head of the Middle Fork of Holston. He received a pension in 1825, William a bounty warrant.

ADDITIONAL

Alexander. James was born in Rowan county, N. C., 1756, entered the army from Lincoln, was at King's Mountain under Campbell, died in Buncombe June 28, 1814. Wife, Rhoda, daughter of Humphrey Cunningham, born 1758, was living 1840.

Anderson. George (1740-1808) was from Laurens county, South Carolina. Was a major and lost a leg in the battle. Married Mollie Saxon, and his son William married Annie Coker. Died in Anderson county, S. C.

William, born 1766, enlisted from Botetourt. Was also at Cowpens, and Eutaw. Wounded in thigh at King's Mountain. Five years service, including three months guarding lead mines in Wythe. Applied for pension in Davidson county, Tennessee, 1839. Affirmation by Colonel John Nesbitt of Dickson county.

Brown. John, born in Spartanburg county, South Carolina, 1765, enlisted under his father Andrew Brown, was at King's Mountain under Colonel Roebuck, and moved to Jefferson county, Alabama, where his widow Jincey applied for pension, 1853, when fifty-eight.

Campbell. John, born 1743, died 1808 at Abingdon, Virginia. Commanded a company from Washington county, Virginia, and was also at Guilford. Married Ruth Edmondson, and his son Richard married Catharine Lewis.

Carr. William enlisted from Mecklenburg county, North Carolina, 1775, was at King's Mountain under Captain Wallace, and also at Musgrove's mill. Applied for pension 1832 in Sullivan county, Tennessee.

Choat (Shoat). Greenbury was born in Virginia 1751, enlisted from Washington county, Tenn., 1779, was at King's Mountain under Captain George Russell. Applied for pension in 1833 from Johnson county, Illinois.

Cobb. Pharoah was born in Northampton county, North Carolina, 1752, enlisted in Watauga settlement 1776, was under Shelby at Musgrove's mill and King's

Mountain.   Pensioned in Hawkins county, Tennessee, 1832.

Cross. Zachreah was born 1761, enlisted from Sullivan county, Tennessee, 1777, serving till 1781. Died in Wayne county, Illinois, 1833. Married Esther Johnson of Logan county, Kentucky, 1792, who died 184—. Pension granted to surviving children: Rachel McDonald, William, Mary Punkhouse, Edna Reeves, James, Oliver, Robert.

Culbertson. Robert was born in Lancaster county, Pennsylvania, 1750, enlisted from Caswell county, North Carolina, 1780, and fought at Camden, King's Mountain, and Cowpens. Applied for pension in Laurens district, South Carolina, 1832.

Duckworth. John was born in Virginia 1759 and died in Burke county, North Carolina, 1843. Enlisted 1776. Was also at Ramseur's mill, where he was wounded in left shoulder. Only surviving child was Alexander of Morganton, North Carolina.

Feimster. William, born 1725-1759 in York district, South Carolina, died in Iredell county, North Carolina 1842, was also at Ramseur's mill and Musgrove's mill. Pensioned as a private in South Carolina. First wife was Mary Sharp, second was Margaret King.

Floyd. John was born in Mecklenburg county, North Carolina, 1758, enlisted 1776, was also at Musgrove's mill, Blackstock, and Guilford, and was pensioned as private. Married Anne Anderson and died 1830.

Gaines. James was born in Culpeper 1741, died 1830, at Kingsport, Tennessee. Was at Musgrove's mill and Cowpens, commanded a company at Guilford, and is said to have been at King's Mountain. Married Elizabeth Southers of Carter county, Tennessee.

Gaston. William was born in Lancaster county, Pennsylvania, 1757, died in Marion county, Illinois, 1838. Enlisted from Chester district, South Carolina, was at King's Mountain under Lacy, and was in other engagements. Pension granted to Mary, widow. Children: John, William, Annie R. Rainey.

Gibbs. Nicholas, said to have been at King's Mountain, received a landgrant from North Carolina for service in the Continental line. This record is in Book B, No. 2, Register's office, Knoxville, Tenn.

Gray. James was born in Augusta county, Virginia, 1755, enlisted in the "Liberty Men" from Rutherford county, North Carolina, served under Cleveland, and applied for pension in Rutherford, 1832.

Guest. Moses was born 1750 in Fauquier county, Virginia, and died in Franklin county, Georgia, 1837. Was at King's Mountain under Cleveland, enlisting from Wilkes county. Children by first wife: Susan Hall, Elizabeth Maberry, Joseph. Married Eleanor York of Franklin county, Georgia, 1829, who died 1866. Claim allowed 1833.

Hampton. Joel enlisted from Wilkes county, North Carolina, 1779, and was in service till 1783, fighting at King's Mountain and in other battles. Died in Logan county, Kentucky, 1832. Married Hannah Mitchell 1783, who applied for pension. Her sisters were Peninah Mitchell and Temperance Greer, her living children were James, Joshua, William, Andrew, Sally, Ally, and Hannah.

Helms. John was born in Botetourt 1761, applied for pension in Lincoln county, North Carolina 1833, and died 1838. Served from 1775 to 1781. Married Annie Okerman of Rowan county, about 1783, widow receiving pension. Children: John, Jacob, Peter, Amy, Eliza, Barley, born, respectively, 1788, 1793, 1798, 1800, 1803, 1810.

Henry. Joseph served under Captain Samuel Martin of Chronicle's battalion, and was pensioned in Buncombe county, 1832, when about seventy.

Joseph enlisted from Lincoln county, North Carolina, was wounded at King's Mountain, and was in other engagements. Applied for pension 1844 in Carroll county, Indiana, when eighty-eight. Granted to widow, Mary.

John and Moses, brothers to second Joseph, were killed at King's Mountain.

Houston. James, born in Augusta county, Virginia, 1757 was pensioned in Blount county, Tennessee, 1832. Enlisted 1776, was at King's Mountain under Campbell, moved to Tennessee, and was a member of its first Constitutional Convention. Built Houston Station on Little River, six miles north of Maryville. Son of Samuel and

Elizabeth (McCroskey) Houston. First wife, Esther, daughter of Matthew, an uncle. Second wife, Polly Gillespie.

Johnson. Samuel was a lieutenant at King's Mountain under Captain Joel Lewis, and was wounded, being pensioned therefor by North Carolina about 1798. Married Mary Hammons in Wilkes county, 1781, who applied for federal pension. Her father was William, a Baptist minister. The father of Samuel was Jeffrey, who died in Wilkes county. Ambrose, a son of Samuel. Affidavits by Jesse Franklin of Surry county, James Gray of Wilkes, Sterling Rose of Wilkes, John Sparks of Wilkes, William Spicer, of Wilkes, Nancy Gambell, George Johnson, a cousin and son of William Johnson.

Jones. Joshua was born 1764, and died in Knox county, Tennessee, 1840. Was under Captain Joel Lewis at King's Mountain, was wounded in the left arm and side, and taken to his home in Wilkes. Wife, Valencia. Applied for pension, 1832.

Kelly. John of Fairfield district, South Carolina, was under Hampton, and died in Fairfield in 1842. Hampton and Frost were sons.

Willaim was born in Union district, South Carolina, 1757, was also in battle of Stony Point, and applied for pension in McMinn county, Tennessee, 1832. Married Elizabeth ————— in 1817-82, to whom pension was granted. Children: Joshua, Rockwell, Nancy, Esther, Jane, Judah, Dinah, Daniel, William, Alcey, Richard, Elizabeth, Samuel, John.

Lane. Aquila was born 1755, served under Shelby, and died 1819. In 1780 married in Washington county, Tennessee, Agnes Fitzgerald, born 1763. Children: Esther, Garrett, Ransom, James, Theny, born, respectively, 1782, 1784, 1786, 1789, 1791. Samuel, brother to Aquila, was too young for service.

Long. Robert was born in county Antrim, Ireland, about 1763, and was pensioned in Laurens district, South Carolina, 1832. In service, 1778-80. His father's people were Covenanters and fled to Ireland in the reign of Charles II.

Love. John was born in Brunswick county, Virginia, 1762, and was pensioned 1832, when living in Wilkes county, North Carolina. Was at King's Mountain under Cleveland, a substitute for his father, James.

McCorkle. Francis was born in Scotland 1740, and died in Salisbury, North Carolina, 1802. He was also at Ramseur's mill and Cowpens. He married Sarah Work in Rowan county and had five children. He was over six feet tall and had red hair and a florid complexion.

McGaughey. Samuel was born in York county, Pennsylvania, 1763, and died in Lawrence county, Alabama, 1842. He served 1778-91, being also at Eutaw, Tiger River, Pacolet River, and on scout duty. Widow applied for pension in 1842.

McLain. John was born 1760 in Pennsylvania, and died in Rabun county, Georgia, 1844. He served 1775-81, and was also at siege of Ninety-Six. He married Mary ————— in 1748, who died 1844. Children: David, John, Charles, Ephraim E., James N., Margaret McLure, Jane Porter, Ann, widow of Alexander Mouldin. Applied for pension for North Carolina Service, 1834.

Massengale. Henry was born 1758, enlisted in North Carolina, served two years five months, and died in Sullivan county, Tennessee, in 1837, where he married Elizabeth Emmart, to whom pension was allowed.

Michael was born in Northampton county, North Carolina, 1756, and applied for pension in Grainger county, Tennessee, 1832. He lived on the Watauga in the Revolution, and was also at Musgrove's mill and Blackstock.

Martin. Samuel was born in Ireland 1752, and died in Lincoln county, North Carolina 1836. He was at Biggin's bridge, siege of Charleston, King's Mountain, and Eutaw. His children were Jane, Margaret Kerr, Thomas, George (wife Martha), Joseph. Grandchildren were June Martin, William Kerr, Rev. William Martin. Pension allowed, 1833.

Mayes. Samuel was born in Sumter district, South Carolina, 1759, and died in Maury county, Tennessee, 184—. He was at Savannah, Cowpens, King's Mountain, and Blackstock. His wife was Mary Frieson.

Newton. Benjamin was born in Caroline county, Virginia, 1752, enlisted from Caswell county, North Carolina, was at Cowpens, King's Mountain, and Yorktown, and applied for pension in Norris county, Kentucky.

Prather. Thomas was a private under Cleveland and applied for pension in Jackson county, Indiana, 1823. Basil was a son.

Pruitt. Martin enlisted in Washington county, Virginia and served two years. He was pensioned at Madison, Illinois, where he died 1841, aged ninety-two. Married in North Carolina, 1771, Martha Woods (died 1807.)

Reed. John enlisted in Washington county, Virginia, served as an express, was at King's Mountain and Guilford, and died 1826. The widow Keziah was allowed pension in 1844, and in 1849, when eighty-two, was living at Tulip, Texas. The only surviving child was Mrs. Charles H. Smith.

Reeves. Asher was born in Virginia, 1757, and died in Ohio. He enlisted from Wilkes county, North Carolina, and applied for pension in 1833.

Reynolds. Elisha died in Wilkes county, North Carolina, 1836, and was in service 1776-81. In 1786 he married Judith Edwards, who was allowed pension 184—.

Riggs. Bethiel was born at Towbridge, New Jersey, 1757, and enlisted in that state, 1776. He moved to Wilkes county, North Carolina, and took Cleveland's place at King's Mountain, when the latter was wounded. After the battle his company guarded the prisoners to the Moravian town. He was a Baptist minister.

Sarter (Sorter). William was at Blackstock, King's Mountain, and Cowpens, and died in Union district, South Carolina, leaving a large family, one of whom was Thomas. The widow applied for pension in 1839.

Smith. David was born in Anson county, North Carolina, 1753, was at King's Mountain and the siege of Augusta, and died in Harris county, Texas, 1835. He was first married to Sarah Terry of Virginia, who died 1772, and in Kentucky, 1791, he married Obedience Fort of North Carolina, who died 1847. His son Jackson, applied for pension, 1852.

Edward served 1775-81. After the battle of King's Mountain he and William Snodgrass were sent back to direct the militia following on foot to halt, which they did. In Washington county, Virginia, he married Hannah Crabtree, 1787, to whom pension was allowed. When living in Estill county, Kentucky, 1856, and eighty-eight years old, she applied for bounty land.

Starnes (Starns.) Nicholas enlisted under Arthur Campbell in 1775 for service against tories and Indians on New River. After King's Mountain, where he was under William Campbell, the wounded were placed in his care. Later the same fall he served against the Cherokees, the expedition burning sixteen towns. He was born in Cecil county, Maryland, 1756, and at the beginning of the Revolution the family were in Washington county, Virginia. He married Barbara Winters, 1816, in Rhea county, Tennessee, and died 1835. Pension was allowed the widow.

Steele. Joseph was born in Ireland 1759, and died in York county, South Carolina in 1795. He was in Marion's brigade, and at King's Mountain under Lacy.

Stribling. Clayton was in service 1777-83, and was under Brandon at King's Mountain. He was born 1762, and married Margaret ———— 1787, who applied for pension 1850, when eighty-three. He died 1831. The children were Thomas, John, Elizabeth, Samuel, Lucy, Fanny, Mary, Nancy. Thomas was the only soldier of that name, according to the Pension Office.

Taylor. Isaac was born 1757, and died in Carter county, Tennessee, 1844. He enlisted 1780, was in several other battles, and in 1781 was a lieutenant. He married Elizabeth Brown, 1814, who was allowed pension when seventy years old.

Andrew was a private in David McNabb's company of Sevier's regiment. He was born 1765 and was pensioned in Carter county, Tennessee, 1832.

James substituted in Surry county, North Carolina, serving in the Third North Carolina. In 1796 he moved to Blount county, where pension was allowed 1832.

Topp. Roger and five brothers were in the battle.

Utterly. William was born in Connecticut, and died in Wake county North Carolina 1794. He served under Colonels Hunter and Cleveland at Cowpens, King's Mountain, and Guilford.

Wallace. Thomas was born in Maryland 1745, and died in Montgomery county, Alabama, 1830. He served under Shelby. He married Rebecca Milligan, who applied for pension 1839, and died 1840 aged ninety-one. The children, Joel, Thomas, William, and Ruth, died before 1862.

Walling. William was at King's Mountain and served 24 months between 1777 and 1781, being pensioned in Sullivan county, Tennessee, in 1832, when 73 years old. After the Revolution he served 18 months against the Indians.

Walton. William enlisted in Wilkes county with his father William in John Brown's company. In the severe winter of 1779-80 there was wheat in the mountains, and he was drafted by Captain Loving to pack it to the mills to be ground into flour for the army. A wagon could not be used and the grain was carried by sled or packsaddle. He was thinly clad and barefoot much of the time. With his father he volunteered for service in South Carolina, and was present at the defeat of Gates. He applied for pension in Green county, Alabama, 1833, when sixty-six.

Welchel. John was born in Albemarle county, Virginia, 1766, and enlisted from Union district, South Carolina. At King's Mountain he was under Williams. He also served against the Cherokees. At Cowpens he received four saber cuts on the head, but was present at Eutaw. He married Abigail Davis 1784, and applied for pension in 1832 from Hall county, Georgia.

Francis, David, and William, brothers to John, were also in the battle, as was also their father Francis, who cared for the sick and wounded.

White. William was born in Ireland 1753, enlisted from Chester district, South Carolina, 1776, serving till 1782, and being present at Fishing Creek, Blackstock, King's Mountain, and other engagements. He came to America 1766, married Jane ————— in 1779, and died 1833, pension having just been allowed. His children were John, Samuel, Hugh, William, Abraham, Francis, and Gardner.

Williams. Benjamin was living six miles from Abingdon in 1776, where he volunteered under Colonel Christian, and was in several skirmishes in the vicinity. He applied for pension in Knox county, Tennessee, 1832, when ninety-one years old, and died the following year. In 1829 he married Nancy————.

Wyley. James was born in Mecklenburg county, North Carolina, 1762, and while very young moved to Montgomery county, Virginia, where he volunteered as a private in Preston's cavalry. He was pensioned in Blount county, 1833, and died 1851. He married Mary Mittenbarger of the same county, 1826, who applied for pension in 1853, when fifty-two.

Young. Thomas was born in Laurens district, South Carolina, 1764, enlisted 1780, and was in the affairs at King's Mountain, Orangeburg, and Ninety-Six. At Cowpens he received several wounds and was captured, but escaped. He was a nephew to Colonel Brandon, and is referred to in 1828 as Major Thomas Young. He was allowed invalid pension 1838.

William enlisted from Greenville district, South Carolina, 1775, and was at Brier Creek, Stono, Augusta, King's Mountain, Musgrove's mill, and Cowpens. He married Mary Salmon 1789, and died 1826, in Greenville, South Carolina, aged sixty-seven. Pension granted the children in 1850. They were William, Robert, Julia G. Caldwell, Hamilton, Emily Rosamond, Mary Wallace, James.

APPENDIX

SUPPLEMENTARY LISTS
REVOLUTIONARY PENSIONERS
Federal Office, Knoxville, Tennessee

Note: All are privates unless otherwise mentioned. All counties are in Tennessee.

Name Rank	County	When put on pension list	Died
Allen, Richard	Roan	1833	
Allgood, John	Monroe	1833	
Aiken, James	Roan	1833	
Armstrong, Isaac	Anderson	1833	
Atchely, Thomas	Sevier	1833	
Anderson, James	Morgan	1833	
Adcock, Thomas		1833	
Brewer, William	Blount	1833	
Bryant, James	Grainger	1833	July 2, 1839
Bowen, Charles		1833, transferred to Indiana.	
Brown, George	Jonesboro	1833	
Beeler, Jacob	Jonesboro	1833	
Bowman, Sparkling	Jonesboro	1833	
Beard, Robert	Jonesboro	1833	
Bowers, Leonard	Jonesboro	1833	
Boyd, William	Roan	1833	
Brimer, William	Sevier	1833	
Bassett, Nathaniel		1833	
Brooks, Thomas	Hawkins	1833	
Briggs, John	Jonesboro	1833	April 11, 1833
Brown, Isaiah		1833	
Brown, Benjamin		1833	
Bingham, Benjamin	Blount	1833	
Brown, Stephen	Bledsoe	1833	August 31, 1837
Backwell, David	Claiborne	1833	
Brakshears, Mattis	Roan	1833	
Brown, Thomas	Grainger	1833	
Burns, Laird	Roan	1833	
Box, Samuel	Jefferson	1833	May 16, 1836
Bowman, William		1839	
Brooks, David		1839	September 5, 1840
Breden, John		1841	August 3, 1840
Breakbill, Peter		1840	
Creswell, Andrew	Sevier	1833	July 1st, 1838
Campbell, Jermiah	Jonesboro	1833	
Cross, Elijah, Sergt.,	Jonesboro	1833	
Campbell, Jermiah	Jonesboro	1833	October 24, 1838
Clark, James	Blount	1833	
Carmichal, John		1836	
Carrell, William	Roan	1833	
Compton, Jermiah H.	Sevier	1833	
Chapman, Benjamin	Roan	1833	
Collinworths, John	Grainger	1833, Transfered to Ill., 1834	
Clayborn, John	Knox	1833	Died Sep. 4, 1838
Childress, John	Knox	1833	
Childress, Mitchell	Knox	1833	
Caunice, Nicholas		1837	

Chitwood, James	Campbell	1833	
Coleman, Spence		1833	
Chapman, John H.	Roan	1833	
Cardwell, Perrin	Knox	1833	
Covey, Samuel	Knox	1833	
Cox, Curd	Knox	1833	
Coal, Willis	Fentress	1833	
Cathcart, Joseph	Monroe	1833	Nov. 27, 1835
Cummings, Andrew	Blount	1833, Nov. 27, 1835. (1840 wi-	
Crenshaw, John	Roan	1833	dow receiving pension)
Copland, Zacheus	Jefferson	1833	
Campbell, Joseph	Hamilton	1833	
Clay, William	Hamilton	1833	
Coop, Horatia		1833	
Caruthers, James	Blount	1833	
Carter, Charles		1833	April 11, 1833
Duncan, John	Blount	1833	
Dobkins, Jacob	Claiborne	1833	
Doherty, George, Sr.	Jefferson	1834	
Dunn, William	Knox	1833	Dec. 19, 1837
Dyer, Manoah, Drum'r,	Monroe	1833	
Dalton, John	Bledsoe	1833	
Davis, William	Jonesboro	1833	
Davis, Andrew, Lieut.,	Bledsoe	1833	
Davis, John	Blount	1833	
Davis, Joel		1833	Feb. 12, 1848
Duncun, Thomas	Monroe	1833	
Dodd, William	McMinn	1833	
David, Azariah	Rhea	1833	
Duglass, Edward	Jefferson	1833	
Davis, Robert	Marion	1833	July 8, 1834
Davis, William	Cocke	1833	
Dave, Thomas		1838	
Douglass, Robert	McMinn	1834	July 10, 1837
Evans, Ardin	Roan	1833	
Edgman, William	Roan	1833	
Everett, William	Marion	1833	
Evans, Andrew	Rhea	1833	
Ewing, George		1833	July 4, 1840
England, Joseph		1833	Nov. 13, 1834
Fitch, John	Jonesboro	1833	
Furgason, James	Rhea	1833	
Ford, John, Sergt.	Bledsoe	1832	
Fulkner, David	Knox	1833	
Forrister, Robt., Sergt.,	McMinn	1833	
Gaspeuson, John	Anderson	1833	
Garner, John F.	Blount	1833	
Gorsage, John	Jonesboro	1833	
Gillespie, Jacob	Knox	1833	
Griffith, Joseph	Morgan	1834	
Grantham, Richard, Sergt.		1833	
Gammon, Harris	Knox	1833	
Geren, Solomon		1833	
Graves, Boston	Knox	1833	
Goodman, Henry, Sergt.		1833	June 11, 1833
Graham, William	Anderson	1833	
Hendricks, Solomon	Jonesboro	1833	

Hunter, Thomas, Sergt., Blount		1833	
Hamilton, Joshua	Jonesboro	1833	
Hughs, Peter	Jonesboro	1833	
Harper, Richard	Claiborne	1833	
Hall, John	Jonesboro	1833	
Houston, James, Ensign	Knox	1833	
Hall, Thomas	Knox	1833	
Hotchkiss, Jared	Roan	1833	
Hall, David	Anderson	1833	
Hooper, Ennis		1833	Feb. 4, 1833
Huffacre, George	Knox	1833	
Houston, John	Knox	1833	March 30, 1835
Hamby, William	Blount	1833	
Haddon, George	Blount	1833	
Hancock, Stephen	Roan	1833	
Hankins, Abraham	Knox	1833	
Henry, John	Jefferson	1833	
Hale, John	Bledsoe	1833	
Hancocke, Joseph	Anderson	1833	
Housley, Robert	Jefferson	1833	
Holloway, John	Morgan	1833	April 4, 1837
Hedrick, William	Sevier	1833	
Holdway, Timothy		1838	
Hamilton, Thomas	Rhea	1833	
Hank, Michael	Monroe	1833	
Harrison, Nathaniel	Blount	1833	
Hobbs, Thomas	Claiborne	1833	
Hardy, Thomas	Claiborne	1834	
Hale, William		1833	
Ivy, Henry	Jefferson	1833	July 7, 1834
Johnson, James	Knox	1833, transferred to Ind., 1834	
Jack, James	Jonesboro	1833	
Johnson, Robert	Knox	1833	
Jones, James	Marion	1833	
Jenkins, James	Sevier	1833	Aug. 26, 1839
Jamison, John	Grainger	1833	Feb. 28, 1839
James, John	Marion	1833	
Jones, David	Knox	1833	
James, Rolling	Campbell	1833	
James, Martin	Franklin	1833	
Jackson, Churchwell	Monroe	1833	
Johnson, James	Fentress	1833	
King, John	Jonesboro	1833	
Kindle, William	Jonesboro	1833	
Kitchen, John	Anderson	1833	
Keys, Matthew	Knox	1833	
Kendred, Thomas	Morgan	1833	
Kelley, William	McMinn	1833	March 1, 1837
King, Andrew	Claiborne	1833	Sep. 4, 1833
Liture, Harman	Jonesboro	1833	
Landrum, James	Jonesboro	1833	
Liles, David	Roan	1833	
Lain, Charles	Roan	1833	
Lesley, Thomas	Monroe	1833	Feb. 23, 1839
Love, Hezekiah		1833	June 11, 1833

Love, Nancy, widow of Hezekiah pension was transferred to Hunts-ville, Ala., 1841

Lawson, John	Morgan	1833	Jan. 14, 1838
Landrum, Thomas		1833	
Lewallen, Michael		1834	May 8, 1833
Lane, James	Grainger	1833	Feb. 4, 1835
Lyman, Jacob	Sevier	1833	
Lusk, Joseph	McMinn	1833	Sep. 4, 1836
Larrimore, Hugh	McMinn	1833	transferred to Mo., 1839
Lane, Isaac	McMinn	1833	
Lay, Thomas	Grainger	1833	
Long, Nicholas	Jefferson	1833	
Levi, Rice	Anderson	1833	
Lannim, Joseph	Anderson	1833	Nov. 11, 1837
Lengley, William		1840	
McBee, Israel	Grainger	1833	
McCoy, Robert, Sergt.	Blount	1833	
McLemore, John, Sergt.	Knox	1833	
McCormick, Thomas	Jonesboro	1833	
Millen, John	Jonesboro	1833	
Moore, Thomas	Rhea	1833	
Moser, Abraham	Anderson	1833	
Miller, Martin	Claiborn	1833	Aug. 9, 1838
Manson, William	Jefferson	1833	July 3, 1838
McFarland, Robt., Lt.,	Jefferson	1833	
McCallister, William	Bradley	1834	Sep. 4, 1841
McCampbell, Soloman		1833	Removed to Mobile, Ala.
McCormick, Jos., Jackson, Ala.		1834	
Malaby, John	Bledsoe	1833	
Massingill, Michael	Grainger	1833	
Miller, John H.	Knox	1833	
Madonough, Andrew	Bledsoe	1833	
Murphy, John	Jefferson	1833	Feb. 17, 1837
Murphy, William	Jefferson	1833	Transferred to Mo., 1840
Miliken, James	Cocke	1833	
McWheeler, And., Putman, Ind		1833	Oct. 7, 1834
Marney, Amos		1833	Aug. 28, 1837
Manley, Amos	Anderson	1833	
Mason, Edward	McMinn	1833	Aug. 22, 1833
McCallon, James	Blount	1833	
McPeters, Joseph	Morgan	1833	
McMillen, Joseph	Knox	1833	
McCormick, Robert	McMinn	1833	
Moore, William	Blount	1833	
McKamey, James	Blount	1833	
Mosier, Francis	Monroe	1833	Oct. 22, 1836
McCroskey, John	Sevier	1833	
Martin, Robert	Marion	1833	
Metcalf, William	Marion	1833	
Neel, John	Blount	1833	
Neal, Zephaniah		1833	Transferred to West Tenn.
Newman, Jacob	Blount	1833	
Norton, Alexander	Blount	1833	
Nuanly, Henry		1833	
Norman, William	McMinn	1833	July 1, 1841
Nelson, ————	Knox	1833	
Phillips, Joseph		1833	
Panter, Adam	Jonesboro	1833	
Parry, John	Roan	1833	

Porter, Mitchell	Sevier	1833	
Porter, Penelope, widow of Mitchell, paid pension after Mar. 4, 1836			
Portwood, Page, Segt., Anderson		1833	
Perry, Jesse, Ensign		1833	
Patton, Jacob	Monroe	1833	Mar. 4, 1840
Phillips, Clemmon	Morgan	1833	
Palmer, Thomas	Rhea	1833	
Patton, Joseph	Morgan	1833	
Peck, Able	Knox	1833	
Price, John	Granger	1833	
Peters, William	McMinn	1834	
Pollard, Chattin		1841	
Quarles, Francis	Knox	1833	
Queener, John	McMinn	1833	
Russell, Moses	McMinn	1833	
Rutherford, William	Knox	1833	Nov. 16, 1833
Reed, David	McMinn	1833	
Rogers, William	Hamilton	1833	
Richardson, Amos	Rhea	1833	
Rutherford, Absolm	Knox	1833	
Rogers, Benjamin	Campbell	1833	
Riggins, James	McMinn	1833	
Rudd, Burlingham	Sevier	1833	
Reed, Lovett	Bledsoe	1833	Nov. 9, 1838

(Note: Libby Reed, widow of Lovett paid pension Mar. 1, 1841)

Roberts, Joshua	Morgan	1833, Transferred to Mo., 1837	
Robertson, Joseph	Blount	1833	
Rains, John, Capt.	Bledsoe	1833	Jany 28, 1835
Richardson, James	Monroe	1833	
Reed, Abraham	Monroe	1833	
Roper, Drury	Jefferson	1833	
Robertson, Thomas	Monroe	1833	
Roberts, Edmund	McMinn	1833	
Scott, John	Jonesboro	1833	
Sevier, James	Jonesboro	1833	
Stephens, Mashack	Marion	1833	
Stone, Ezekial	Marion	1833	
Scott, Arthur	Knox	1833	
Sterling, Robert	Blount	1833	
Smith, Obediah		1833	
Smith, Henry	McMinn	1833	
Steed, Thomas	McMinn	1833	
Sellers, James	Bladley	1833	
Smith, Ransom	Marion	1833	
Stone, Soloman	Marion	1833	
Steele, Samuel	Monroe	1833	
Simms, James	Blount	1833	
Smith, Laton	Marion	1833	
Smallwood, William	Sevier	1833	
Smith, Edward	Knox	1833	
Sarrett, Allen	Cocke	1833	
Sutherland, David	Bledsoe	1834	
Sharp, Samuel	Knox	1833	Sep. 4, 1849
Stone, Conway	Monroe	1833	Nov. 19, 1834
Smith, William	Jefferson	1833	Jan. 24, 1836

(Note: Sep. 24, 1759 paid to the 24th of Jany. 1836 to two of four children, to-wit: Hester Smith and Jane Wild.   See the letter June 16, 1860.)

Stansfiels, Jas., Sergt., McMinn		1834	
Scott, James	Knox	1833	
Stellars, James	Grainger	1833	
Stencipher, Joseph	Morgan	1833	
Swadley, Mark	Monroe	1834	
Sims, John	Blount	1833	
Siske, Bartlett		1834	
Smith, Harnet	Knox	1833	
Smith, Phillip	Monroe	1833	
Shever, Frederick	Green	1833	
Sample, Samuel	Knox	1834	
Sumpter, Thomas, Fifer, Knox		1833	
Taylor, Andrew	Jonesboro	1833	
Taylor, Isaac, Lieut., Jonesboro		1833	
Thompson, Sam'l, Sergt., Blount		1833	Jany. 8, 1839
Taff, George	Jefferson	1833	
Trail, James	Jonesboro	1833	
Tate, David	Grainger	1833	Aug. 7, 1838
Thatcher, Benjamin	Roan	1833	
Thurman, Philip	Bledsoe	1833	Sept. 25, 1840
Thurman, Charles	Bledsoe	1833	
Trail, James	Jonesboro	1833	
Thomas, John		1833	
Trice, James	Blount	1833	
Tulloch, Magnus, Fifer, Blount		1833	
Tedford, Robt., Sergt., Blount		1833	
Trexal, Jacob	Marion	1833	
Thompson, Thomas	McMinn	1833	
Trowell, James	Anderson	1833	
Truce, Michael	Jefferson	1833	
Taylor, Daniel	Grainger	1833	
Thompson, Stephen	Marion	1834	
Tyner, Damsey	Hamilton	1833	
Wiser, George	Claiborne	1833	
Williams, John J.	Claiborne	1833	
Williams, John	Morgan	1833	
Wood, Obadiah	Anderson	1833	

(Note: Transferred to Arkansas, May 4, 1835.)

Woddy, John	Roan	1833	
Williford, Jacob	Grainger	1833	Feb. 18, 1839
Williams, Benjamin	Knox	1833	June 5, 1835
Williams, Shadrack	Grainger	1833	July 15, 1839
Welch, Robert	Grainger	1833	
Walker, John	Blount	1833	

Note: Paid to children, Aug. 6th, 1837.)

Walling, John	McMinn	1833	April 26, 1836
Whitman, John	Campbell	1833	
Woods, John	Blount	1833	
Wyley, James	Blount	1833	
Wear, John	Sevier	1833	

(Note: Transferred to Indiana, Sept. 4, 1834.)

Walker, George, Sergt., Bledsoe		1833	
Wooton, Turner		1833	Nov. 23, 1833
White, William	Anderson	1834	Jany. 8, 1835
Wiette, Edward	Anderson	1833	

Williams, Matthew	Morgan	1833	
Wiley, Alexander	Anderson	1833	July 4th, 1833
Wees, Peter	Roan	1833	
Willis, Smith	Morgan	1833	
White, Benjamin	Maury	1830	
Walker, Robert	Bedford	1832, Age 77	
White, Gordon	Blount	1833, Age 72	
Waddle, Martin	Green	1833, Age 71	
Wolever, Philip	Green	1833, Age 83	
Walling, William	Hawkins	1833, Age 75	
Willia, John	Hawkins	1833, Age 64	
Winstead, Francis	Hawkins	1833, Age 74	
Young, Isham	Roan	1833	
Yader, Joseph	Grainger	1833	Dec. 25, 1834
Yancey, Ambrose	Grainger	1833	
Young, Samuel	McMinn	1832	
Yates, Samuel	Cocke	1833	

B

Acor, Jacob
Archerm, Isaac
Acre, Cronanmus
Abbott, John, Sergeant
Boyd, John
Brocus, John (died Apr. 14, 1824)
Banard, Jonathan
Brummett, Thomas

Bayless, John (Dead)
Beaty, Walter
Baker, Henry B.
Bright, James
Bowman, John
Britten, Joseph, Lieutenant
Boston, Christopher

Invalid

Bushong, George
Berry, John

Bates, Isaac
Barlow, Henson

Half Pay

Bailey, Mary, Guardian of the heirs of John Bailey, private. (Note: Cash paid to the Hon. John Cocke, your att. at the office of the Auditor, as per letter from Peter Hagner of the 21st of Jany. 1824 $182.27 being the amount of pension due to the 4th of Sept. 1823.)

Clark, John
Carr, William
Childress, David
Coleman, John
Carter, Thomas
Clark, Thomas (dead)
Crews, Gideon (dead)
Conway, James
Chandley, William, Sergeant

Cooper, Richard
Crow, Robert
Crawford, Moses
Carr, William, 2nd (dead)
Copinger, Higgins
Courtney, Michael
Cunningham, Valentine (transferred from West Tenn.)

Invalid

Caldwell, John
Craighead, Robert
Dawson, James
Desern, Frederick

Draper, Robert
Dixon, George
Dunkin, Daniel

Invalid

Dunlap, James
Dunham, Washington
Evens, Samuel
Ethridge, John, Transferred from West Tenn.
Falls, John

Fitzergerald, George
Floid, Perry
Fant or Fain, George
Fuller, George
Fry, Gabriel

Invalid
Fain, John

Grant, James (Died Jan. 21, 1824)
Givens, Jalrick
Graves, Stephen
Grant, David
Goings, Williams
Goings, Daniel
Godsey, William
Green, Samuel
Gregory, George, Captain
Godfrey, Zachriah
Harrison, William

Hays, William
Hines, James
Honey, John A.
Holliway, Billey
Harbison, John
Harper, Thomas
Henwood, Robert
Harris, Hugh
Horton, Isaac
Hood, Jacob

Invalid

Harton, Howell

Heater, William

Half Pay

Harmon, Jacob, Guardian of the heirs of Jon Goforth, a private at & 4 per mo.

Hemmill, Henry, Guardian of the heirs of John Davis, a private, & per month.

Hawkins, Joseph, Guardian of the heirs of Jethroe Reynolds, private.

Hickman, Henry, Guardian of the heirs of James Keeney, private.

Jordon, John	Jackson, Jonthan
Jackson, William	Jones, Joseph
Johnson, William	Kilborn, Benjamin
Johnson, Peter	Kelly, Charles, Sergeant

Invalid

Kilgore, Charles (Died June 17, 1823)	Kennedy, Andrew
	Kelley, Allen

Liles, John, (died April 15, 1824)	McRoberts, David
Leay or Lee, William	Mann, Ebenezer
Leonard, John	McElroy, Daniel
McEntire, John (died)	May, George
Mann, Robert	McVey, Eli
Morgan, John	McDonald, John, Mus. N.
	Mackey, William
McLain, Thomas (Died April 11, 1824)	McDonald, James
	Minton, Ebenezer

Invalid

Matlock, Henry	Malloy, Timothy
Montgomery, John	Morrint, Joseph
Montgomery, James	

Half Pay

McClintock, James, Guardian of the heirs of Barclay Reams or Rheams, private.

Norton, George	Price, James
Nelson, John	Peterson, Daniel
Northern, Solomon	Pearce, Joshua
Nixon, John	Parsons, George
Neeley, John	Pratt, Thomas
Norris, William	Petty, John
O'Bar, Robert	Price, John
Osburn, Nathaniel, Captain	Porterfeild, Richard
Parsons, Thomas, (died Feb. 15, 1825)	

Invalid

Posey, Harrison	Pannel, John
Parks, James	

Robinson, James	Rock, John
Ross, Robert (died Jan. 23, 1825)	Rector, Uriah
Rhodes, Samuel, Transferred to Mo., 1822.	Rogers, Willonburghby

Invalid

Rhea, Luna	Reed, Joseph
Rhea, Robert	Russell, John

Half Pay

Rowlin, Lory, Guardian of the heirs of Thomas Rowland, private.

Rhea, Henrietta, Guardian of the heirs of John Rhea, private.

Staples, John	Slaughter, Jacob
Sitton, William	Sexton, Timothy

Simmons, James
Spears, Samuel
Smith, Robert Sergeant
Spragon, Thomas

Stephens, Henry

Smith, John A.
Stansbury, Luke
Smith, Caleb

Invalid
Seals, Hezekiah

Thomas, Jacob, transferred to West Tennessee

Tarrant, Henry, Transferred to West Tennessee

Invalid

Thonburgh, John Sergeat
Tipton, William

Titlow, Philip, Sergeant

Half Pay
Thankenley, Sarah, Guardian of Walker, John
the heirs of William Tankenley, private.

Williams, Alexander
Whelan, Richard
Walker, Samuel, Captain

Wright, William
Wheeler, Samuel

Walker, John, Sergeant Major
Wees, Michael
Wells, Zachariah
Invalid
Waddle, David
Webb, Jesse

BIBLIOGRAPHY
Of Principal Books Consulted.

North Carolina—State Record.

Pension Lists—Virginia, North Carolina, South Carolina, Kentucky, Georgia, Tennessee, Missouri, Alabama, Mississippi.

Lineage Book, D. A. R., Volumes 1-60.

Lineage Book, S. A. R.

History of Mecklenburg County, N. C.—J. B. Alexander.

History of Mecklenburg County, N. C.—D. A. Tompkins.

Early Hopewell Settlers—J. B. Alexander.

History of Halifax County, N. C.—W. C. Allen.

Dropped-Stitches of Tennessee History—John Allison.

County of Illinois—C. W. Alvord.

Scotch-Irish of Pennsylvania—W. C. Armor.

Notable Families of the South—Zella Armstrong.

History of Watauga County, N. C.—J. P. Arthur.

Western North Carolina—J. P. Arthur.

Chronicles of the Scotch-Irish families in Augusta County, Va.—Lyman Chalkley.

Early Settlers of Rowan County, N. C.—Eugene Bean.

History of the German Settlements in North and South Carolina—G. D. Bernheim.

Scotch-Irish pioneers in Ulster and America—C. K. Bolton.

First Settlements in Tennessee—J. W. Breaxeale.

Southwest Virginia and the Shenandoah Valley—Thomas Bruce.

The South in the Revolution—J. W. Caldwell.

History of Tennessee—W. H. Carpenter.

Historical Collections of South Carolina—B. R. Carroll.

Interesting Revolutionary Incidents—E. W. Caruthers.

Historic Sumner County, Tennessee—J. G. Cisco.

Notes on the War in the South—N. H. Claiborne.

History of Davidson County, Tenn.—N. W. Clayton.

Historical Sketches of Kentucky—Lewis Collins.

History of Pioneer Kentucky—R. S. Cottrell.

Life of Davy Crockett—By Himself.

Historical Collections, Joseph Habersham Chapter, D. A. R., Ga.

Historic North Carolina Troops, North Carolina Line —C. L. Davis.

Affair at King's Mountain—J. W. DePeyster.

King's Mountain and Its Heroes—L. C. Draper.

Shelby and His Men—J. N. Edwards.

Revolutionary Soldiers of Virginia—H. J. Eckenrode.

The State of Franklin—W. E. Fitch.

Sketches of North Carolina—W. H. Foote.

Sketches of Virginia—W. H. Foote.

The Scotch-Irish in America—H. J. Ford.

John Sevier—J. R. Gilmore.

Historic Families of Kentucky—T. M. Green.

Civil and Political History of Tennessee—John Haywood.

Sketches of Western North Carolina—C. L. Hunter.

History of Sweetwater Valley—W. B. Lenoir.

History of Georgia—McCall.

Battle of King's Mountain—F. B. McDowell.

Some Tennessee Families—Selden Nelson.

Pioneer Settlers of Grayson County, Va.—B. F. Nuckolls.

Annals of Tennessee—J. G. M. Ramsay.

History of Rowan County, N. C.—Jethro Rumple.

Loyalists of the American Revolution—Lorenzo Sabine.

History of Orangeburg County, S. C.—A. S. Salley.

Records of the Revolutionary War—W. T. R. Saffell.

Historic Sullivan County, Tenn.—Oliver Taylor.

Tennessee Historical Magazine.

History of McNair County—M. J. Wright.

Virginia Magazine of History and Biography.

Annals of Augusta County—J. A. Waddell.

Historical Sketches of North Carolina—J. H. Wheeler.

Historical Collections of Georgia—George White.

Upper South Carolina—J. B. C. Landrum.

Draper Manuscripts of North Carolina, Virginia, and Tennesse History.

INDEX

www.ingramcontent.com/pod-product-compliance
Lightning Source LLC
Chambersburg PA
CBHW031119020426

42333CB00012B/149